Energy and Environment in the Korean Economy

Energy and Environment
in the Korean Economy

---

by Eui-Soon Shin

Published by the Yonsei University Press
134 Shinchon-dong, Sodaemoon-ku, Seoul 120-749, Korea
TEL : (82-2) 392-6201, 361-3381～2 FAX : (82-2) 393-1421
E-mail : ysup@yonsei.ac.kr.
http://www.yonsei.ac.kr/press

Price ₩20,000

ISBN 89-7141-655-6 93320

Printed and bounded in Seoul, Korea

Energy and Environment in the Korean Economy

Eui-Soon Shin

2005년도
대한민국학술원
기초학문육성
“우수학술도서”
선정

YONSEI UNIVERSITY PRESS

Contents

PART III. Environmental Policy and Environmental Cooperation

Preface

Korean economy grew from one of the poorest in the world to the 11th largest in 2004. Korea has scarce indigenous energy resources with only hydro and small amounts of anthracite coal available. As a result, Korea imports more than 97 per cent of its energy needs from abroad. The impact of the two oil crises in the 1970s seriously hampered the Korean economy and resulted in a minus growth rate in 1980, which was the first time since Korea started its first five-year economic development plan in 1962. Since then, a stable supply of oil became the core of the Korean energy policy. During the 1980s and 1990s, the world oil market was more or less favorable to Korea. However, the deterioration of the situation in Iraq, together with the rapid growth of China, is disrupting the international oil market again. Rapidly diminishing non-OPEC producers' crude oil reserve will increase Korea's dependence on the geopolitically unstable Middle East, which will trigger price hike and threaten Korea's energy security. This fear has drawn increased interest in energy cooperation in Northeast Asia.

Korea, with its dense population and industries in limited land space, has experienced serious environmental quality deterioration as its economy grew rapidly. Air pollution in large cities is common and water pollution in the four largest rivers is threatening the health of Korean people. Yellow dust and acid rain from China have raised trans-boundary air pollution issues. The upcoming implementation of the Kyoto Protocol will require energy conservation and will promote energy substitution into new and renewable energy sources. Korea faces the delicate task of continuing its economic growth while trying to secure stable energy supply and to resolve domestic and regional environmental problems.

This volume is a collection of my papers on economic analyses of contemporary energy and environmental issues in Korea since 1980. I hope this volume could provide stimulus and inspiration to those who believe that Korea, a country with scarce natural resource and poor environmental capacity, should follow the path of sustainable development by setting its first priority to energy and environmental security.

Part I of this volume contains six papers on energy security and energy cooperation. The topics covered are energy demand and inter-energy substitution in Korea; comparison of energy supply policies between Korea and Japan; energy cooperation in Asia-Pacific and Northeast Asia; and restructuring of the Korean electric power industry. Part II deals with water-use conflicts and natural resource endowment in Korea. It contains three papers on water-use conflicts in the Seoul Metropolitan Region and natural resources and environmental management in Korea. Part III examines environmental policy and environmental cooperation. The topics covered are environmental policy of Korea; categorization and valuation of urban environmental problems; economic analysis of trans-boundary air pollution in Northeast Asia; environmental cooperation between South and North Korea; and tax policy options to prepare for the Kyoto Protocol.

Some of the papers in this volume are reprinted with modifications from their previous publications. Others are printed here for the first time. I wish to acknowledge the financial as well as spiritual support of the Economics Department of the University of Washington, the Institute of East and West Studies and the Institute of Unification at Yonsei University, the East-West Center in Hawaii, United Nations Centre for Regional Development in Nagoya, OECD, UNEP, the World Bank, Nautilus Institute in San Francisco and the Korea Science Foundation. I also want to thank the Yonsei University Press for generously agreeing to publish this monograph and Jae-ho Pyung for his excellent editorial support. Finally I would like to thank my wife, Sunhee, for her endurance and ardent support during the course of my academic career.

Eui-Soon Shin
Seoul, Korea
June 2004

PART I

Energy Security and Energy Cooperation

1. Inter-Energy Substitution in Korea, 1962-1975*

I. Introduction

Korea is poorly endowed with energy sources. Coal is the only indigenous fossil fuel discovered so far, and its reserve is very limited.[1] So the increase in energy demand following rapid industrialization made it inevitable for Korea to increase the import of energy from abroad. In 1972, Korea imported 52.3 percent of energy consumed in that year. This was a big jump from the import share of 10.7 percent in 1962. Out of 22.8 million tons of coal equivalent energy import in 1972, only 42,000 tons were coal and the rest were crude oil. The 1973-74 world oil crisis quadrupled the price of crude oil in two years. This dramatic increase in the

* "Inter-Energy Substitution in Korea, 1962-1975," *Journal of Economic Development*, Vol. 6, No. 1 (July 1981), pp. 33-46.

1) Estimated total exploitable coal reserve in Korea was 600.42 million tons in 1975. At the 1975 production rate of 13.57 million tons, the estimated reserve will last for 44 years.

price of oil seriously affected Korea which imported all of its required crude oil from abroad. From 1972 to 1974, expenses for the import of crude oil rose as much as five times from 221 million to 1,108 million and the cost share of crude oil among total import rose from 8.8 percent to 16.2 percent.

Up to the early 1960s, wood and charcoal were the main energy sources in Korea. In 1961, wood and charcoal composed 56.7 percent of total energy consumption while coal composed 33.4 percent, oil 8.2 percent, and hydro electricity 1.6 percent.[2] During the first five-year economic planning period of 1962 to 1966, wood and charcoal were gradually replaced by coal and oil. In 1966, coal composed 46.9 percent, wood and charcoal 34.6 percent, oil 16.6 percent, and hydro electricity 1.8 percent of total energy consumption. During the second five-year economic development planning period of 1967 to 1971, oil replaced coal as the chief energy source in Korea. In 1971, oil composed 52.7 percent of total energy consumption compared to 27.5 by coal, 18.3 by wood and charcoal, and 1.5 percent by hydro electricity.

The change in the composition of energy consumption through time could have been the result of rapid industrialization, changes in government energy policy, changes in life style, etc. But one of the most important reasons is the change in the relative price of energy sources. This paper examines how the mix of energy consumption can be affected by changing relative energy prices. For

2) The share of each energy source among total energy consumption is compared in converted kilo calorific values. (1 kilo calorie = 3.968 Btu.) See Table 2 of Shin (1980) for more information.

this purpose, a translog cost function is employed to a system of derived demand equations. Section 2 discusses the model. Section 3 explains how the data are constructed for the translog analysis. In section 4, estimated price elasticities are reported with the results of various tests. Section 5 is the concluding remarks.

II. The model

Suppose there is a twice differentiable aggregate production function for the Korean economy as follows :

$$Y = F(E,\ O,\ C,\ \underline{X}), \qquad (1)$$

where Y is gross national product, E is electricity, O is fuel oil, C is coal, and $\underline{X}$ is a vector of all other inputs.[3] If the energy inputs are homothetically weakly separable from all other inputs, the aggregate production function can be written as

$$Y = H(R^{*}(E,\ O,\ C),\ \underline{X}), \qquad (2)$$

where R^{*} is an energy input function. Dual to this energy input function is an energy cost function :

$$V = J(R,\ P_E,\ P_O,\ P_C), \qquad (3)$$

where V is total cost of energy, R is aggregate energy input, and

3) Wood and charcoal are excluded from the analysis. Beside the fact that they are not one of modern energy sources, the published data were not suitable to use for the present study.

P_E, P_O, P_C are prices of electricity, fuel oil, and coal, respectively. If the energy input function is a positive, non-decreasing, positively linear homogeneous, concave function, then the energy cost function can be written as

$$V=R \cdot G(P_E,\ P_O,\ P_C), \tag{4}$$

where G is a unit cost function satisfying the same regularity conditions and is a function of energy prices only.

To investigate the substitution possibilities among energy sources in Korea, a translog cost function is employed.[4)] The translog cost function does not place *a priori* restrictions on Allen partial elasticities of substitution and provides a second order approximation to an arbitrary functional form. The translog unit energy cost function will be as follows :

$$\begin{aligned} \ln G = {} & \alpha_G + \alpha_E \ln P_E + \alpha_O \ln P_O + \alpha_C \ln P_C \\ & + 1/2\, \beta_{EE} (\ln P_E)^2 + \beta_{EO} \ln P_E \ln P_O + \beta_{EC} \ln P_E \ln P_C \\ & + 1/2\, \beta_{OO} (\ln P_O)^2 + \beta_{OC} \ln P_O \ln P_C \\ & + 1/2\, \beta_{CC} (\ln P_C)^2 \end{aligned} \tag{5}$$

By differentiating equation (5) logarithmically, we get

$$\frac{\partial \ln G}{\partial \ln P_i} = \frac{\partial G}{\partial P_i} \cdot \frac{P_i}{G} = \alpha_i + \sum_j \beta_{ij} \ln P_j, \qquad i,\ j = E,\ O,\ C \tag{6}$$

According to Shephard's lemma,

---

4) See Christensen, Jorgenson, and Lau (1971, 1973) for the early development of the translog function.

$$\frac{\partial G}{\partial P_i} = \frac{X_i}{R}, \quad \left(\frac{\partial V}{\partial P_i} = \frac{\partial (R \cdot G)}{\partial P_i} = R \cdot \frac{\partial G}{\partial P_i} = X_i\right), \tag{7}$$

where X_i represents the cost minimizing energy demand when aggregate energy input R is held constant. By substituting (7) into (6), we get

$$\frac{\partial \ln G}{\partial \ln P_i} = \frac{P_i X_i}{\sum_i P_i X_i} = M_i = \alpha_i + \sum_j \beta_{ij} \ln P_j, \quad i, j = E, O, C, \tag{8}$$

where M_i is the cost share of energy input i.

The system of cost share equations is as follows :

$$\begin{aligned} M_E &= \alpha_E + \beta_{EE} \ln P_E + \beta_{EO} \ln P_O + \beta_{EC} \ln P_C + u_E, \\ M_O &= \alpha_O + \beta_{OE} \ln P_E + \beta_{OO} \ln P_O + \beta_{OC} \ln P_C + u_O, \\ M_C &= \alpha_C + \beta_{CE} \ln P_E + \beta_{CO} \ln P_O + \beta_{CC} \ln P_C + u_C, \end{aligned} \tag{9}$$

where the disturbance term is added for each cost share equation to allow for randomness in the cost minimizing behavior. As the cost shares sum to unity, the following restrictions are imposed on (9) :

$$\begin{aligned} &\alpha_E + \alpha_O + \alpha_C = 1, \\ &\beta_{EE} + \beta_{OE} + \beta_{CE} = 0, \\ &\beta_{EO} + \beta_{OO} + \beta_{CO} = 0, \\ &\beta_{EC} + \beta_{OC} + \beta_{CC} = 0. \end{aligned} \tag{10}$$

Parameter estimates of any two cost share equations generate the parameter estimates of remaining one equation due to the restriction (10). Furthermore, the cross equation symmetry restriction leaves only five out of twelve parameters free of restriction. Imposition of the cross equation symmetry restrictions on the B_{ij} together with the adding up restrictions ensures that the unit cost function is linear homogeneous in its prices. Cost share equations to be estimated after adding up and symmetry restrictions being imposed are as follows :

$$M_O = \alpha_O + \beta_{EO}(\ln P_E - \ln P_O) + \beta_{OC}(\ln P_C - \ln P_O) + u_O,$$
$$M_C = \alpha_C + \beta_{EC}(\ln P_E - \ln P_C) + \beta_{CO}(\ln P_O - \ln P_C) + u_C. \qquad (11)$$

Estimates of α_E, β_{EE}, β_{OO}, and β_{CC} are calculated from (10). But an arbitrary choice of two equations for estimation will result in varying parameter estimates. To avoid this problem, the iterative Zellner efficient (IZEF) method is used. Parameter estimates by this procedure converge to maximum likelihood estimates which are invariant to the equations chosen.[5)]

Following Uzawa,[6)] Allen partial elasticities of substitution between energy input i and j are

$$\sigma_{ij} = \frac{G \cdot G_{ij}}{G_i \cdot G_j}, \qquad i = E, O, C, \qquad (12)$$

where G is a unit energy cost function and G_i and G_{ij} are first and second derivatives of the unit cost function with respect to energy prices. $\sigma_{ij} = \sigma_{ji}$ follows from (12). These Allen partial elasticities of

5) See Zellner (1962), and Oberhofer and Kmenta (1974) for discussions on this subject.

6) Uzawa utilized a unit cost function to derive this condition. Berndt and Christensen (1973) extended the idea to the case of a homothetic production function.

substitution can be calculated from the estimated cost share equations of (11) as follows :

$$\sigma_{ii}=\frac{\beta_{ii}+M_i^2-M_i}{M_i^2}, \qquad i=E, O, C, \tag{13}$$

$$\sigma_{ij}=\frac{\beta_{ij}+M_iM_j}{M_iM_j}, \qquad i, j=E, O, C, \quad i\neq j. \tag{14}$$

Allen has shown that Allen partial elasticities of substitution are related to the price elasticities of demand for factors of production as follows :[7)]

$$E_{ii}=\frac{\partial X_i}{\partial P_i}\cdot\frac{P_i}{X_i}=M_i(\sigma_{ii}-\eta), \qquad i=E, O, C, \tag{15}$$

$$E_{ij}=\frac{\partial X_i}{\partial P_j}\cdot\frac{P_j}{X_i}=M_j(\sigma_{ij}-\eta), \qquad i, j=E, O, C, \ i\neq j \tag{16}$$

where $\eta=\frac{\partial R}{\partial P_R}\cdot\frac{P_R}{R}$ denotes price elasticity of demand for aggregate energy. If R is held constant, η becomes zero and this guarantees the following relations :

$$E_{ii}=M_i\sigma_{ii}=\frac{\beta_{ii}+M_i^2-M_i}{M_i}, \qquad i=E, O, C, \tag{17}$$

$$E_{ij}=M_j\sigma_{ij}=\frac{\beta_{ij}+M_iM_j}{M_i}, \qquad i, j=E, O, C, \quad i\neq j. \tag{18}$$

Since the elasticities of substitution and the price elasticities are functions of cost shares, they will be different across the sample. If the price data are scaled at the means, the estimated constants α_i

---

7) See Allen (1938), p. 508.

($i=E$, O, C) become equal to the fitted cost shares at the means. In this paper, the price elasticities will be calculated at the means of the data by replacing M_i and M_j in (17), (18) by α_i and α_j.

A cost function is well behaved if cost increases monotonically with its input prices and if it is concave to input prices. As the translog cost function does not satisfy these conditions globally, we have to check the conditions separately. Monotonicity requires $\partial G / \partial P_i > 0$. Since $M_i = (\partial G / \partial P_i) \cdot (P_i / G)$, and P_i and G are always positive, the fitted unit cost function increases monotonically in its input prices if the fitted cost shares are positive. Concavity of the translog unit cost function can be checked by the Hessian matrix which is made of second partials of the unit cost function. If the Hessian matrix is negative semidefinite for each observation, the concavity condition is satisfied. This means that the principal minors alternate in sign starting from negative sign. As a measure of goodness of fit, "pseudo-R^2" is calculated. Pseudo-R^2 can be calculated as $1 - \exp(2(L_1 - L_2) / T)$, where L_1 is the logarithm of the maximum likelihood function when the coefficients of all the right hand variables are constrained to zero, L_2 is the logarithm of the maximum likelihood function when the coefficients are unconstrained, and T is the number of observations. The value of pseudo-R^2 is invariant to the choice of equation omitted from the system of cost shares.[8)]

8) See Berndt and Khaled (1977).

III. Data

The data used are national aggregate time-series data ranging from 1962 to 1975. To estimate the cost share equations which are derived from the translog unit cost function, prices and cost shares of three energy sources are constructed from the raw data. The prices for electricity (P_E) are weighted average prices of electricity, where the shares of electricity sale by kinds are used as weights. The prices of oil (P_O) are divisia price indexes of fuel oil. The types of fuel oil used to get the divisia price indexes of fuel oil are gasoline, kerosene, diesel, heavy fuel, bunker-C, propane, and jet fuel. For the prices of coal (P_C), the prices of anthracite coal from government-owned mines are used as an approximation. All the nominal price data are converted into 1970 constant prices using wholesale price indexes. Total cost for energy is the summation of price multiplied by quantity for three energy sources. Cost shares for each energy source are calculated by dividing the expenses for each energy source by total energy cost.

As this paper investigates inter-energy substitution at national aggregate level, national energy consumption data should be adjusted properly to avoid double counting. Oil and coal are the main sources of fuel in generating thermal electricity. So the amounts of heavy fuel oil, diesel oil, and coal which were sold to the electric utilities were subtracted from total consumptions of those respectively to get net consumption data.[9] In Table 1, total

9) In 1975, 21.3 percent of oil and 4.6 percent of coal consumptions were for the

| Table 1 | Total Energy Cost and Cost Shares of Electricity, Fuel and Coal

Year	Total	Cost Shares		
	Energy Cost[a,b]	Electricity	Fuel Oil	Coal
1962	.160	.266	.370	.364
1963	.151	.256	.354	.389
1964	.133	.291	.333	.375
1965	.178	.307	.360	.333
1966	.208	.355	.342	.323
1967	.391	.225	.590	.185
1968	.317	.347	.424	.230
1969	.397	.330	.451	.218
1970	.479	.330	.480	.190
1971	.578	.292	.541	.167
1972	.666	.287	.561	.152
1973	.804	.273	.572	.155
1974	1.210	.211	.682	.106
1975	1.464	.263	.642	.095

[a] Wood and charcoal are not included.
[b] In 1970 billion dollars.

energy cost and cost shares of electricity, net fuel oil, and net coal are reported. Column 1 of Table 1 shows that from 1962 to 1975, expenses for the three energy sources increased more than nine times from $0.160 billion to $1.464 billion. Annual cost share of oil shows continuous rises except in 1975. This trend in oil is

generation of electricity. In 1962, the composition of oil and coal used for the generation of electricity were 12.2 percent and 10.0 percent, respectively. For further information, see Table 15 of Shin (1980).

sharply contrasted to the continuous fall in the cost share of coal. The cost share of electricity rose during the 1960s in general but fell continuously in the 1970s. In 1975, the combined cost shares of electricity and net fuel oil comprised more than 90 percent of the total energy cost.

IV. Empirical Results

Parameter estimates and asymptotic errors with and without the cross equation symmetry restrictions imposed are shown in Table 2. The calculated pseudo-R^2 was 0.754. The cost shares, M_i, are equal to $\partial \ln G / \partial \ln P_i$, which are the percentage changes in the unit cost of energy with respect to the percentage changes in the prices of energy sources. At the means of the data, α_i in Table 2 show the elasticities of unit energy with respect to the energy prices. Table 2 shows that the change in the price of fuel oil had the greatest effect in changing unit cost of aggregate energy.

The likelihood ratio test was performed to check the significance of the cross equation symmetry restrictions. Minus twice the logarithm of a likelihood ratio ($-2\log\lambda$), where λ is the ratio of the maximum value of the likelihood function with the cross equation symmetry restrictions imposed to that without the restrictions imposed, is distributed asymptotically as chi-squared with the degrees of freedom equal to the number of restrictions being tested.[10] The null hypothesis of cross equation symmetry is rejected if and only if the test statistic exceeds the critical value. As

| Table 2| Parameter Estimates of Translog Cost Function

Parameters	Symmetry Constrained	Symmetry Unconstrained
α_E	.287	.287
	(.009)	(.008)
α_C	.234	.234
	(.022)	(.017)
α_O	.479	.479
	(.027)	(.020)
β_{EE}	−.038	.039
	(.038)	(.066)
β_{EC}	.127	.035
	(.042)	(.068)
β_{CE}	.127	.371
	(.042)	(.141)
β_{EO}	−.087	−.077
	(.027)	(.025)
β_{OE}	−.087	−.409
	(.027)	(.167)
β_{CC}	−.108	−.441
	(.071)	(.147)
β_{CO}	−.021	−.016
	(.068)	(.053)
β_{OC}	−.021	.406
	(.068)	(.174)
β_{OO}	.108	.094
	(.083)	(.063)
pseudo-R^2	.754	

* Figures in parentheses are asymptotic standard errors.

10) See Theil (1971), p. 98 and p. 396.

shown in Table 3, the cross equation symmetry restriction was not rejected at the 0.01 significance level. Monotonicity of the unit cost function was checked by the fitted values of the cost shares. Since all 42 fitted cost shares were positive, the monotonicity condition was satisfied. Concavity of the unit cost function was checked by examining the signs of the principal minors at each observation. First and second ordered principal minors had the correct signs in all but one observation. In addition to the tests of regularity conditions, the test to see if there is a significant difference in the estimation results of translog and Cobb-Douglas functions was performed and the result is shown in the right column of Table 3. The test result shows that the translog functional form gives significantly more information than the Cobb-Douglas functional form.

| **Table 3** | Test of Hypotheses

	Cross-Equation Symmetry of B_{ij}	Cobb-Douglas Functional Form
Test Statistic	8.30	19.62
Degrees of Freedom	3	6
χ^2 Critical Value[a]	11.34	16.81
Test Results	Not rejected	Rejected

[a] At the .01 significance level.

The estimates of the price elasticities at the means of the data are shown in Table 4 together with asymptotic standard errors. These estimates show the responses of energy consumption to the changes in the prices of energy sources when total energy is

| Table 4 | Estimates of Price Elasticities (Total Energy Constant)

Elasticity	Estimates
E_{EE}	−.853
	(.132)
E_{CC}	−1.221
	(.311)
E_{OO}	−.297
	(.175)
E_{EC}	.678
	(.147)
E_{CE}	.829
	(.184)
E_{EO}	.175
	(.098)
E_{OE}	.105
	(.058)
E_{CO}	.391
	(.292)
E_{OC}	.192
	(.144)

* Figures in parentheses are asymptotic standard errors.

constant.[11] All the estimated own price elasticities have correct signs. The estimated price elasticity for coal is greater than one, and the estimated price elasticities for electricity and fuel oil are less than one. All the estimates of the cross price elasticities have

11) If total energy is allowed to vary, own price elasticities will be greater in absolute values and cross price elasticities will be smaller than the estimated results of Table 4. For further discussion on this topic, refer to Shin (1981).

positive signs, implying that all three energy sources are substitutable.

V. Concluding Remarks

The translog cost function was employed for the analysis of inter-energy substitution in Korea. The model performed well satisfying most of the conditions checked. Estimated cross price elasticities showed that electricity, coal, and oil are all substitutable. Among these energy sources, electricity and coal turned out to be the best substitutes. As most of the coal consumption in Korea was by residential and commercial sectors, this finding suggests that the increasing energy demand in the residential and commercial sectors can best be met by increasing the supply of electric energy. With limited hydro resources and poor coal reserves, and under the increasing burden of oil import, the construction of nuclear power plants is one of few choices available to Korea. Of course, the environmental effects of nuclear power plants should be considered carefully when planning future energy policy.

Three comments on the interpretation of the present study are in order. First, the data used for the analysis were highly aggregated national time-series data which could not allow for variations across different sectors and industries. If proper data were available, disaggregated studies in the manufacturing industry or at the individual industry level would produce more fruitful results. Second, as the consumption data for coal and oil were net of the amounts sold to electric utilities, the estimated cross elasticities show substitution possibilities among secondary energy sources. The results should not be used to get an insight into the problem of substitution among primary energy sources. Third, the analysis is partial in that total energy consumption is kept constant. If unit energy cost changes, relative prices among labor, capital, and energy will change and substitutions among factors of production will take place.

Appendix : Sources of Data

Annual Statistics of Korea Electric Company (1978) : Korea Electric Company.

Economic Statistics Yearbooks (1967–1976) : The Bank of Korea.

Energy Summary : The Korea Atomic Energy Research Institute, 1976.

Korea Statistics Yearbooks (1962–1976) : Economic Planning Board.

Price Summaries (1968, 1977) : The Bank of Korea.

The Comprehensive Energy Policy : Ministry of Energy and Natural Resources, 1978.

The Comprehensive Plan for Energy Supply–Demand to the Year 2000 : Ministry of Energy and Natural Resources, 1978.

References

Allen, R. G. D., *Mathematical Analysis for Economists*, London, McMillan,

1938, pp. 503-509.

Berndt, E. R. and L. R. Christensen, "The Internal Structure of Functional Relationships : Separability, Substitution, and Aggregation," *Review of Economic Studies*, July 1973, pp. 403-410.

______, and M. S. Khaled, "Economies of scale and Bised Productivity Gains in U.S. Manufacturing, 1947-71," Discussion Paper No. 77-23, University of British Columbia, August 1977.

______, and D. O. Wood, "Technology, Prices and the Derived Demand for Energy," *Review of Economics and Statistics* 57, August 1975, PP. 259-268.

Christensen, L. R., D. W. Jorgensen, and L. J. Lau, "Conjugate Duality and the Transcendental Logarithmic Production Function," *Econometrica* 39, July 1971, pp. 255-256.

______, "Transcendental Logarithmic Production Frontiers," *The Review of Economics and Statistics* 55, February 1973, pp. 28-45.

Halvorsen, R., "Energy Substitution in U.S. Manufacturing," *The Review of Economics and Statistics*, November 1977, pp. 381-388.

______, *Econometric Models of U.S. Energy Demand*. Lexington, Lexington Books, 1978.

Hulten, C. R., "Divisia Index Numbers," *Econometrica* 41, November 1973, pp. 1017-1026.

Oberhofer, W., and J. Kmenta, "A General Procedure for Obtaining Maximum Likelihood Estimates in Generalized Regression Models," *Econometrica* 42, May 1974, pp. 579-590.

Shin, E., *Impact of the 1973-74 Oil Crisis and Energy Substitution in Korea*, unpublished Ph. D. dissertation, University of Washington, 1980.

______, "Elasticities of Substitution and Firm Behavior," Social Sciences

Working paper, California Institute of Technology, 1981.

Theil, H., *Principles of Econometrics*, John Wiley and Sons, Inc., 1971.

Uzawa, H., "Production Functions with Constant Elasticities of Substitution," *Review of Economic Studies* 29, October 1962, pp. 291–299.

Zellner, A., "An Efficient Method of Estimating Seemingly Unrelated Regressions and Tests for Aggregation Bias," *Journal of American Statistical Association* 57, June 1962, pp. 348–368.

2. The Impact of the First Oil Crisis on Energy Demand in Korea*

This paper investigates how the first oil crisis affected energy demand in Korea. First, annual growth rates in energy consumptions for pre-and post-crisis periods are compared. Second, the price and income elasticities of energy sources estimated from the 1961-72 and 1961-76 observations are compared. Third, F-test is performed with an oil demand equation to see whether a structural change in oil demand occurred after the first oil crisis. The author concludes that the impact of the first oil crisis in Korea was not serious enough to cause a structural change in oil demand.

I. Introduction

The two unhappy experiences of the world oil crisis in the 1970s

* "The impact of the first oil crisis on energy demand in Korea," *Energy Economics*, Vol. 4, No. 4 (October 1982), pp. 259-267.

changed people's perception of oil as cheap and the best available energy source in the world. Oil might still be hailed as one of the most environmentally acceptable energy sources, but it is no longer cheap. The first oil crisis of 1973-74 quadrupled the price of oil in two years and the second oil crisis of 1978-79 tripled it in two years. Consequently, importing countries have to pay as much as $34.00 for a barrel of crude oil today while they paid less than $3.00/bbl up until the outbreak of the 1973-74 oil crisis.

After the first oil crisis, various studies investigated the impact of the higher oil prices on energy consumptions in oil importing countries.[1] However, most of these studies centered around the OECD countries and little, if any, is known about the impact of the 1973-74 oil crisis on less developed countries. To fill the gap, this paper examines how the 1973-74 oil crisis affected energy consumption in Korea.

II. Energy Demand in Korea

Korea achieved a remarkable economic growth through a successful series of five-year economic development plans. The first five-year economic development plan of 1962-66 brought an annual GNP growth rate of 7.8% and the second five-year economic development plan of 1967-71 resulted in an annual growth rate of 10.5%. Influenced by the 1973-74 oil crisis, GNP

1) For example, Bundy, Fried and Schultze, and Nordhaus.

growth rate stayed at 8.7% in 1974 and 8.3% in 1975. But Korea fully recovered from the impact of the oil crisis in 1976, realizing a 15.2% GNP growth rate.

The rapid economic growth in Korea was made possible by rapid industrialization. In 1961, the agricultural sector composed 44.1% while the industrial sector composed 11.9% of total value added. By 1975, the composition of the industrial sector increased to 29.1%, exceeding the agricultural sector's 25.7%. This rapid industrialization was accompanied by a rapid growth in energy consumption. As Korea is poorly endowed with energy resources, the increase in energy demand made an increase in energy imports inevitable. In 1962, Korea imported only 10.7% of total energy, but this rose to 52.3% in 1975.

Table 1 shows the share of each energy source in total energy consumption.[2)] Up to the early 1960s, wood and charcoal had been the dominant energy sources in Korea. In 1961, wood and charcoal composed 56.7% of total energy consumption. But the Korean government began to curb the use of wood and charcoal as energy sources to protect forest resources and encouraged the production and consumption of coal. During the first five-year economic development plan of 1962-66, the consumption of coal increased at the annual rate of 14.3%, composing 46.9% of total energy consumption in 1966. During the second five-year economic devel-

---

2) In Table 1, the share of electricity shows only the quantity of energy supplied by hydro power plants. However, while hydro power plants supplied 1.2% of total energy consumption in 1973, total electricity consumption composed 11.5% of total energy consumed in that year.

opment plan of 1967–71, the consumption of oil increased at the annual rate of 40.9% while coal consumption grew only 0.5% a year. In 1971, oil composed 52.7% while coal composed 27.5% and wood/charcoal composed 18.3% of total energy consumption. As a result, oil became the dominant energy source in Korea from the beginning of the 1970s.

|**Table 1**| Composition of Energy Consumption by Source (%).[a]

Year	Coal	Oil	Electricity[b]	Wood/Charcoal
1961	33.4	8.2	1.6	56.7
1962	38.0	9.8	1.7	50.5
1963	42.2	10.3	1.6	45.9
1964	44.3	9.6	1.6	44.5
1965	45.1	12.0	1.4	41.4
1966	46.9	16.6	1.8	34.6
1967	42.3	26.0	1.6	30.0
1968	34.8	34.9	1.4	28.9
1969	31.9	42.4	1.9	23.8
1970	29.7	48.4	1.5	20.5
1971	27.5	52.7	1.5	18.3
1972	26.7	54.9	1.5	17.0
1973	28.8	56.6	1.2	13.4
1974	28.8	56.7	1.7	12.7
1975	28.8	59.0	1.5	10.7
1976	28.2	60.6	1.4	9.8

Source : The Comprehensive Energy Policy, pp. 22–25.

[a] Compared in kilo calorie (1 kilo calorie = 3.968 Btu).

[b] Hydro only.

|**Table 2**| Changes in Energy Consumption (%)

	Average annual growth rate		Percentage change from previous year			
	1962-66	1967-71	1973	1974	1975	1976
Electricity[a]	20.5	24.3	23.7	14.1	17.9	18.0
Coal[b]	14.3	0.5	24.5	2.7	5.9	9.8
Oil[c]	23.4	40.9	19.5	1.6	8.5	14.8
Wood/Charcoal[d]	−3.9	−2.2	−8.0	−4.0	−12.1	2.4
Petrol(gasoline)	25.6	24.6	6.7	−32.9	−4.9	26.2
Kerosene	19.2	40.4	1.3	−18.6	63.1	10.5
Diesel	26.0	31.4	21.4	2.8	14.1	23.3
Heavy oil	3.9	4.6	21.7	−0.3	0.3	14.7
Bunker-c	na	65.7	20.2	3.7	8.6	10.9
LPG	na	70.6	56.4	33.8	26.7	8.7
JET	na	46.4	−15.1	7.3	9.9	14.3

[a] Total electricity consumed (compared in kWh).
[b] Total coal consumed (compared in metric ton).
[c] Total oil consumed (compared in barrel).
[d] Compared in barrel of oil equivalent.
na : Data during this period are not available.

Table 2 compares the change in energy consumption rates during the first and second five-year economic development planning periods and the post-crisis period. Electricity consumption has grown at lower rates since 1974 compared to the pre-crisis periods, but the difference was not large compared to other energy sources. One reason for this is that there are no good substitutes for electricity. Another reason is that the price of electricity did not rise as high as the price of oil.[3)]

Coal consumption increased 24.5% in 1973, which was a significant departure from the annual growth rate of 0.5% during the second economic development planning period. This sudden increase in coal consumption in 1973 was made possible by depleting accumulated coal inventory. But coal consumption has grown at only moderate rates since 1974.

In 1974, oil comumption increased only 1.6%. This was a dramatic drop compared to the annual growth rate of 40.9% during the 1967–71 period. The impact of higher oil prices on oil consumption is more clearly reflected by the decrease in the consumption of petrol, kerosene, and heavy oil after the oil crisis.

III. Energy Demand Equations and Data

1. Electricity

The demand equation shows the response of quantity purchased to the changes in the prices of own and closely related goods and income. If the prices and income are exogenously given, ordinary least squares estimation of a double-log demand equation will give consistent estimates of the elasticities of demand. But the use of declining bloc rates for electricity makes the unit price of electricity a function of quantity purchased.[4] It means that the price and

3) From 1972 to 1976, the price index of electricity rose from 114 to 254 while the price index of oil rose from 157 to 714.

4) The electric bill in Korea is composed of two parts. One is monthly basic charge

quantity purchased of electricity are simultaneously determined in the system of demand and price equations. The specifications of structural demand and price equations of electricity used in this study are

$$\ln Q_E = a_0 + a_1 \ln P_E + a_2 \ln Y + U \qquad (1)$$
$$\ln P_E = b_0 + b_1 \ln Q_E + b_2 \ln P_A + V, \qquad (2)$$

where Q_E is the quantity of electricity purchased, P_E is the price of electricity, P_A is the production cost of electricity, and U and V are disturbance terms. In the electricity demand Equation (1), a_1 is the own price elasticity with negative expected sign and a_2 is the income elasticity with positive expected sign. In the electricity price Equation (2), the expected sign of b_1 is negative due to the declining bloc rates for electricity. The expected sign of b_2 is positive as the price of electricity would change to the same direction as the cost of production.

2. Oil and coal

Oil and coal are used as energy sources for the production of

---

and the other is pro-rated monthly use charge. So the price of electricity per kWh decreases as more electricity is purchased, and the more the price of electricity is different for different sectors and time of day. While declining block rates are applied to the industrial sector, an inverted rate structure is applied to the residential sector. As the industrial sector composes more than 80% of total electric energy consumption in Korea, it can be generalized that the declining bloc rates are applied in Korea. For more information on electricity in Korea, see Jang(1977).

various commodities and services. Some is used to generate electricity in thermal power plants. In 1961, 4.4% of oil and 13.7% of coal were consumed for the generation of electricity. But in 1976, the shares of oil and coal were 21.6% and 5.8% respectively. As considerable portions of oil and coal are used for the generation of electricity, we need to check the sensitivity of estimated demand elasticities when gross and net consumption data are used.

Considering this, we specified and estimated oil and coal demand equations for the following three categories : gross demand, net demand, and the demand for the generation of electricity which will be called generating demand hereafter. The gross and net demand equations for oil and coal are

$$\ln Q_i = C_{i0} + C_{i1} \ln P_i + C_{i2} \ln P_j + C_{i3} \ln Y + Z_i \,, \quad (i, j = oil,\ coal,\ i \neq j) \tag{3}$$

where Q_i is a gross consumption for gross demand and a net consumption for net demand, P_i is own price, P_j is the price of substitute, Y is income, and Z_i is a disturbance term. In the gross and net demand Equations (3), the coefficients of $\ln P_i$, C_{i1}, are the own price elasticities with negative expected signs, the coefficients of $\ln P_j$, C_{i2}, are the cross price elasticities with positive expected signs, and C_{i3} are the income elasticities with positive expected signs.

The generating demands for oil and coal are derived demands from electricity production function. So the generating oil and coal demand equations are factor demand equations as follows :

$$\ln Q_i^E = d_{i0} + d_{i1} \ln P_i^E + d_{i2} \ln P_j^E + d_{i3} \ln Q_E + V_i, \quad (4)$$
$$(i, j = oil, coal, i \neq j)$$

where P_O^E and P_C^E are the prices of oil and coal which are used in thermal power plants, Q_E is total electricity generated from thermal power plants, and V_i is disturbance term.[5] In the generating oil and coal Equations (4), d_{i1} and d_{i2} are the own and cross factor price elasticities and their expected signs are negative and positive, respectively. The expected signs of d_{i3} are positive if oil and coal are not inferior factors in generating electricity.

Besides the aggregate oil demand equations specified above, demand equations for major oil products are specified as follows :

$$\ln Q_i = \alpha_0 + \alpha_1 \ln P_i + \alpha_2 \ln P_j + \alpha_3 \ln Y + \varepsilon_i, \quad (5)$$

where Q_i is the quantity demanded of individual oil product i, P_i is own price, P_j is the price of the best substitutable fuel including coal, Y is gross national product, and ε_i is a disturbance term. The expected signs of α_1, α_2, α_3 are respectively negative, positive and positive.

---

5) The correct specification of the factor demand equation for oil would be $Q_O^E = f(P_K, P_L, P_C, P_O, Q_E)$, where P_K and P_L are respectively the rental price of capital service and wage rate in generating the electricity. P_K and P_L are not included in the specification for lack of data availability. Fuel cost composed 55.4% of production cost and 20.2% of supply cost in 1972. In 1975, fuel cost composed of 85.1% of production cost and 53.4% of supply cost.

3. Data

Energy consumption data used for the estimation of energy demand equations are national time-series data. The prices of electricity, oil, and coal (P_E, P_O, P_C) used in the aggregate oil and coal demand equations are annual energy price indices published in the *Economic Statistics Yearbook*.

The appropriate price variable to be included in the electricity demand equation is marginal price. However, as Halvorsen(1975) has shown, the estimated elasticities obtained by average price data are identical to those obtained by marginal price data. In the present study, the electricity price index is utilized for P_E. For the production cost of electricity, P_A, the Divisia price index of heavy oil, diesel oil, and coal which are fuels for electric generation is used as a proxy variable. The Divisia price index for fuel is derived from

$$\log P_t - \log P_{t-1} = \sum_{i=1}^{n} \frac{1}{2}[S_{i,t} + S_{i,t-1}] \times [\log \dot{P}_{i,t} - \log P_{i,t-1}],$$

(i=heavy oil, diesel oil, and coal ; t=time)

where

$$S_{i,t} = P_{i,t}\, q_{i,t} \,/ \sum_{i=1}^{n} P_{i,t}\, q_{i,t} \,,$$

which is relative share of *i*th fuel in period *t*. The weight shown above is arithmetic weight. But we can alternatively use geometric weight or combined weight instead. The change in the logarithm of Divisia price index is a weighted average of the changes in the logarithm of the individual fuel prices. By normalizing and taking antilogarithms, we can get the Divisia price index for fuel.[6)]

Energy cost shares of each fuel for thermal electric generation are shown in Table 3. Coal was the main fuel for thermal electric generation in Korea up to the first half of the 1960s, reaching its peak in 1965 with the energy cost share of 73.1%. But the importance of coal as a fuel for electric generation has diminished

Table 3 Energy Cost Share of Fuel in Thermal Power Plants (%).

Year	Heavy oil	Diesel oil	Coal
1961	20.8	0.5	78.7
1962	40.5	7.6	51.9
1963	43.5	2.8	53.7
1964	40.9	3.0	56.1
1965	25.4	1.5	73.1
1966	36.9	1.6	61.5
1967	41.7	15.8	42.4
1968	37.0	30.6	32.4
1969	50.8	22.3	26.9
1970	74.3	10.0	15.7
1971	83.1	3.9	13.0
1972	84.3	2.1	13.6
1973	83.5	1.4	15.2
1974	93.1	3.7	3.2
1975	94.9	1.8	3.2
1976	94.3	1.8	4.0

* Energy cost share= $\frac{P_iQ_i}{\sum_i P_iQ_i}$ (i=heavy oil, diesel oil, coal)

6) Refer to Hulten for further discussion on Divisia index numbers.

since 1965 as relatively cheap oil replaced coal, composing only 4.0% of total energy cost for thermal electric generation in 1975. On the other hand, the energy cost share of heavy oil (mostly bunker-C oil) rose to 94.3% in 1976 from a mere 20.8% in 1961. The share of diesel oil was less than 10% except for the period of 1967 to 1970.

For the price of oil in the generating oil demand, P_O^E, Divisia price index of heavy oil and diesel oil is used. The prices used for the major oil product equations are actual prices per kilolitre. All the nominal price data are converted to 1970 real price data using wholesale price indices. The data used for income, Y, are 1970-constant gross national product data.[7] In the following section, we will discuss the regression results of the energy demand equations estimated with 1961-76 data.

IV. Estimation Results

1. Electricity

The electricity demand equation is estimated by the ordinary least squares (OLS) as well as by the two-stage least squares (TSLS). The estimation results are shown in Table 4. All the signs of estimated coefficients in the electricity price equation matched our prior expectations. The estimated coefficient of production cost approxi

7) For the source of data, see Shin(1980).

Table 4 Electricity Demand Equations

(1) Electricity demand equation (OLS)

$$\ln Q_E = -0.25 - 0.16 \ln P_E + 1.97^a \ln Y$$
$$(0.54) \quad (0.24) \qquad (0.07)$$

$R^2 = 0.991$ $DW = 0.75$

(2) Electricity demand equation (TSLS)

$$\ln Q_E = 3.07 - 2.11 \ln P_E + 1.60^a \ln Y$$
$$(2.68) \quad (1.71) \qquad (0.35)$$

$R^2 = 0.944$ $DW = 1.13$

(3) Electricity price equation (OLS)

$$\ln P_E = 1.68^a - 0.11^a \ln Q_E + 0.07 \ln P_A$$
$$(0.50) \quad (0.03) \qquad (0.07)$$

$R^2 = 0.479$ $DW = 0.98$

(4) Reduced form equation for quantity purchased (OLS)

$$\ln Q_E = 0.70^b - 0.20^a \ln P_A + 2.09^a \ln Y$$
$$(0.28) \quad (0.04) \qquad (0.04)$$

$R^2 = 0.997$ $DW = 2.56$

(5) Reduced form equation for price (OLS)

$$\ln P_E = 1.79^a + 0.09 \ln P_A - 0.23^a \ln Y$$
$$(0.51) \quad (0.07) \qquad (0.07)$$

$R^2 = 0.492$ $DW = 0.95$

Note : The numbers in the parentheses are standard errors.
[a] Significant at the 0.01 level.
[b] Significant at the 0.05 level.

mated by Divisia price index for fuel was positive as expected. The negative sign of the estimated coefficient of $\ln Q_E$ confirmed the declining rate structure for the unit price of electricity. The value of R^2 for the electricity price equation was 0.48. The reason for this low value of 'goodness of fit' is because several variables such as labour and capital costs were not considered in approximating the production cost of electricity for lack of data. The estimated results of the reduced form equations for both quantity purchased and price also matched the expected signs as derived from the coefficients of the electricity demand and price equations.

The electricity demand equation estimated by TSLS using $\ln P_A$ and $\ln Y$ as instrumental variables show significantly different results from the one estimated by OLS. The two-stage least squares resulted in an estimated price elasticity of −2.11 while the ordinary least squares generated −0.16. The estimated income elasticities were elastic, both significant at the 0.01 level. Even though the t-value for the estimated price elasticity was higher in the estimation by the two-stage least squares, the estimation result of the structural price equation was not good enough to totally accept the estimated coefficients by the TSLS.

The possibility of serial correlation in error terms was checked by the Durbin-Watson test. The null hypothesis of serial independency in error terms was rejected in the electricity demand equation estimated by ordinary least squares. When estimated by two-stage least squares, the null hypothesis was accepted at the 95% confidence level.

2. Oil

Oil demand equations estimated by OLS are shown in Table 5.

|**Table 5**| Demands for Gross and Net Oil

	Gross		Net	
	$\ln Q_0$	$\ln Q_0$	$\ln Q_0^N$	$\ln Q_0^N$
Constant	-11.53^a (0.52)	-6.13^a (1.18)	-10.96^a (0.50)	-5.67^a (1.07)
$\ln P_0$	-0.60^a (0.08)	-0.41^a (0.06)	-0.58^a (0.08)	-0.42^a (0.05)
$\ln P_C$	1.41^a (0.28)	1.21^a (0.22)	1.48^a (0.27)	1.10^a (0.21)
$\ln Y$	2.64^a (0.07)	1.49^a (0.26)	2.54^a (0.07)	1.38^a (0.23)
Lag ln	×	0.41^a (0.09)	×	0.44^a (0.09)
R^2	0.993	0.998	0.993	0.998
Degrees of freedom	12	10	12	10
DW	1.98	1.85	1.82	2.59

Note : The numbers in the parentheses are standard errors.
[a] Significant at the 0.01 level.
x : not included in the specification.

All the estimated coefficients were significant at the 0.01 level and the signs were all as expected. In all the static oil demand equations, the null hypotheses of no serial correlation in error terms were accepted at the 95% confidence level.[8)]

In the static gross oil demand equation, the own price elasticity was −0.60, the cross price elasticity of oil with respect to the price

8) The Durbin-Watson test for serial correlation can be used only when the regression equation does not have a lagged dependent variable in the right hand side of the equation.

of coal was 1.41, and income elasticity was 2.64. The estimated elasticities from static equations are believed to generate medium-run elasticities. To get the short-and long-run elasticities separately, we need to estimate the dynamic equations which include lag-dependent variables in the specification.

In the gross dynamic oil demand equation, the short-run own price elasticity of oil was −0.41, and the short-run income elasticity was 1.49. The long-run price and income elasticities, calculated as short-run elasticities divided by one minus the estimated coefficient of lag term, were respectively −0.69 and 2.53. These values of long-run elasticities calculated from the dynamic oil demand equation were very close to the short-run elasticities estimated from the static oil demand equation.

The estimated elasticities from the net oil demand equations were virtually the same as those from the gross oil demand equations. This result shows that there is little difference in the estimates of price and income elasticities whether we use gross or net consumption data.

The estimation results of the generating oil demand equation are shown in Table 6. The estimated own price elasticity was correct in sign and was significant at the 0.05 level. The estimated cross price elasticity with respect to the price of coal was positive, but was insignificant. The estimated output elasticity was elastic, significant at the 0.01 level.

3. Coal

The estimation results of the coal demand equations are shown

|**Table 6**| Generating Demands for Oil and Coal

	Generating oil $\ln Q_0^E$	Generating coal $\ln Q_C^E$
Constant	-9.58^a (2.27)	19.74^a (2.01)
$\ln P_0^E$	-0.42^b (0.17)	-0.06 (0.15)
$\ln P_C^E$	0.30 (0.79)	-1.73^c (0.70)
$\ln Q_E$	1.41^a (0.10)	-0.03 (0.09)
R^2	0.959	0.456
Degrees of freedom	12	12
DW	1.67	1.57

Note : The numbers in the parentheses are standard errors.
[a] Significant at the 0.01 level.
[b] Significant at the 0.05 level.
[c] Significant at the 0.10 level.

in Table 7. In all the static coal demand equations, the null hypotheses were accepted at the 95% confidence level.

In the static gross coal demand equation, the estimated own price and income elasticities were correct in signs and were both inelastic at the 0.01 significance level. But contrary to our expectation, the estimated cross price elasticity of coal with respect to the price of oil was negative. Nevertheless, the low level of t -value does not allow the acceptance of the estimated sign. In the dynamic gross coal demand equation, the cross price elasticity of coal turned out to be positive, confusing its true sign.

I suspect that this low robustness of the estimated value of cross

|**Table 7**| Demands for Gross and Net Oil

	Gross		Net	
	$\ln Q_C$	$\ln Q_C$	$\ln Q_C^N$	$\ln Q_C^N$
Constant	4.33[a] (0.39)	3.06[a] (0.87)	3.71[a] (0.38)	3.27[a] (0.81)
$\ln P_C$	−0.82[a] (0.21)	−0.35 (0.23)	−0.73[a] (0.21)	−0.29[a] (0.21)
$\ln P_O$	−0.06 (0.06)	0.03 (0.06)	−0.05 (0.06)	0.03 (0.06)
$\ln Y$	0.65[a] (0.05)	0.30[c] (0.14)	0.72[a] (0.05)	0.43[b] (0.16)
Lag ln	×	0.42[c] (0.19)	×	0.29 (0.21)
R^2	0.937	0.950	0.950	0.960
Degrees of freedom	12	10	12	10
DW	1.63	2.04	1.85	2.11

Note : The numbers in the parentheses are standard errors.
× : not included in the specification.
[a] Significant at the 0.01 level.
[b] Significant at the 0.05 level.
[c] Significant at the 0.10 level.

price elasticity of coal is due to the unique pattern of coal consumption in Korea. Coal consumption in Korea had increased through 1967 substituting wood and charcoal. But the energy modernization policy abruptly changed the trend of coal consumption, resulting in a decrease in the absolute amount of coal consumption in 1968. From then on, the level of coal consumption stayed nearly constant until the outbreak of the 1973–74 oil crisis. Therefore, the coal consumption data during the period of 1967 to

1972 does not accord with the theoretical equilibrium quantity of coal purchased at the market clearing price. As the government's energy policy restricted the use of coal for a considerable period of time, it could not function as a substitute for oil in the normal sense.

The distinctive difference between the estimates of oil and coal demand equations can be found in the income elasticity. While the estimated income elasticity was elastic for oil, it was inelastic for coal. This empirical evidence signifies the popularity of oil as a preferred form of energy as income level increases.

The estimation result of the generating coal demand equation is shown in Table 6. The result showed poor fit, with R^2 value of only 0.46 and low t-values for the estimates. With this poor fitting of the equation in mind, the negative sign of the estimated output elasticity could be interpreted that coal has become an inferior factor in generating thermal electricity.

The estimated short-run price and income elasticities from the dynamic gross coal demand equation were −0.35 and 0.30, respectively. The t-values of the estimates were considerably lower than the estimates of the static demand equation. The long-run price and income elasticities were calculated as −0.60 and 0.52, respectively. The net coal demand equations resulted in similar estimates to those of gross coal demand equations.

4. Oil products

In specifying the oil product equation, we included only the price of the best substitutable fuel besides own price and income to save degrees of freedom. The fuels selected as the best substitutes in each equation are diesel oil for the petrol demand equation, petrol for the diesel oil demand equation, and coal for the kerosene demand equation. Coal is selected as the best substitute for kerosene because most of the kerosene (91.0% in 1970 and 84.8% in 1973 of total kerosene consumption) had been used in the residential sector, where coal was an important energy source.

Oil product demand equations are estimated by the Cochrane–Orcutt procedure as well as by the ordinary least squares considering possible serial correlation in the variables left out of the specification. If there is a serial correlation in error terms, the ordinary least squares method does not generate the best linear unbiased estimates even if they are unbiased. The Cochrane–Orcutt procedure is an alternative to the ordinary least squares method when there is a problem of serial correlation. If the variables left-out are important ones, the estimates of the equation will also be biased.

The estimation results are shown in Table 8. Petrol and diesel oil demand equations were better with the Cochrane–Orcutt procedure while the kerosene demand equation showed a better result with the OLS method. All the estimated elasticities were correct in signs and values of R^2 were satisfactorily high in all equations. The estimated own price elasticity was elastic for petrol while it was inelastic for diesel and kerosene, all significant at the 0.01 level. The estimated cross price elasticities were all inelastic. Only the cross price elasticity of kerosene with respect to the price of coal was significant

|Table 8| Demands for Gasoline, Diesel, and Kerosene

	$\ln Q_G$	$\ln Q_D$	$\ln Q_K$
Constant	-5.06^b (1.96)	-6.74^a (0.48)	-6.03^a (0.69)
$\ln P_G$	-1.16^a (0.30)	0.10 (0.10)	
$\ln P_D$	0.50 (0.54)	-0.75^a (0.19)	
$\ln P_K$			-0.87^a (0.10)
$\ln P_C$			2.07^a (0.34)
$\ln Y$	2.06^a (0.26)	2.26^a (0.05)	2.15^a (0.08)
R^2	0.962	0.991	0.985
Degrees of freedom	11	11	12
DW	1.64	2.15	1.87

Note : The numbers in the parentheses are standard errors. Petrol and diesel demand equations are estimated by the Cochrane-Orcutt procedure and the kerosene demand equation is estimated by ordinary least squares.

[a] Significant at the 0.01 level.
[b] Significant at the 0.05 level.

at the 0.01 level. The estimated income elasticities were greater than two in all the equations and were significant at the 0.01 level. The values of the estimated income elasticities in the oil products equations were in fact very close to the estimated income elasticities from the aggregate oil demand equations reported in Table 5. The estimated own price elasticities were slightly higher in the oil products equations than in the aggregate oil demand equations.

V. Impact of the 1973-74 Oil Crisis on Energy Demand Elasticities

The estimated price and income elasticities of various energy sources are reported in Table 9. The entries under '1961-72 data' show the price and income elasticities estimated by the pre-crisis observations. These elasticities show the historical trends which would have continued without the interruption of the 1973-74 oil crisis.

The entries under '1961-76 data' reveal the changes in the price and income elasticities from the historical trends when the four post-crisis observations including 1973 are added to the data base.

|Table 9| Estimated Elasticities by 1961-72 and 1961-76 Data

	1961-72 data		1961-76 data	
	Price	Income (GNP)	Price	Income (GNP)
Electricity	×	2.09[a]	×	1.60[a]
Aggregate oil	−0.47[b]	2.78[a]	−0.60[a]	2.64[a]
Aggregate coal	−0.58[b]	0.40[a]	−0.82[a]	0.65[a]
Petrol	−0.99[b]	2.62[a]	−1.16[a]	2.06[a]
Kerosene	−0.64[a]	2.38[a]	−0.87[a]	2.15[a]
Diesel	−0.62[b]	2.35[a]	−0.75[a]	2.26[a]

Note : Electricity demand equation is estimated by the two-stage least squares, petrol and diesel demand equations are estimated by the Cochrane-Orcutt procedure, and the rest are estimated by ordinary least squares.

[a] Significant at the 0.01 level.

[b] Significant at the 0.05 level.

[c] Significant at the 0.10 level.

× : Not compared for lack of credibility.

By comparing the price and income elasticities from the two estimations, we can get an idea about whether the oil crisis has changed the pattern of energy consumption in Korea. While most of the estimated elasticities in Table 9 are significant at the 0.01 level, the estimated price elasticities for electricity were poor in t-value, so they are not included.

The comparison of the estimated own price elasticities from the two data sets shows that the energy consumption in Korea became more price responsive as a result of the oil crisis. All the estimated own price elasticities became greater in absolute values when the four observations were added. The comparison of estimated income elasticities shows another interesting fact. While the income elasticities became smaller for electricity and oil when the four post-crisis observations are added, the income elasticity for coal became greater with the inclusion of the four additional data. This result reveals that the oil crisis made coal a relatively more favoured energy source compared to the pre-crisis period. But still the income elasticity for coal was inelastic while other energy sources were elastic.

Table 9 shows clearly the direction of changes in price and income elasticities when the four post-crisis observations are added. However, the comparison is not sufficient to show whether there was a structural change in energy consumption due to the oil crisis. In the following analysis, we will perform an F-test to see whether a structural shift has taken place in energy consumption in Korea between pre-and post-crisis periods. In the present study, only the oil demand equation will be subjected to the test because none of the other equations gave satisfactory estimation results either in signs or t -values of the estimated coefficients.

The oil demand equation :

$$\ln Q_0 = a_0 + a_1 \ln P_0 + a_2 \ln P_C + a_3 \ln Y + \varepsilon$$

can be separately written for pre-and post-crisis periods using matrix notation as follows :

$$y_1 = X_1 \beta_1 + \varepsilon_1 \qquad (6)$$

$$y_2 = X_2 \beta_2 + \varepsilon_2 \qquad (7)$$

Equation (6) is for the pre-crisis period with 12 observations, where y_1 is a (12×1) column vector, X_1 is a (12×4) matrix, and β_1 is a (4×1) vector of coefficients. Equation (7) is for the post-crisis period with 4 observations. The null hypothesis to be tested is

$$\beta_1 = \beta_2,$$

which implies no structural change in oil demand between the pre- and post-crisis periods.

As the number of additional observations in the post-crisis period is not greater than the number of parameters to be estimated, we will utilize the test method developed by Chow. Before performing the Chow-test, the predicted values of the dependent variable calculated using the estimated coefficients of the Equation (6) are compared to the actual values.

As shown above, all the predicted values of oil consumption are upward biased. It is because the estimated own price elasticity of oil by the 1961-72 observations was too small in absolute value to

	Logarithms of actual oil consumption	Logarithms of predicted oil consumption	Actual value minus predicted value
1973	9.70382	9.88833	−0.18451
1974	9.71987	9.74080	−0.02093
1975	9.80168	9.96955	−0.16787
1976	9.93943	10.35903	−0.41960

fully predict the conservation effect caused by the higher oil prices. At the same time, the estimated income elasticity was too big, so the increase in oil consumption due to the increased GNP was over predicted. This result is consistent with the implication obtained when we compared the price and income elasticities estimated separately by the 1961–72 and 1961–76 data. The residuals of estimated dependent variables are relatively large compared to the standard error of the regression which is 0.08336 and the deviation of the predicted from actual oil consumption grew annually since 1974. This fact can be interpreted to show the change in the course of oil consumption after the oil crisis.

The F-statistic to be used for the Chow-test is

$$F = \frac{(B-A)/m}{A/(n-k)},$$

where A is the residual sum of squares from the regression estimated by the 1961–72 observations, with (12–4) degrees of freedom ; B is the residual sum of squares from the regression estimated by the 1961–76 observations, with (16–4) degrees of freedom ; n is the number of the pre-crisis observations which is 12,

m is the number of the post-crisis observations which is 4, and k is the number of parameters in the regression which is 4 in the oil demand equation.

The values of A and B from the two regressions are 0.5559 and 0.1457, respectively. So the F-statistic was 3.24, with (4, 8) degrees of freedom. The critical value of F at the 5% level of significance is 3.84. As the computed F-statistic is less than the critical value, the null hypothesis of no structural change could not be rejected in the analysis.

However, this is not the end of the test. So far in this analysis, we designated 1961–72 as the pre-crisis period and 1973–76 as the post-crisis period mainly because coal consumption increased dramatically in 1973. But a noticeable change in oil consumption occurred in 1974. As the value of F-statistic depends not only on the residual sum of squares but also on the degrees of freedom between the pre-and post-crisis periods, we have to check the sensitivity of test result to the partitioning of pre-and post-crisis observations. In the alternative analysis, we considered 1961–73 as the pre-crisis period and 1974–76 as the post-crisis period. The estimation result of oil demand equation by 1961–73 observations is given below :

$$\ln Q_0 = -\underset{(0.74)}{11.54^a} - \underset{(0.15)}{0.64^a} \ln P_0 + \underset{(0.25)}{1.39^a} \ln P_C + \underset{(0.09)}{2.64^a} \ln Y$$

$$R^2 = 0.994$$

The estimated coefficients above by the 1961–73 observations are very close to those estimated by the 1961–76 observations.

Following is the comparison of the actual and predicted values of dependent variable :

	Logarithms of actual oil consumption	Logarithms of predicted oil consumption	Actual value minus predicted value
1974	9.71987	9.51097	0.2089
1975	9.80168	9.72834	0.0733
1976	9.93943	10.1018	−0.1624

While the predicted values from the previous analysis resulted in upward bias, the present analysis with the 1961–73 observations as pre-crisis period resulted in downward bias in the predicted values in 1974 and 1975. On the contrary, the predicted value brought upward bias in 1976.

If the estimation results of the alternative regression with the 1961–73 observations represented more closely the true relation between oil consumption and explanatory variables in Korea than the previous regression with the 1961–72 observations, the following explanation can be given as a probable answer to the discrepancy between the predicted and actual values. As the oil demand equation used for prediction was a static equilibrium model whose estimated coefficients show medium-term elasticities, the estimated price and income elasticities were too big to predict short-term adjustment. Especially, as the price index of oil rose from 181 in 1973 to 520 in 1974, the application of medium- term price elasticity of −0.64 would have resulted in too much downward pressure on the 1974 predicted value. In 1975, the size of the residual decreased significantly.

In 1976, the predicted value showed upward bias contrary to the previous two years' results. This is because the static oil demand equation could not deal with the distributed lag adjustment effect on oil consumption caused by the 1973–74 oil price change. From 1974 to 1975 the price index of oil rose from 520 to 662 and from 1975 to 1976 the oil price index rose from 662 to 713. So the effect of oil price change on energy consumption was not significant during these periods, but the lagged effect of the 1973–74 oil price hike still prevailed in 1976.

The residual sum of squares from the regression by 1961–73 observations was 0.0746. So the F-statistic from the alternative analysis brought the value of 2.86 with (3.9) degrees of freedom. As the critical value, corresponding to (3.9) degrees of freedom at the 5% significance level is 3.86, we could not reject the null hypothesis of no structural change in the alternative analysis either.

VI. Concluding Remarks

We investigated in this paper how the dramatic increase in the price of oil in 1973–74 affected the pattern of energy demand in Korea. First, we compared the annual growth rates in energy consumption between pre- and post-crisis periods. Second, we compared the estimated price and income elasticities from the regressions by 1961–72 and 1961–76 observations. And then we performed an F-test for oil demand to see whether there was a structural change in oil demand in Korea after the 1973–74 oil crisis. The calculated F-statistic was close to the critical value at the 5% significance level, but the null hypothesis of no structural change could not be rejected in the test. To check the sensitivity of the test result to the classification of pre- and post-crisis periods, we alternatively included 1973 in the pre-crisis period, leaving 1974–76 as post-crisis period. We could not reject the null hypothesis in this alternative analysis either.

The conclusion of this analysis is that the pattern of energy demand in Korea has not changed significantly since the 1973–74 oil crisis. The abrupt decline in the growth rate of oil consumption in 1974 was the normal response to the sudden surge in the price of oil. As the price of oil resumed its stability after 1975, the consumption of oil started to grow again. In 1972, Korea spent $221million for the import of crude oil, 2.26% of GNP. In 1976, the import of crude oil cost $1,492 million, 5.96% of GNP.

In spite of the increased burden of oil import, Korean economy continued to grow at a fast rate, realizing a 15.2% GNP growth rate in 1976. The share of oil in total energy consumption increased from 54.0% in 1972 to 60.6% in 1976. On the other hand, the share of coal changed only slightly during the period from 26.7% to 28.2%.

The statistical evidences described above coupled with the test results of this study show that even though the 1973–74 oil crisis increased the financial burden of oil import in Korea, the impact was not so serious as to bring a structural change in energy demand or to jeopardize the momentum of rapid economic growth. This lack of responses to the signalling of the first oil crisis in developing countries as well as in developed countries plunged the world into a second worldwide oil crisis in the winter of 1978.

References

Bundy, William P., ed, *The world Economic Crisis*, W. W. Norton and Co, Inc, New York, NY, USA, 1975.

Chow, Gregory C., 'Tests of equality between sets of coefficients in two linear regressions', *Econometrica*, Vol 28, July 1960, pp 591-605.

Fried, Edward R., and Charles L. Schultze, eds, *Higher Oil Prices and the World Economy : The Adjustment Problem*, The Brookings Institution, Washington, DC, USA, 1975.

Halvorsen, Robert, 'Residential demand for electric energy', *Review of Economics and Statistics*, February 1975, PP 12-18.

Hulten, Charles R., 'Divisia index numbers', *Econometrica*, Vol 41, November 1973, pp 1017-1026.

Jang, Young S., *Analysis of Electricity Demand and Price in Korea*, Korea Development Institute, Seoul, Korea, March 1977.

Johnston, J., *Econometric Methods*, Second Edition, McGraw-Hill, New York, 1972.

Nordhaus, William D., ed, *International Studies of the Demand For Energy*, North-Holland Publishing, Amsterdam, 1977.

Shin, Euisoon, *Impact of the 1973-1974 Oil Crisis and Energy Substitution in Korea*, unpublished Ph.D. thesis, University of Washington, 1980.

______, 'Inter-energy substitution in Korea, 1962-1975', *Journal of Economic Development*, Vol 6, No 1, July 1981, pp 33-46.

3. Energy Supply Policies in Korea and Japan*

I. Introduction

The economies of Korea and Japan are highly dependent on imported energy sources, especially oil. So, the two countries' main energy policy objectives have been the stable supply of energy and the reduced dependence on imported oil. Accordingly, Korea and Japan have adopted similar energy policies as follows :

On the supply side, they diversified the region and the method of crude oil imports to reduce their dependence on the Middle East. Also they promoted oil development activities inland and overseas to raise self-sufficiency ratios. Oil storage facilities were constructed and they increased the level of oil stockpiles to prepare against the sudden disruption of the imported oil supply.

On the demand side, they encouraged the substitution of oil for

---

* "Energy Supply Policies in Korea and Japan," in Dalchoong Kim and Euisoon Shin (eds.), *Energy Policies in Korea and Japan*, Yonsei University Press, September 1986, pp. 1-45.

non-oil energy sources such as coal, nuclear power, LNG, etc. Also they endeavored to conserve energy through improved energy efficiency and structural change in industries. Institutionally, Korea and Japan adopted various energy tax and subsidy policies deeply influencing their domestic energy markets even if the level of intervention was different.

This paper compares the energy supply policies of Korea and Japan and investigates possible ways of energy cooperation between the two countries. After the introduction, section 2 analyzes the energy supply trend of the two countries since 1960s and compares their long-term energy plans. Section 3 compares the oil development policies and section 4 compares the oil stockpile policies of Korea and Japan. Lastly, section 5 summarizes the analysis and suggests possible energy cooperation between the two countries.

II. Energy Supply and Energy Policy

1. Korea

(1) Energy Supply

Up to the early 1960s, major energy sources in Korea were coal and firewood. In 1962, the two energy sources composed 88.6% of total energy consumption while oil comprised only 9.8%. However, the pattern of energy consumption in Korea started to change following the successful progress of the economic development plan. Oil became a major energy source in the late 1960s and the share of oil in total primary energy consumption increased to 62.9% in 1979. The dependence ratio on imported energy was only 10.5% in 1964, but with the replacement of coal by oil as a major energy source, the dependence on imported energy, mostly on oil, grew rapidly and reached 47.5% in 1970 and 74.8% in 1983.

The increased oil consumption naturally increased the imports of crude oil. The import price of crude oil was $2.65 in 1964 but it jumped to $35.58 in 1981, a 16.5 fold increase during the period. As Korea had not produced any domestic oil, the total amount of crude oil needed should have been imported from overseas.

Table 1 shows that the total amount of crude oil imports was $13 million in 1964, only 3.2% of the total import. However, due to the increase in import quantity and the unit price of imported oil, total amount of crude oil imports increased rapidly and reached $6.5 billion in 1981 composing 24.9% of total import. In 1983, 192.9 million barrels of crude oil and 21.7 million barrels of oil products

|Table 1| Oil Import of Korea

Year	Oil Import			Total Import (million $) (B)	A/B (%)
	Crude Oil		Oil Products		
	(1,000 Bbl)	(million $) (A)	(1,000 Bbl)		
1964	5,835	13	2,785	404	3.2
1970	69,150	119	88	1,984	6.0
1974	112,703	1,105	1,617	6,852	16.1
1978	166,532	2,174	3,540	14,972	14.5
1981	182,816	6,504	13,161	26,131	24.9
1983	192,969	5,768	21,697	26,192	22.0

Source : Ministry of Energy and Resources. Office of Customs Administrations.

were imported at a cost of $6.4 billion.

From 1978 to 1981, the amount of crude oil imports increased by only 9.8% while the payments for imports increased by 199.2% due to the rise in the price of crude oil caused by the second oil crisis. After the second oil crisis, the burden of the rapidly rising payments for imported crude oil and the funds for nuclear power plants were heavily financed by foreign debts. For this reason the foreign debt in the energy sector increased rapidly and it reached $6.6 billion in 1983, composing 16% of Korea's total foreign debt.

Up to 1978, Korea imported crude oil mainly from the Middle East. Saudi Arabia, Kuwait, and Iran supplied 95.8% of the total oil imports in 1978. Since the outbreak of the second oil crisis, the Korean government initiated a policy aimed at diversifying the sources of Korea's crude oil imports. As a result, the share imported from the Middle East countries decreased to 74% in 1983. The share of the three Middle East countries dropped to 57.5% and the number of countries from where crude oil was imported increased to eleven in 1983.

The international oil majors initially participated in the oil refining business of Korea through equity participation. So most of the crude oil imported up to the second oil crisis was based on long-term contracts between domestic oil companies and the oil majors. However, the major's position in the world oil market was weakened after experiencing the two oil crises and a significant change occurred in the method of crude oil imports in Korea as shown in Table 2.

In 1980, the crude oil imports based on long-term contracts

accounted for 97% of the total crude oil import and more than half of them were through the majors. However in 1984, the share of the import through the majors decreased to 9.0% while the share of the direct deal (DD) increased to 53.4%. The import of crude oil from the spot market increased from 5.6 million barrels in 1980 to 63.2 million barrels in 1984 and the share increased from 3.1% to 31.7% accordingly.

|Table 2| Method of Crude Oil Import in Korea

Method / Year	G - G	D - D	Major	Spot	Total (1,000 Bbl)
1980	29.2%	16.3%	51.4%	3.1%	182,860
1981	33.5%	28.1%	35.8%	2.6%	182,816
1982	23.0%	42.6%	26.5%	7.9%	178,369
1983	10.4%	48.2%	13.4%	28.0%	192,969
1984	5.9%	53.4%	9.0%	31.7%	199,681

Source : Korea Petroleum Development Corporation, *Petroleum*, June 1985 (Vol. 24), p. 41.

(2) Energy Policy

Up to the 1950s, Korea remained an agricultural society. Firewood had been the main energy source and the government encouraged the production of domestic coal to replace firewood. During the first five-year economic development plan which started in 1962, Korea concentrated on the construction of oil refineries and electric power generation facilities. This period was a cheap oil period and the consumption of oil increased at a fast rate.

During the second five-year planning period of 1967-1971, oil consumption grew at an annual rate of 40.9%. After the first oil crisis, the oil consumption growth rate dropped to 1.6% in 1974, but it started to increase again and recorded 8.5% in 1975 and 14.8% in 1976. GNP growth rate dropped to 7.7% in 1974 and 6.9% in 1975 from 14.1% of 1973. However, thanks to the Middle East construction boom which followed the first oil crisis, the Korean economy recovered easily from the impact of the oil shock and regained the momentum of continued economic growth from 1976 realizing 14.1% GNP growth rate. The government of Korea took no specific measures to deal with the upsurge in oil prices and the wholesale price index increased 42.1% in 1974. Even after the first oil crisis, the share of oil among total energy consumption had increased steadily until 1978 and Korea was left vulnerable to the upcoming second oil crisis.

In January 1978, the Ministry of Energy and Resources was established in Korea. However, the second oil crisis struck the Korean economy before the Ministry of Energy and Resources set up a long-term energy policy. The impact of the second oil crisis was deeper and longer compared to the first oil crisis. In 1978, Korea realized an annual GNP growth rate of 9.7%. In 1979, the GNP grew moderately at 6.5% but it plunged to minus 5.2% in 1980. The second oil crisis also affected Korea's trade balance seriously. From 1978 to 1979, total imports increased $5,367 million while total exports increased by only $2,345 million. As a result, Korea recorded a trade deficit of $4,396 million in 1979. In 1977, the trade deficit was only $477 million.

In September 1979, Ministry of Energy and Resources announced a long-term comprehensive energy plan. The energy policy in Korea since the second oil crisis (1979-1981) emphasized the following three major objectives. The first objective was to secure a stable supply of energy sources. For this purpose, the Korean government encouraged maximum production of domestic anthracite coal. Also, the government strongly promoted overseas direct development of energy sources and oil stockpiling policies. To support these policies, the petroleum business fund which included the petroleum stockpile fund was instituted in 1979. The second objective was the reduction of the oil dependence ratio. Construction of nuclear power plants, fuel switching from oil to bituminous coal in electric companies and cement industry, development of new energy sources, and the import of LNG and LPG were the policies carried out to reduce the oil dependence ratio. The third objective was energy conservation. To support energy conservation, the energy use rationalization law was enacted in December 1979. Also the Energy Management Corporation was established in 1980 and has been managing the energy use rationalization fund.

In 1982, oil consumption growth rate was minus 0.2% while GNP grew 5.3% from 1981. The Korean government encouraged the rational use of energy through improved energy efficiency rather than through a simple reduction in energy consumption. The substitution of oil for bituminous coal in the domestic cement industry was completed by 1983. Korea made a long term contract with Indonesia to import LNG for 20 years from 1987 and established the Korea Gas Corporation in 1983. The government's continued efforts dropped the oil dependence ratio to 56.2% in

1983 from 62.9% of 1979.

The Ministry of Energy and Resources announced a long-term energy outlook in 1985. According to the 'outlook', total demand for primary energy sources in 2001 will be 124.2 million TOE (tons of oil equivalent), 2.6 times greater than the 1983 level. Energy demand is expected to grow at the average annual rate of 5.2%, slower than the trend so far. Energy demand grew at an annual rate of 9.9% from 1966 to 1973 and at a rate of 13.0% from 1976

|Table 3| Long-Term Energy Supply and Demand Outlook in Korea

Item	1983 (actual)	1991	1996	2001
Primary Energy Demand	49.7 million TOE	79.1 million TOE	99.9 million TOE	124.2 million TOE
Energy Source	Quantity (%)	Quantity (%)	Quantity (%)	Quantity (%)
Coal (million tons)				
Anthracite	21.7 (20.3)	21.3 (12.8)	19.8 (NA)	18.7 (7.1)
Bituminous	9.6 (12.8)	20.9 (17.4)	34.9 (NA)	51.1 (27.2)
Oil (million Bbl)	191.3 (56.2)	267.1 (47.4)	305.3 (NA)	349.6 (39.7)
LNG (million tons)	−(−)	2.0 (3.3)	5.0 (NA)	5.0 (5.2)
Hydro (1,000 GWH)	2.7 (1.4)	4.1 (1.3)	4.2 (NA)	5.1 (1.0)
Nuclear (1,000 GWH)	8.9 (4.5)	47.3 (15.0)	58.7 (NA)	82.6 (16.6)
New and Reproduced Energy, etc. (million TOE)	2.4 (4.8)	2.2 (2.8)	2.8 (NA)	3.9 (3.2)
Final Energy Demand	41.6 million TOE	62.5 million TOE	76.8 million TOE	92.9 million TOE

NA : not available.

Source : Ministry of Energy and Resources, *Long Term Energy Outlook and Strategy for the 2000s*, 1985.

to 1979. From 1981 to 1983, the energy demand growth rate was 4.1% because of the economic recession during the period.

The share of oil in total energy consumption will decrease continuously in the future and the increasing energy demand will mostly be met by the increasing supply of electricity from nuclear and bituminous coal power plants and by fuel substitution in the industrial sector from oil to coal. However, the absolute amount of oil demand will increase from the present level of 0.52 million B/D to 1 million B/D in 2001, about a 1.9 fold increase. So the stable supply of oil will remain as one of Korea's most important energy policy objectives. The trend of rapid increase in the demand for light oil will be intensified in the future following the substitution of heavy oil for bituminous coal in electric power generation and industrial sectors and the expansion of city gas in the residential sector. The share of light oil products in total oil demand was 52% in 1983, but it is expected to increase to 71% in 2001.

The share of anthracite coal which is mostly used for residential purposes will decrease as LNG replaces coal in the latter part of 1980s. The structure of energy demand and supply in the 2000s will be more diversified and stable than the present. As shown in Table 3, oil will compose 39.7%, bituminous coal will compose 27.2%, and nuclear power will compose 16.6% of total energy consumption in 2001.

2. Japan

(1) Energy Supply

Up to 1960, the major sources of energy in Japan were coal and hydroelectric power. Since 1960, the Japanese government has encouraged the import of oil to replace coal as a major energy source. The supply of cheap crude oil from the Middle East heavily benefitted Japan's rapid economic growth since the 1960s. The share of oil in Japan's total energy supply increased from 38% in 1960 to 75% in 1972, and the energy dependence on imported sources increased from 44% to 86% during the period.

In 1973, Japan paid 1,633 billion yen to import oil, 18.09% of the total imports. Japan paid 5,504 billion yen in 1974 for oil imports and the share in the total imports increased to 35.08%. Despite the decrease in crude oil imports since the first oil crisis, Japan has had to pay 13,905 billion yen in 1980 for the import of crude oil and oil products, nearly 8 times more than the oil bill of 1973. The oil bill accounted for 43.46% of total imports in 1980.[1] In 1982, Japan imported 207 million kl of crude oil which cost 11,443 billion yen. When 2,070 billion yen for the import of oil products are added, the 1982 total oil bill amounted to 13,513 billion yen, 41.38% of the total imports. The share of oil in total imports is shown in Table 4.

Since the first oil crisis, Japan tried hard to reduce the dependence on Middle East oil by diversifying the origin of the

1) MITI, *Energy-'84* (in Japanese), 1984, p. 74.

|Table 4| Oil Import of Japan

Year	Oil Import				Total Import (B) (100 million yen)	A/B (%)
	Crude Oil		Oil Products (100 million yen)	Total (A) (100 million yen)		
	(million kl)	(100 million yen)				
1964	74.2	3,344	962	4,306	28,575	15.07
1970	204.9	8,048	2,356	10,404	67,972	15.31
1973	288.6	16,330	2,488	18,817	104,044	18.09
1974	275.9	55,039	8,371	63,410	180,764	35.08
1978	275.4	49,803	7,263	57,066	167,276	34.11
1979	277.1	73,775	13,812	87,587	242,454	36.13
1980	249.2	120,114	18,942	139,056	319,953	43.46
1981	230.2	116,877	18,860	135,737	314,641	43.14
1982	207.4	114,427	20,697	135,124	326,563	41.38
1983	212.8	95,060	21,203	116,263	300,148	38.74

Source : JNOC, *Oil Development Data*, 1985, p. 5.

crude oil imports. As s result, the dependence ratio on the Middle East oil decreased steadily in Japan. In 1976, crude oil imports from the Middle East countries composed 79.5% and those from Southeast Asia composed 16.7%. Together the two regions supplied 96.2% of total crude oil imports. In 1982, the Middle East supplied 70.4%, Southeast Asia supplied 18.8%, Middle and South America supplied 4.6% and the Communist Bloc and Africa supplied the rest. Major oil exporters to Japan were Saudi Arabia who supplied 68 million kl, 32.9% of the total crude oil imports, Arab emirates who supplied 14.7%, and Indonesia who supplied 14.5%.[2)]

For a long time the crude oil supply had been dominated by the multinational oil majors. However, since the Middle East War of 1973, the oil producing countries have gradually increased their control over the export of crude oil to foreign countries. Accordingly, the share of crude oil imports from major oil companies has dropped and the share of direct imports from oil producing countries has increased. As shown in Table 5, foreign oil companies (mostly majors) supplied 82.3% of Japan's crude oil imports in 1973, but their share dropped to 35.6% and state-owned enterprises of oil producing countries supplied 53.3% of total crude oil imports in 1983. This means that the form of oil imports was changed from the majors to direct deal (DD) with the state-owned enterprises of oil producing countries and the government to government (GG) deals based on inter-governmental agreement. Japanese oil companies participating in oversea oil development have supplied about 10% of Japanese crude oil imports.

Since the reduction of the crude oil price in the spring of 1983, the share of crude oil imports from the spot market has increased significantly. In 1984, Japan imported 834,000 B/D from the spot market, while spot market imports in 1982 were 334,000 B/D. Accordingly, the share of the crude oil imported from the spot market increased from 9.0% in 1982 to 22.6% in 1984 as shown in Table 6.

---

2) MITI, *Energy Demand and Supply Outlook in the 21st Century* (in Japanese), 1984, p. 147.

|Table 5| Crude Oil Imports by Supply Source

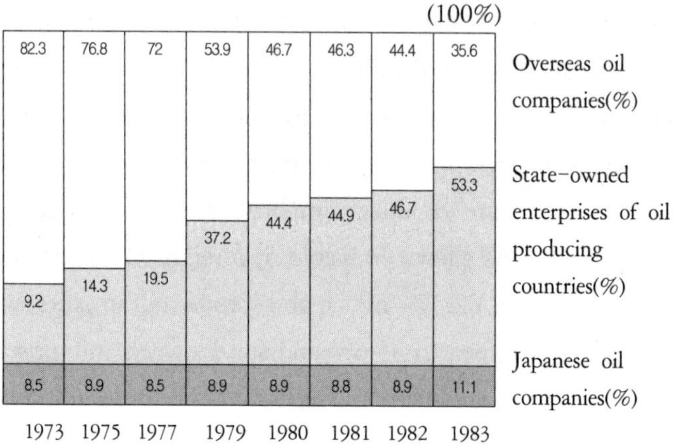

Source : MITI, Energy in January 1985, p.15.

|Table 6| Trend of Crude Oil Import from Spot Market in Japan

	Import from Spot Market (1,000 B/D)	Share in Total Crude Oil Import(%)
1977	257	5.4
1978	193	4.1
1979	377	7.8
1980	444	10.1
1981	223	5.6
1982	334	9.0
1983	642	17.9
1984	834	22.6

Source : Korea Petroleum Development Corporation, *Petroleum News*, 1985, 3.

(2) Energy Policy

Japanese economic policy is based on a group consensus among bureaucrats and industry leaders. The central government agency for Japanese energy policy is MITI. The Agency for Natural Resources and Energy within MITI was established just before the first oil crisis of 1973 and has played a leading role in formulating Japanese energy policy. The second major group is industry leaders. Private industry leaders reflect their concerns through government advisory committees and industrial federations. The large Japanese trading companies are one of the key voices in energy policy making. They actually handle 60% of Japan's energy imports and exports.

The Japanese response to the first oil crisis was most likely a panic. They rushed to hoard daily commodities in fear of continued oil disruption and the government rushed to placate Arab oil-producing countries. After the crisis, Japan had to change the definition of "resource diplomacy" and energy became a major concern of Japanese economic policy. After the first oil crisis Japan adopted demand-restraint policies and the Japanese economy achieved economic equilibrium based on smaller scale industrial and import activities.[3)]

After the first oil crisis, the main targets of Japanese energy policy were reduction in oil consumption and increase in energy efficiency. For this purpose Japan aimed to reduce dependence on imported oil from the Middle East and to develop alternative energy

3) Ronald A. Morse, "Japanese Energy Policy", in *After the Oil Crisis*, ed. by Wilfred L. Kohl, D. C. Health and Company, 1982.

sources. The highly motivated Japanese energy policy dramatically changed the trend of oil consumption in Japan. Since 1960, the oil consumption in Japan increased continuously up to 1973. This trend came to a sudden end in 1974 and the Japanese crude oil import in 1978 stood at 275.3 million kl, even less than the 1973 level of 288.6 million kl.

The impact of the second oil crisis of 1978–1979 was much milder than the first oil crisis. It was because Japan had learned a valuable lesson from the experience of the first oil shock, that energy security was essential for solid and steady economic growth. After the second oil crisis, MITI announced a long term energy supply and demand outlook in August 1979. In the outlook, total energy demand in 1990 was projected to be 700 million kl of oil equivalent.

In April 21, 1982, MITI announced a revised outlook. In the August 1979 outlook, it was assumed that GNP would grow at an annual rate of 5.5% from 1979 to 1985 and 5% from 1985 to 1990. However, the actual GNP growth rate was 5.3% in 1979, 3.7% in 1980, and 2.7% in 1981. So Japan had to adjust her prediction of GNP growth rate downward to 5.0% during 1985 and 1990. That was the first reason for the revision of the outlook.

The second reason was that Japanese industries have performed better than expected in achieving energy conservation and have become less dependent on oil. In 1981, the steel industry used only 86% of the energy used in 1973 to produce one ton of steel and the cement industry used only 76% to produce one ton of cement. These industries also significantly reduced their dependence on oil during the period. The steel industry reduced its use of oil to 32%

level and the cement industry to 10% of the 1973 level.

The third reason was that the structural change which took place in Japanese economy reduced the energy intensity. After the oil crisis, the Japanese economy gradually moved towards technology intensive industries such as fabrication and assembly from energy intensive industries such as chemicals and pulp and papers. This structural change improved energy productivity. In 1980, 220 liters of oil equivalent was needed to produce commodities worth 100 million yen, which was a 21% reduction compared with the 283 liters needed in 1973.

Japan adjusted her long-term energy supply and demand outlook downward in 1982 while keeping the policy objectives of the 1979 outlook. Those objectives were (1) to conserve energy nationally, (2) to reduce dependence on oil, and (3) to promote the introduction of alternative energy sources. In the new outlook, the total energy demand in 1990 was estimated to be 590 million kl of oil equivalent. That was a 15.7% reduction from the 1979 outlook. Among the various energy sources, oil and new energy sources were the main targets of the reduction in total demand. On the other hand, no significant reduction was made with regard to coal and LNG. This represented MITI's intention to reduce the dependence on oil still further.[4)]

After the second oil crisis, structural change in the Japanese economy into energy saving industries and the successful progress of

---

4) Industrial Bank of Japan, *Long-term Energy Supply and Demand Outlook in Japan*, June 1982.

the energy conservation policy reduced energy consumption significantly. In 1982, energy consumption in Japan was recorded at 388 million kl, which was the lowest since the oil crisis and 48 million kl less than the consumption level of 1979.

In 1982, Japan's dependence on oil was reduced to 62%. This was made possible mainly through a fuel switch from oil to alternative energy sources such as coal, natural gas, and nuclear power in the electric power generation and industrial sectors. The supply of coal increased 2.3 times from 1973 to 1982 as a result of massive fuel switching in the electric power generation and cement industries. During the same period, the supply of natural gas increased 7.5 times due to the increased use of natural gas for electric power generation and city gas. The share of electricity generated from nuclear power plants expanded from 2.4% of 1973 to 19.5% in 1982.

In March 1983, the official price of crude oil was cut $5 per barrel from $34/B to $29/B reflecting decreased oil demand in the world oil market. In addition, the increased cost of energy since the oil crisis imposed unbearably large burden on the Japanese economy. A series of such changes made the 1982 outlook far apart from reality. Under such a situation, the Advisory Committee for Energy prepared a report, "Japan's Long-Term Energy Supply and Demand Outlook and Future Energy Policy" in November 1983 as a guide to the energy policy of Japan in the new period.[5)]

5) Demand and Supply Subcommittee of Advisory Committee for Energy, *An Interim Report on an Outlook for the Long-term Demand and Supply of Energy*, November 16, 1983.

|Table 7| Long-Term Energy Supply and Demand Outlook in Japan

November 16, 1983

Item	FY 1982 (actual)		FY 1990		FY 1995		FY 2000 (estimate)	
Energy demand	388 million kl		460 million kl		530 million kl		(Approx.) 600 million kl	
Energy source	Quantity	(%)	Quantity	(%)	Quantity	(%)	Quantity	(%)
Coal	94.5 million tons	18.5	108 million tons	17.5	128 million tons	18	160-170 million tons	20
(Domestic coal)	(18.3 million tons)		(18-20 million tons)		(18-20 million tons)			
(Steam coal)	(28.4 million tons)		(43 million tons)		(58 million tons)			
Nuclear	17.3 GW	6.9	34 GW	10.8	48 GW	14	62 GW	16
Natural gas	27 million kl	7.0	56 million kl	12.1	61 million kl	12	64-66 million kl	11
(Domestic natural gas)	(2.1 billion m^3)		(4.3 billion m^3)		(5 billion m^3)			
(LNG)	(17.6 million tons)		(36.5 million tons)		(40 million tons)			
Hydro		5.4		5.0		5		5
(Conventional)	19.4 GW		2 GW		24 GW		26.5 GW	
(Pumped-up)	14 GW		18 GW		19.5 GW		22 GW	
Geothermal	0.4 million kl	0.1	1.5 million kl	0.3	3.5 million kl	1	6-7 million kl	1
New fuel oils, new energy Source, etc.	0.9 million kl	0.2	8 million kl	1.7	19 million kl	4	35-55 million kl	6-9
Oil	240 million kl	61.9	240 million kl	52.5	250 million kl	48	250-260 million kl	42
(Domestic oil)	(0.48 million kl)		(1.5 million kl)		(1.9 million kl)			
(LPG)	(15.7 million tons)		(19 million tons)		(21 million tons)			
Total supply	388 million kl	100.0	460 million kl	100.0	530 million kl	100	600 million kl	100

Source: MITI, *Energy in Japan*, 1985.

The report proposed the following three guidelines for Japan's future energy policy : (1) insure energy security, (2) reduce the cost of energy, (3) realize the optimum structure of energy demand and supply balancing the security and cost. The noticeable change in the new outlook was the consideration of energy costs in addition to reduction in oil dependence and insurance of energy security. The energy policy before the first oil crisis considered only the cost of energy. The energy policy before the first oil crisis can be named a first generation energy policy. The second generation energy policy which appeared after the first oil crisis emphasized energy supply security above all things. The third generation energy policy which appeared with MITI's 1983 energy outlook considered security and economic efficiency at the same time, a synthesis of the two previous energy policies.[6)]

The 1983 new outlook predicted that the energy demand in 1990 would be 460 million kl, 22% lower than the 1982 outlook. The new outlook projected that the energy demand in 1995 would be 530 million kl. The energy demand will grow at an annual rate of 2.2% up to 1990, significantly lower than the 3.2% projected by the 1982 outlook and the actual growth rate of 3.4% realized during the period from 1975 to 1979.

With a stable supply of energy and reduction in the cost of energy as its main policy objectives, the new outlook recommended continued efforts to develop and introduce oil substituting energy sources. It proposed that future growth in energy demand would be

---

6) MITI, *Energy-'84*, pp. 28-32.

met by alternative energy sources, thus keeping the level of oil consumption virtually unchanged from the 1982 consumption level of 240 million kl. From 1982 to 1995, the increase in energy demand will be 142 million kl of oil equivalent. Out of this, only 10 million kl will come from oil. Energy dependence on oil will decline steadily from 61.9% in 1982 to 52.5% in 1990 and 48% in 1995. The share of oil in total energy demand in 1990 was revised slightly upward to 52.5% in the new outlook from the 49.1% in the previous outlook. This change reflects the increased competitiveness of oil compared to other energy sources due to the lowered price of crude oil.

3. Comparison and Findings

The comparison of government responses to the oil crises by Japan and Korea gives a clue to the cause of serious damage Korea experienced after the second oil crisis. When the first oil crisis occurred, Japanese government pushed the policy to catch the accelerating inflation at the cost of accepting slowed economic growth. In December 1973, direct government controls were imposed on the prices of major commodities and on the consumption of oil and electricity. The Bank of Japan took several measures to reduce the money supply and the government spending for 1974 fiscal year was cut back significantly. By the end of March, the prices of oil products were allowed to increase by an average of 62% and the price control on other commodities was thereafter removed.[7)]

In 1974, Japan realized minus 0.4 percent real GNP growth.

Negative economic growth in 1974 and slow growth in subsequent years stabilized energy consumption in Japan. In addition to various other measures Japan took to reduce energy consumption since the first oil crisis, technology intensive industries such as electric machinery and transport equipment grew rapidly and the growth of energy-intensive industries such as pulp, paper and paper products, basic metals, and energy products slowed down. Japan made every effort to reduce dependence on oil and Japan's oil consumption in 1979 was only 16.8 percent greater than the 1973 level. Japan's steady economic growth after the second oil crisis was the result of wise government policies taken after the first oil crisis.

The government's response to the first oil crisis was more or less optimistic in Korea. Korea continued to pursue expansionary policies rather than take restrictive measures to absorb the impact of the increased oil prices. Actually, the Korean economy remained healthy ever after the oil crisis. In 1974, the trade deficit increased to $1,937 million from $566 million in 1973. But the deficit decreased to $477 million in 1977 and the improved trade balance falsely indicated to Korean government officials that their expansionary policy was the right choice. Throughout the 1970s, Korea invested a lot of money to foster capital and energy intensive heavy industries. From 1973 to 1979, oil consumption in Korea grew by 94.2%. As a result, Korea was virtually defenseless against the blows of the second oil crisis. The government of Korea adopted more restrictive fiscal and monetary policies after the second oil

7) Ronald A. Morse, *op. cit.*.

crisis and inclined to slower growth on the basis of stable prices.

III. Oil Development Policy

1. Korea

(1) Overseas Energy Development

Korea is poorly endowed with energy resources. There are no known reserves for oil and bituminous coal in South Korea. The only indigenous fossil fuel is anthracite coal, with about a 30 years reserve. A few uranium ore deposits have been discovered, but the grade is too poor to develop commercially.

After the second oil crisis, Korea realized that a stable supply of energy was essential for national security and steady economic growth, so Korea strongly promoted overseas direct development of energy sources. Pohang Steel Company (POSCO), a government owned corporation, began investing in Tanoma Coal Mines in America in 1980 and started producing coal in September 1982. In addition to this, POSCO is participating in the development of bituminous coal at Mt. Thorley Mines in Australia and at Greenhills Mines in Canada with 20% shares in both projects. In addition to these projects, five more ongoing overseas coal development projccts were launched in 1984, two of them are at the development stage and three of them are at the exploration stage. There are also three other overseas resource development projects of which two are in uranium and one is in tin. The outline of Korea's overseas bituminous coal development is shown in Table 8.

In 1983, Korea imported 10.1 million tons of bituminous coal at 588 million dollars and 0.364 tons of uranium at 29 million dollars. Directly developed bituminous coal in 1983 amounted to 1.27 million tons. By 1991, it is expected that coal imports will increase to 24 million tons and uranium imports will increase to 1.4 tons. By the 1990s, Korea plans to supply 30% of the required coal and uranium from overseas direct development.

Major institutional provisions made to promote overseas resource development are as follows : the Department of Energy and Resources was established in January 1978 for systematic and long-term planning and execution of government policies related to energy and resources. In January, 1979 the Overseas Resource Development Promoting Law was enacted. The Overseas Mineral Resources Developing Fund was established by the Korea Mines Promoting Corporation. Overseas resource developing firms also receive loans through an overseas investment fund supplied by the Korea Import and Export Bank. The Korean government has a reserve fund prepared against overseas investment losses and runs an investment fund accumulation system.

(2) Oil Development Policy

In 1968, a physical survey of the Yellow Sea and the East China Sea by the Ocean Research Institute of America indicated the possibility of oil fields in the western sea-bed of Korea. Korea enacted the Sea-Bed Mineral Resources Development Law in January 1970 and established seven sea-bed mining areas along the

|**Table 8**| Overseas Bituminous Coal Development Project of Korea (1984. 12.)

Country and Mine	Company	Main Partner (a)	Korean Share (%)	Estimated Investment (b)(million $)	Remarks
Tanoma (U.S.A.)	POSCO	-	100	68.5	· started production from '82.9 (imported 676,000 tons by '84.11)
Mt. Thorley (Australia)	POSCO	R.W.Miller	20	49	· started production from '82.4 (imported 1.61 million tons by '84.11)
Greenhills (Canada)	POSCO	Westar Mining Ltd.	20	60	· started production from '83.9 (imported 859,000 tons by '84.11)
Drayton (Australia)	Hyundai, Daesung	C.S.R.	5	15.5	· started production from '83.8 (imported 215,000 tons by '84.11)
Usibelli (U.S.A.)	Sunil Shipping Co.	U.C.M	-	1	· expected to import from 1985

(a) the firm with the highest equity participation.
(b) the estimated investment by Korean firms shown in the project plan.
Source : Ministry of Energy and Resources, *Long Term Energy Outlook and Strategy for the 2000s*, 1985.

continental shelf of Korea. As Korea lacked sufficient capital and technology to undertake exploration activities alone, concessions were given to international oil development companies. Since the Shell Oil Company began the first drilling operation at the 6th mining area in November 1972, eleven holes have been drilled but no oil field has been discovered yet.

Korea's overseas oil development activity was initiated by

KODECO Energy in 1981. KODECO Energy is a subsidiary company of the Korea Development Company which developed timber in Indonesia from 1968. KODECO Energy jointly with Pertamina, the Indonesian national petroleum company, drilled several holes in the Madura mining area and struck commercially feasible oil fields. KODECO started to produce oil in 1985.[8)]

As of 1984, Korea is involved in five ongoing overseas oil development projects as shown in Table 9. In particular, the Maridu mining area in North Yemen, where the consortium of Hyundai, Korea Petroleum Development Company, Samwhan, and Sunkyung operate with Hunt Company of America, shows promising signs of commercially feasible oil fields.

The Korean government instituted the oil development fund in June 1983 to promote domestic and overseas oil development activities. The Fund is supported by 10 cents per barrel dues levied on imported crude, diesel, and Bunker-C oil, and $1.16 per barrel dues on imported LPG. Funds are then loaned to oil developers for their exploration and preliminary drilling activities.

Once the oil well is found, additional capital required for development and production activities can be raised through standard loans from the Korea Import and Export Bank or the Korea Industry Bank granted on the basis of reserves and the economic feasibility of the project. The oil development fund is mainly used for exploration activities, but it also can be used for the purpose of

8) Madura oil field has 22 million Bbl of recoverable reserve of crude oil and 400.6 billion ft^3 (69 million Bbl of oil equivalent) of gas.

|Table 9| Overseas Oil Development Project of Korea (1984. 12.)

Company	Area	Operator	Korean Share	Remarks
KODECO	Madura (Indonesia)	KODECO (KOREA)	50%	· started production from 1985
Daeshin Oil	Oklahoma (U.S.A.)	LAMIE (U.S.A.)	75%	· under exploration drilling
PEDCO, Hyundai, Samwhan, Sunkyung	Maribu (N. Yemen)	Hunt (U.S.A.)	24.5%	· under estimation drilling
Lucky, PEDCO, Honam Oil	Adang (Indonesia)	Jackson (U.S.A.)	25%	· under exploration drilling
Samsung	Sarawak (Malaysia)	Husky (U.S.A.)	35%	· under contract negotiation

Source : Korea Institute of Energy and Resources, *A Study on the Overseas Resource Development Strategies of Selected Developed Countries*, 1984.

repayment guarantees on the loans provided for development and production activities.

Korea utilizes a success repayable loan system similar to West Germany and Japan. If the project fails, the loaned amount can not be collected, but if the project succeeds, some royalties are collected in addition to the principal and interest as a mechanism to preserve the fund. A maximum of 80% of the capital required for exploration and drilling activities can be loaned by the fund to private companies. But the expenses for preliminary surveys, bonuses, premiums, expenses for branch management, and operating expenses of the main office are not eligible. Compared to the Japanese loan limit of 70–80%, Korean limit is somewhat higher, but Japan excludes only the operating expenses for the main office from the eligible loans.

The repayment period for the loan is 18 years including a maximum 8 years grace period, a term identical to Japan's. The annual interest rate of 8% is lower than that of an export loan or overseas resource development loan, but higher than Japan's 6.75% and West Germany's 5% for the same type of loan.

It is expected that the present oil glut situation will end before 1990 and the price of oil will begin to rise at that time. In preparation for the upcoming tight oil market of the 1990s, Korea plans to increase overseas oil development activities and secure 10% of oil needed for domestic consumption through direct development by 2001.

In 1982, Korea Oil Drill Company was established and the first oil drilling ship in Korea named the Doosung, was built in 1984. Korea Petroleum Development Corporation (PEDCO) is the biggest share-holder with 51%, followed by Deawoo with a 34% share, with the remaining 15% shared evenly by three other companies.

As shown in Table 9, with the exception of KODECO, all the operators of the oil development projects where Korea is participating are foreign oil companies and the Korean equity participation ratios are mostly 25–35%. As Korea is at the beginning stage in the oil development business and lacks development funds, the government will encourage the participation through the consortium and restrict the equity participation ratio.

The Korean government plans to make several organizations

specialize in specific activities in order to raise the self development capabilities of Korea. The Korea Petroleum Development Corporation will specialize in exploration and development activities, and the Korea Institute of Energy and Resources will specialize in physical survey activities. The Korea Oil Drill Company will actively participate in development activities on the Korean continental shelf, and the private companies will accumulate techniques and experience in overseas operations.[9)]

2. Japan

(1) Brief History

Before the Second World War, the Japanese government enacted the Oil Resource Development Law in 1938 for national defense purposes and established the Imperial Oil Company in 1941, investing half of the capital. After the war, the Imperial Oil Company was reestablished as a private company. In 1955, the Japan Petroleum Exploration Company (JAPEX) was established as a government corporation under the Oil Resource Development Corporation Law. The Japanese government began to finance the overseas oil exploration fund in 1964 and established the Japan Petroleum Development Corporation in 1967 (later renamed the Japan National Oil Corporation (JNOC) in 1977).[10)]

The first oil imports from direct overseas development came in

---

9) Korea Ministry of Energy and Resources, *Long-Term Energy Outlook and Strategy for the 2000s* (in Korean), 1985.

10) 千田広志, *Energy Industry* (in Japanese), 1982, pp. 119-123.

1960 from the Kafji oil field at the neutral zone between Saudi Arabia and Kuwait. In 1973, 24.6 million kl of oil was imported from overseas direct development and it composed 8.5% of the total oil imports. In 1978, due to the tight oil supply caused by the second oil crisis, oil imports from overseas direct development increased to 29.7 million kl, the highest amount ever recorded. However, the quantity of oil imports from direct development decreased consistently from 1979 and was recorded 18.5 million kl in 1982. Japanese oil companies' preference for oil imports from the spot market at a discounted price accounted for the trend of decreasing imports from direct overseas development. In 1983, reflecting the decrease in the official price of crude oil, the oil imports from overseas direct development increased again to 23.6 million kl.

In 1983, the crude oil imported from 17 overseas oil development projects accounted for 11.1% of Japan's total crude oil import. The share of the major overseas oil developing projects were Arabia Oil 52%, Nippon Oil Development 18%, and Indonesia Oil 11%. Recently, Japan has been increasing exploration activities in the sea areas surrounding China.

(2) Oil Development Policy

Japan started "Five-Year Development Plan of Indigenous Oil and Gas Resources" in 1955 and has renewed the plan five times since then. In 1983, Japan produced 2.49 million kl of oil equivalent ; 0.26 million kl from the sea and 2.23 million kl from the land. During the 6th five-year development planning period,

Japan plans to find 40 million kl of oil and gas, 15 million kl from the sea and 25 million kl from the land. Japan expects to double the annual production of indigenous oil and gas to 5.8 million kl by 1990, of which 2.15 million kl will be produced from the sea and 3.65 million kl will be produced from the land. According to the 1983 MITI outlook, total oil and natural gas demand in 1990 will be 296 million kl, making the supply of oil and gas from domestic sources around 2% of total demand.[11)]

The Japan National Oil Corporation plays a leading role in the basic physical survey and drilling activities in Japanese islands and the nearby continental shelf. JNOC invests or lends up to 80% of the capital required for exploration activities on the nearby Japanese continental shelf, and also subsidizes domestic indigenous natural gas explorers within 50% of the required capital. The Japan Development Bank lends up to 70% of the capital required for the development and production of indigenous oil and gas.[12)]

Since the oil producing countries started to consolidate their control over the oil resources within their territory, Japan has increased the development investment in oil producing countries to raise the share of oil imports from direct development. Japan plans to secure 1.2 million B/D of crude oil by 1995 from overseas direct development.[13)]

Japanese oil development companies have drilled about 1500 wells overseas for the past ten years. From 1967 to 1981, Japan

11) JNOC, *Oil development Data*, 1985, p. 13.

12) *Ibid.*, p. 11.

13) MITI, *Energy-'84*, pp. 17-18.

invested 980 billion yen for exploration activities which included exploration around the Japanese continental shelf. During this period, investment for the drilling of production wells and the construction of offshore production facilities totaled 770 billion yen.[14)]

So far Japan has participated in the oil development project through partnership with the powerful western oil companies. However, from now on Japan plans to increase her exploration and development activities in China, Oman, and Indonesia as a sole operator.

The leading roles played by the Japan National Oil Corporation (JNOC) and the Japan Import and Export Bank are a special feature of the Japanese oil development policy. JNOC invests or lends up to 80% for the exploration activities around the Japanese continental shelf and 70% for overseas exploration activities. For overseas development and production activities, the Japan Import and Export Bank lends up to 80% of the required capital. JNOC also guarantees up to 60% of the development funds borrowed by oil developing companies.

The annual interest rates for loans by the JNOC to the oil companies participating in exploration activities are over 6.5% and the repayment period is 18 years with an eight-year grace period. From 1967 to 1983, JNOC invested 354 billion yen and loaned 561 billion yen for exploration activities. JNOC guarantees the repayment of loans provided by banks, banking organizations, and foreign

---

14) Energy-Resource Problems Study Group (ed.), *Energy War Period* (in Japanese), 1983, pp. 87-91.

countries to Japanese overseas oil development activities. The total amount of the repayment guarantee is within 25 times of the government financed debt surety fund. From 1967 to 1983, the total amount of the debt surety fund was 18.5 billion yen. Based on this fund, 665.4 billion yen of surety service has been provided and the remaining surety service balance is 447.5 billion yen.[15]

During the period from 1967 to 1981, 65% of the funds spent for very risky exploration activities came from JNOC and 35% were supplied by private investments and loans. This kind of government supported oil development pattern is expected to be intensified further in the future as the resource-related companies are suffering from low profitability due to the oil surplus and declining oil prices. Also, the leasing and sharing policies of oil producing countries became more beneficial to the host countries and this change made the development activities of private firms more difficult.

Japanese overseas oil development policy presently faces the following problems : (1) how to secure the enormous amount of funds needed for very risky exploration and development activities, (2) how to encourage private oil development companies, and (3) how to guarantee the sale of directly developed oil from overseas. Possible solutions to these problems include reserve funds against losses from foreign investment and reduction of oil taxes for developed oil.

15) JNOC, *op. cit.*, pp. 17-18.

|Table 10| Japanese Oil Import from Overseas Direct Development

(Unit : million kl)

Year	Directly Developed Oil (A)	Total Oil Import (B)	A/B (%)
1962	4.9	47.3	10.5
1967	16.0	125.1	12.7
1973	24.6	288.6	8.5
1974	27.5	275.9	10.0
1975	23.3	262.8	8.9
1976	24.0	275.8	8.7
1977	23.7	277.5	8.5
1978	29.7	275.4	10.8
1979	24.9	277.1	9.0
1980	22.2	249.2	8.9
1981	20.3	230.2	8.8
1982	18.5	207.4	8.9
1983	23.6	212.8	11.1

Source : JNOC, *Oil Development Data*, 1985.

3. Comparison and Findings

Japan stared overseas oil development in 1960, appropriated 11.1% of total oil imports from overseas direct development in 1983 and plans to secure 1.2 million B/D of crude oil by 1995. By comparison, the history of Korean investment in overseas oil development projects is very short. Full-scale overseas oil development started after the outbreak of the second oil crisis. Just recently KODECO Energy struck an oil field at the Madura sea area and

Korea started to import directly developed crude oil beginning in 1985.

Japanese private oil development companies are losing enthusiasm for their investments because of decreasing oil consumption and falling oil prices since 1983. On the other hand, the Korean oil development business is booming stimulated by the Madura oil field strike and the promising sign of finding another commercially feasible oil field at the Maribu area of North Yemen.

The following are ways to secure overseas resources : (1) spot market, (2) long-term purchasing contract, (3) acquisition of long-term purchasing right through loan, and (4) direct development through equity participation. Numbers (2) through (4) emphasize the long-term security of a stable supply. However, the long term purchasing contract cannot provide enough supply security as the contract could be easily cancelled by one party. Therefore direct development is the best way to secure a long-term supply of overseas resources. As Korea has a short history of experience in overseas resource development, it is better to participate in the joint ventures with developed countries who have much experience and are equipped with the latest development techniques and management skills.

When deciding on the investments in overseas resource development projects, marketing of the developed resources should be considered in advance. The direct development of overseas oil helped Japan during the second oil crisis by providing a stable supply of oil at the official price without a premium. However, when the oil market was glutted, oil produced from overseas direct development caused marketing problems. Thus government should induce domestic actual users to participate in development projects or at least require that the developing firms should secure domestic demand in advance.

To promote overseas resource development invertments, the government should provide relevant support in each stage of development. The government can collect and distribute various information such as international resource trend, changing investment condition, and policies of the resource owning countries. It can also provide technical assistance at the initial exploration stage. At the development stage, the government should help the developing companies through favorable loans and tax systems.

While continuing the cooperative exploration activities in the Korea-Japan joint development area, it is desirable for Korea and Japan to extend cooperation in overseas oil development activities through joint ventures. Korea can utilize the advanced technology and experience of Japan while Korea can give stimulus to the discouraged Japanese oil developing companies by providing a stable demand market for developed oil and by alleviating the burden of enormous development costs. Especially, the cooperative activities of Korea and Japan in the South Asian countries like Indonesia and Malaysia are critically important as the import of crude oil and gas from these countries is expected to increase continuously in the future. Korea and Japan should realize that cooperation between resource importing countries, whose overseas resource dependence ratios are high, is as important as cooperation with resource owning countries.

IV. Oil Stockpile Policy

1. Korea

The history of Korea's oil stockpile policy is short and the stockpile level has been very low compared to other oil importing countries. After the first oil crisis, most of the developed countries raised their oil stockpile level as a safeguard against another oil crisis. However, Korea did not develop a specific oil stockpile policy even after the first crisis and she faced the second oil crisis unprepared. After the first oil crisis, the Korean government advised the private oil companies to raise their oil stockpile level, but they were reluctant to keep extra oil in addition to their minimum running stocks.

When the second oil crisis broke out, Korean oil companies were keeping only 30 days of running stocks while Japan was keeping 87 days and Taiwan was keeping more than 60 days stockpile level. After the second oil crisis, the Korean government realized that maintaining a proper oil stockpile level is indispensable to protect the national economy from the disruption of oil supply and pushed the government-initiated oil stockpile policy strongly.

The Korea Petroleum Development Corporation (PEDCO) was founded in March 1979 and prepared the oil stockpile plan of Korea. In the plan fixed in June 1980, PEDCO proposed the following policy guidelines : By 1986, 60 days of government stockpile will be accomplished and the required capital will be collected through the oil stockpile fund. The storage facilities will be mostly constructed underground, but ground facilities will also be constructed for initial stockpile purposes. The government will stockpile crude oil and will guide the private oil companies to stockpile oil products. At the same time, the government will direct the oil companies to complete oil storage facilities good for 60 days reserve by 1982 and guide the heavy oil using companies to keep their own stockpiles.

In the second revision of the Oil Business Law in December 1977, a new provision for the establishment of an oil business fund was created. Based on the revised Oil Business Law, dues for the oil business fund were collected beginning in 1979. While general tax is reflected in the budget and spent for general purposes, the oil business fund is collected and spent only for oil related businesses. The sources of the oil business fund are the fees collected from the oil importers and the oil refiners, the dues collected from windfall profits of domestic oil refiners, and the gains from investments. Up to now, the fees collected from oil importers at the time of the import have constituted the fund's main source of income.

The oil business fund was composed of the oil stabilization fund and the oil stockpile fund when it started, but the oil development fund was later added in June, 1983. The three sources of the oil business fund have their own specific uses. The oil stockpile fund is used for the construction of oil storage facilities and for the purchase of crude oil for stockpile purposes. The oil development fund is loaned to the oil developers for exploration and drilling activities and is also used as a debt surety fund. The oil stabilization fund is spent to diversify the origin of crude oil imports and for energy use rationalization projects including domestic coal and electric power development projects.

Table 11 shows the oil business fund fees as of July 1985. Several changes since the establishment of the oil stockpile fund in 1979 resulted in charges of 25 cents per barrel for imported crude and diesel oil, 10 cents per barrel for Bunker-C oil, and $113.84 per ton of LPG.[16)] From 1979 to 1983, 697 billion won of oil stockpile fund was raised and 468 billion won was used for the government oil stockpile. Of the 468 billion won, 33% was used for the construction of stockpile facilities, 66% was used for the import of stockpile crude oil, and the rest was used for maintenance. During the same period, 870 billion won was collected for the oil stabilization fund. In addition, 163 billion won was collected from the windfall gains generated by the reduction in the price of imported crude oil in 1983.

|**Table 11**| Oil Business Fund Fees (as of '85. 7. 31)

Fund \ Oil	Crude, Diesel	B-C	LPG
Stockpile Fund	$0.25/B	$0.10/B	$113.84/ton
Development Fund	$0.10/B	$0.10/B	$1.16/ton
Stabilization Fund	$0.15/B	$0.10/B	$100/ton
Total	$0.50/B	$0.30/B	$215/ton

Source : Korea Petroleum Development corporation

16) In 1986, the three sources of oil business fund were integrated into one and the fees were raised to absorb the windfall gain of the oil importing companies generated by the fall in the price of oil. As of May 1986, the oil business fund fee is $9.04/Bbl for crude oil and $119/ton for LPG.

As shown in Table 12, the oil business fund fees have decreased since 1981 reflecting the decreased oil consumption level. Government reduced the quantity of the target oil stockpile as the annual oil consumption level decreased. The original government oil stockpile plan of 1980 was revised following the fall in the official price of crude oil and the slowdown in the growth rate of domestic oil demand. According to the revised plan, 40.5 million barrels of storage facilities and 41 million barrels of crude oil stockpile good for 68 days will be completed by 1987. Additionally, 1.8 million barrels of oil products, good for 30 days of Seoul area use, will be stockpiled. Also an LPG stockpile plan was instituted in consideration of the rapidly rising LPG demand. According to the plan, 335,000 tons of LPG (the 60 days consumption level) will be stockpiled by 1990 and the LPG stockpile facilities will be constructed from 1985 to 1989. By 1984, 15 million barrels of crude oil and 25,000 barrels of LPG were stockpiled by the government.

|**Table 12**| Trend of Oil Business Fund Fees (Crude and Diesel)

($/B)

	79.7.10	80.8.24	81.11.29	83.6.15	83.10.1	85.4.1
Stockpile Fund	FOB × 3.3%	1.0	1.5	1.0	0.7	0.25
Development Fund				0.1	0.1	0.1
Stabilization Fund	(import price minus domestic official price)		(")+2.3	2.09	2.09	0.15

Source : Korea Petroleum Development Corporation

|Table 13| Outline of Oil Storage Base

Form	Capacity	Construction Period	Remarks
Crude Oil	(million barrel)	(year)	(present storage, million barrel)
Ground Tank (T-1)	13.5	80-82	12.0
Underground Tunnel (U-2)	27.0	80-85	.
Private Facilities	5.0	.	3.0
LPG	(thousand ton)	(year)	(present storage, thousand ton)
Underground (1)	160.0	85-86	.
Underground (2)	160.0	86-87	.
Private Facilities	15.0		25.0

Source : Korea Petroleum Development Corporation

In August 1984, the Korean government required that the five private oil companies of Korea to keep a 26 days level of crude oil in addition to a 20 days level of products. Out of the 26 days of obligatory crude oil stockpile, the government intended to provide loans for 6 days level (3 million barrels) from the oil stockpile fund. However, the Korean government adjusted the targeted private oil stockpile downward to 8 days of crude oil and 18 days of oil products in 1985 to reduce the trade deficit by cutting down crude oil imports.

Korea has retained the target of reaching a 110 days oil stockpile level by 1988. After 1989, the proper level will be maintained after consideration of the performance of the oil development projects, the diversification of oil importing countries, and the world oil market situation. Government expects the positive participation of private oil companies in oil stockpiling efforts in the future.

2. Japan

In response to the increased control of OPEC over their crude oil exports since 1970, the Japanese government initiated the plan to fulfill a 60 days oil stockpile by the end of 1974. After the first oil crisis, Japanese stockpile level decreased to 49 days, but the Japanese government together with the oil companies pushed through an ambitious stockpile plan to minimize the impact of the second oil crisis.

In November 1974, 18 developed countries including Japan organized the International Energy Agency (IEA) and decided to increase the oil stockpile level to 90 days of net imports by 1980 to help each other in case of emergencies. Japan enacted the Oil Stockpile Law in December 1975 and obliged the private oil companies to fulfill the 90 days of oil stockpile by the end of 1979. According to the Oil Stockpile Law, all the refining, marketing, and importing companies who produce, sell, and import oil over a certain level are obliged to keep an oil stockpile above the obligatory amount in the form of crude oil or oil products. The Iran–Iraq war which broke out in 1979 delayed the goal of securing a 90 days private oil stockpile. However, Japan was able to secure 90 days of private oil stockpile by March 1981 thanks to decreased oil consumption and increased oil stockpile caused by slack industrial activities together with increased energy substitution and conservation. The private oil stockpile level of Japan has been maintained over 90 days since then.

The Japanese private oil stockpile level was recorded at 101 days in March 1982, but has decreased since then because the private oil companies have steadily reduced their crude oil stockpile responding to the decreased oil consumption. On the other hand, the government oil stockpile level has been increasing ever since the Japan National Oil Corporation (JNOC) started the government stockpile operation in 1978. JNOC purchases the stockpiling oil from the oil refining companies through the bidding method. It also establishes national oil stockpile companies with the help of private oil companies who have know-hows and experiences in constructing and operating oil storage bases.

JNOC originally set the government oil stockpile target at 10 million kl, but this goal was reached in 1982 and a new goal was set at 30 million kl by 1988. At the end of 1984, the private oil stockpile of Japan was 53 million kl and the government stockpile was 17 million kl, totaling 129 days at the 1983 oil consumption level.

There are four ways to stockpile oil : tanker stockpiling, land tank stockpiling, sea-tank stockpiling, and underground stockpiling. Japan has been using oil tankers and private storage tanks for government stockpile. Since the partial completion of Mutsu Ogawara national oil storage base in 1983, 3.3 million kl have been stockpiled there. Japan is constructing 6 storage bases and plans to accommodate the entire government oil stockpile in government storage bases by 1988.

Oil stockpile policy is vital as a safeguard against unpredicted sudden interruption of oil supplies to Japan as Japan's dependence on foreign oil is nearly 100%. But the oil stockpile policy requires enormous amounts of money and economic cost for its fulfillment. To achieve 90 days of private oil stockpile in Japan, 2,400 billion yen was spent for oil import and storage facilities construction from 1972 to 1980.[17] JNOC's loans to private oil companies for their purchase of stockpile oil amounted to 780 billion yen from 1975 to 1983. Also, JNOC invested 179 billion yen and loaned 818 billion yen for the purchase of land and construction of storage facilities from 1976 to 1983.

Just to maintain the 90 days private oil stockpile, private oil companies should bear enormous costs every year. Even if the government provides loans to the private oil companies for the construction of storage facilities at a rate 2% cheaper than the prime rate, the loan is within 70% of the required capital in case of sole construction and within 80% in case of joint construction. The burden of maintaining a 90 day oil stockpile deteriorated the financial structure of Japanese oil companies. At the end of 1982, the oil companies' equity-capital ratio was about 5.9%, below one quarter of the average ratio of the Japanese manufacturing industries. Japanese private oil companies are asking the government for an increase in government support for their stockpile activities and for the replacement of private company's crude oil stockpile with government stockpile.

According to the Japan's 1982 national budget plan, total revenue from oil taxes amounted to 3,053 billion yen, which

---

17) 岩動道行, *Energy-Its Nature and Strategy* (in Japanese), 通商産業研究社, 1982, pp. 253-256.

|Table 14| Oil Stockpile Trend of Japan

(Unit: million kl)

	Private Reserve						Government Reserve			Total	
	Reserve Target Days	Crude Oil (A)	Semi-Products (B)	Oil Products (C)	TOTAL (A)×0.95+(B)+(C)	Reserve to use Ratio (Days)	Crude Oil		Reserve to use Ratio (Days)	Total	Reserve to use Ratio (Days)
							Crude Oil Base	Oil Products Base			
1978. 4	80	36.61	10.61	14.56	59.93	87	-	-	-	59.93	87
1979. 3	80	34.48	9.56	13.19	55.50	81	5.24	4.98	7	60.48	88
1980. 3	80	37.37	10.04	15.42	60.96	88	5.24	4.98	7	65.93	95
1981. 3	85	39.44	10.40	15.09	62.95	90	7.25	6.89	10	69.84	100
1982. 3	90	41.85	10.18	13.03	62.96	101	11.05	10.50	17	73.46	118
1983. 3	90	33.93	9.94	12.02	54.18	93	12.51	11.88	20	66.06	113
1983. 12	90	31.02	9.68	13.76	51.91	98	13.74	13.05	24	65.96	122
1984. 11	90	28.04	10.33	16.24	53.21	98	17.51	16.63	31	69.84	129

Source: MITI, *Energy Supply and Demand Monthly Statistics*, 1984, 11, p. 53.

accounted for 8% of the total national revenue of 1982. The oil tax, which is levied at several stages, was established in 1978 to provide funds for Japan's oil stockpile and oil development policies. When the oil is imported from overseas, crude oil tariff and oil tax are levied. These two taxes amounted to 579 billion yen in 1982. When the various kinds of oil products are produced from the crude oil, oil products consumption taxes are levied. In 1982, 1,916 billion yen of gasoline tax, 462 billion yen of diesel oil transaction tax, 32 billion yen of petroleum gas tax, and 64 billion yen of jet fuel tax were collected.[18)]

Out of 3,053 billion yen of oil tax revenue, 49 billion yen (about 1.5%) was attributed to general revenue sources and the rest was used for special purposes. About 80% of the total oil tax revenue was used for road construction and maintenance purposes. The share of oil tax revenue attributed to reinforce the oil stockpile of Japan was only 6.0%, 1.3% for private oil stockpiling and 4.7% for government oil stockpiling. For the oil exploration and development activities, another 4.3% was used. Japan seems to have some room to alleviate the burden of private oil companies in stockpiling and developing oil by cutting a certain portion of road-related expenses from oil tax revenues.

Japan was forced to change the oil tax system in 1984 to make up for the reduced revenues caused by the oil price reduction in 1983. The oil tax rate was raised from 3.5% to 4.7% and a new tax system was introduced for LPG and LNG in September 1984.

18) *Ibid.*, pp. 257-259.

The tax rate for LNG and LPG is 1.2% of CIF plus a tariff for imported gas and 1.2% of the gas field price for domestic gas.

3. Comparison and Findings

There are two noticeable differences in the progress of the oil stockpile policies in Korea and Japan. The first difference is that a full scale oil stockpile policy in Korea started after the outbreak of the second oil crisis while Japan initiated the oil stockpile policy in the early 1970s. By 1974 Japan had completed a 60 days private oil stockpile. After the first oil crisis, Japan set the goal of securing a 90 days private oil stockpile by 1980 and reached the goal in 1981. Korea did not even conceive the oil stockpile plan after the first oil crisis. At the end of the 1970s, the Korean government tried to induce private oil companies to increase their oil stockpile besides running stocks, but it failed. Only after the second oil crisis, was the government-initiated oil stockpile plan pushed strongly.

The second difference is the government's role in the early stage of the oil stockpile operations. While the Japanese government started to participate in the oil stockpile activities from 1978 by which time private oil companies had already secured an 87 days oil stockpile, the Korean oil stockpile plan was initiated by the government from the beginning. Korea expects to complete the construction of government oil storage facilities and secure a 68 days government oil stockpile by 1986. The Japanese government stockpiled 17.5 million kl, a 31 days stockpile in 1984 and plans to reach 30 million kl, about a 45 days stockpile by 1988.

The Japanese oil stockpile policy was successful in the sense that it mitigated the impact of the second oil crisis. But enormous amounts of money were spent for the construction of oil stockpile facilities and the import of stockpiling oil. Japanese private oil companies have been keeping more than 90 days stockpile oil since 1981. As long as the worldwide oil glut situation continues and the import of crude oil from the spot market is cheaper than the official price, 90 days obligatory private oil stockpile in Japan will impose a heavy burden on the private oil companies. It seems that Japan should reduce the level of obligatory private oil stockpile and replace it gradually with a government stockpile.

Korea can learn from the Japanese experience that at this time of cheap oil prices it is desirable to secure a basic amount of government oil stockpile first and then adjust the level of private stockpile properly according to the oil market situation. However, as the world oil market is expected to become tight again in the 1990s, Korean private oil companies should establish plans to secure a proper level of private oil stockpile within 4 years.

V. Summary and Suggestions for Cooperation

1. Comparison of Energy Policies and Performances

The energy policies of Korea and Japan for the past ten years or so are very similar in many ways. However, there are many differences in the performance of the energy policies of the two countries due to the different timing of policy initiation. Stimulated by continued rapid economic growth after the first oil crisis, Korea did not seriously consider the necessity of changing the industrial structure of her economy into an energy saving one. As a result, Korea was struck by the second oil crisis unprepared and recorded a minus 5.2% economic growth rate in 1980, the first negative growth rate since the initiation of the five year economic development plan in 1962.

On the other hand, Japan learned after experiencing a minus 0.4% economic growth rate in 1974, that her economy should reduce its dependence on energy, especially on oil in order to attain sustained economic growth. Japan succeeded in achieving a nationwide consensus to mobilize strong energy policies to conserve energy and reduce her dependence on imported oil. Japan secured 90 days oil stockpile and reduced oil consumption through improved energy efficiency in the manufacturing industries and energy conservation in all sectors of the economy. Japan's oil consumption in 1982 was 2.44 billion barrels which was the lowest level since the first oil crisis. Compared to the Japanese performance, the case of Korea was far less successful. Korea invested large amounts of money in heavy and petrochemical industries even after the first oil crisis and the economy became more vulnerable to imported oil. Korea consumed 191.3 million barrels of oil in 1983, which was about twice the consumption level of 1974.

Japan initiated a strong energy policy right after the first oil crisis under the direction of the Agency for Natural Resources and

Energy. However, a full-scale energy policy in Korea was formulated belatedly by the Department of Energy and Resources, established in 1978. As a result, the Japanese economy could easily adapt to the impact of the second oil crisis while the Korean economy suffered from deep economic recession and growing foreign debts.

The main energy policy objectives of Korea and Japan have been the secure supply of energy and the reduction in energy dependence, especially on oil. However, this tradition was slightly modified since OPEC announced a reduction of the official price of crude oil in the spring of 1983. The world oil market has transformed from a seller's market into a buyer's market since the 1980s and this trend has accelerated recently. Responding to this change Japan postponed the development of costly new energy sources and increased the share of oil in the revised long-term energy plan. Korea also expressed concern for the best energy mix which would give a secure supply of energy at the least possible cost in the "Long Term Energy Outlook and Strategy for the 2000s".

2. Suggestions for Energy Cooperation

Both Korea and Japan are poorly endowed with natural resources, so their economies have been heavily dependent upon imported energy sources, especially on imported oil. In this sense, the two countries have common concerns, namely energy security. For the energy importing countries, a close relationship with energy exporting countries is essential to secure a stable long term energy supply. However, the cooperation among the energy importing countries are as much important to stop the arbitrary manipulation of the market by the energy exporting countries and to cope with the unexpected disruption of the energy supply.

As each country has its own life style, stage of economic development and unique energy policy, it is not easy to find mutually acceptable fields of energy cooperation. However, there have been several cooperation efforts among countries not only through the IEA but also on a country-to country basis. For example, Japan and the U.S. have sought governmental level cooperation through the Japan-U.S. energy working group. This kind of energy cooperation has also been discussed through regular meetings of interested organizations of the two countries. As another example of regional energy cooperation, the national oil companies of ASEAN have been sharing their expertise in geology, petroleum engineering, refining, and using their laboratories and training facilities for their common benefit through the ASEAN Council on Petroleum. The ASEAN member countries also have been cooperating in the field of electric power systems.

The U.S. is contemplating a wider range of cooperation on energy matters in the Pacific-Asian region through the World Energy Conference (WEC). The WEC, a non-political, professional organization with a membership from the developed and developing countries, shares information on energy supply and use, planning, technology, economics, operations, maintenance, etc.[19)]

As such it would be worth trying to organize non-governmental

---

19) John E. Gray, "Remarks Presented at the International Symposium on Energy and Development in Asia," Tokyo, Japan, February 1985.

regular meetings between Korea and Japan to identify common concerns and develop ways to enhance mutual benefits in the energy fields. Following suggestions for energy cooperation between Korea and Japan could be considered as possible policy alternatives.

(1) Exchange of Information and Expertise

Korea and Japan can cooperate in setting up their best energy mixes through meetings and exchanges of specialists either on a public or private level. The information sharing system between the Korea Energy Economics Institute and the Institute of Energy Economics of Japan is a good example for this kind of cooperation. Exchange of academic research results between the two countries through international conferences can also enhance mutual understanding by clarifying differences in opinion.

(2) Cooperation in Importing and Developing Energy Sources

The most certain way of securing energy supply is direct development. Japan has been supplying 10% of required oil through direct development from overseas and plans to secure 20% eventually. Korea also plans to secure 10% of her oil demand through direct development by 2001. Naturally, the two countries' development activities in the Asia-Pacific region will increase in the future. Then the terms of contract with the resource-owning countries will be in order. In this case, through regular and recognized meetings between interested parties of two countries, the key issues and options can be identified and an unnecessary waste of time and expenses can be minimized.

For the past several years, Korea and Japan have been cooperating on oil development activities in the joint continental shelf mining area. By extending cooperative efforts into overseas oil development projects through a consortium of private companies, the two countries can diversify the risk of failing, reduce the required capital, and secure the selling market. Especially, Korea can utilize the advanced managing skills and technologies of experienced Japanese oil development companies.

As long as the present oil glut situation continues, overseas oil development will not be hailed as a lucrative business. However, this is the best time for Korea and Japan to invest on overseas oil development as they can acquire concessions from the resource owning countries in better terms and the rental costs of exploration equipments are much cheaper than before.

It takes nearly ten years from the initiation of exploration activities to actual production. As the world oil market is expected to become tight again from early 1990s, this is the right time for Korea and Japan to increase their investments on overseas oil development. While Japan left the distribution of the windfall gain from the lowered import price of oil to the market mechanism, the Korean government decided to collect all the surpluses through the petroleum business fund after lowering the official price of oil products twice in 1986. To prepare against another oil crisis the government of Korea should spare a good sum of the accumulated fund for oil exploration and development activities on the continental shelf of Korea and overseas by private oil companies.

Before starting an actual joint overseas oil development, exchange of technology, expertise, and know-how in the field of oil development between Korea and Japan is desirable. The existing training internship program between PEDCO and JNOC is a successful case and this kind of program should be extended further.

(3) Cooperation in Oil Transporting and Refining

Korea and Japan import oil mostly from the Middle East, one of the most troublesome regions in the world. So the two countries can cooperate by sharing information related to safe transportation of crude oil via sea lanes. They can also cooperate by introducing swap systems of crude oil and surplus oil products considering the differences in oil refining systems and needs of the two countries. This kind of cooperation doesn't have to be restricted to the two countries, but the geographical closeness and similar compositions of the origin of oil imports will especially enhance the benefits from mutual cooperation.

Korea plans to construct oil cracking facilities to meet the increasing demand of light oil products. However, the OPEC countries are increasing their investments on downstream areas and some of the Asia-Pacific region countries are suffering from excess refinery capacities. So the development of a crude oil consignment refining system can be considered as a way of saving refining costs before constructing expensive oil cracking facilities separately. Korea and Japan can cooperate especifically on this matter.

(4) Cooperation in Oil Stockpile

Oil stockpile is the surest way to cope with the sudden disruption of the oil supply. Korea and Japan learned from the two oil crises of the 1970s that a stable supply of energy sources, especially oil, is vital to the economic stability and national security of the two countries. While the direct development of oil is an active way to secure a stable oil supply, oil stockpile policy is considered a passive way. However, direct development of oil is a very risky business and does not guarantee a timely supply of required oil. So a certain amount of oil stockpile has to be kept as a safeguard despite the considerable cost.

Japan has been keeping more than 120 days of oil stockpile and plans to increase the stockpile level further. Korea also plans to eventually stockpile 110 days of oil, so the exchange of information and expertise between Korea and Japan on oil stockpile will be desirable. Moreover, the sharing system of stockpiled oil between the two countries can be considered a possibility. The member countries of IEA and the six countries in the Persian Gulf have already been cooperating in this field respectively.

The world oil market is expected to tighten again in the 1990s. The increasing consumption of oil by the developing countries will be held partly responsible for this transition. So it will be to the benefit of the developed countries in the long run if they are able to help the developing countries diversify their energy consumption mix and increase oil exploration and development activities. The energy cooperation between Korea and Japan can be developed as a sample case of regional cooperation for the upcoming Asia-Pacific economic era.

References

Agency for Natural Resources and Energy, MITI, *Energy in Japan : Facts and Figure*, January, 1985.

International Energy Agency, *Energy Policies and Programmes of IEA Countries*, OECD, 1984.

Korea Institute of Energy and Resources, *International Oil Seminar : Changing Market Signals and Consumer Country Strategy*, December, 1984.

Korea Petroleum Association, *Oil Policies and Oil Industries (1945-1983)*, April 1984.

Korea Ministry of Energy and Resources, *Long-Term Energy Outlook and Strategy for the 2000s*, Seoul, 1985.

Morse, Ronald A., "Japanese Energy Policy", in *After the Second Oil Crisis*, ed. by Wilfred L. Kohl, D.C. Health and Company, 1982.

______(ed.), *The Politics of Energy Strategy*, Berkeley ; University of California, 1981.

Oshima K., T. Suzuki, and Matsuno, "Energy Issues and Policies in Japan", *Ann. Rev. Energy*, 1982, pp. 87-108.

Yager, Joseph A., *the Energy Balance in Northeast Asia*, 1984.

石油公団, 石油鉱業連盟共著,「石油開発資料」, 1985.

経済企画庁編,「省資源・省エネルギーと これからの 暮らし」, 1979.

通商産業省,「エネルギ生産・需給統計月報 : 石油, 石炭」, 1984.

経済企画庁 経済研究所,「エネルギー需給の 計量分析」, 1983.

通商産業省編,「21世紀への エネルギー需給展望」, 1984.

通商産業省編,「エネルギー'84」, 1984.

通商産業省,「80年代 エネルギーの 需給展望」, 1981.
岩動道行著,「エネルギーその 本質と 迫られる 戰略」, 1982.
日本経済研究センタ偏,「石油危機の 時代」, 1983.
干田広志著,「エネルギー産業界」, 1982.
岩部成良著,「石油業界」, 産業界シリ-ズ No. 327, 1983.
省 エネルギーセシタ(財),「省エネルギー便覧」, 1984.
エネルギ-資源問題研究会 編著,「エネルギー戰国時代」, 1983.

4. Energy Cooperation in the Asia-Pacific Era*

I. Introduction

The two oil crises which struck the world in the 1970s share at least two common characteristics. One of them is unusually high price increase which can't be expected in a normal market situation. The other is the significant impact of the oil price increase on the world economy. The crude oil price quadrupled during the first oil crisis and it tripled during the second oil crisis. Many developed countries such as the United States, Japan, West Germany, and the Great Britain experienced negative economic growth after the first oil crisis, and the Republic of Korea together with some developed countries recorded negative economic growth in 1980. Especially the world-wide economic recession after the second oil crisis was regarded as one of the worst since the great depression of the 1930s

---

* "Energy Cooperation in the Asia-Pacific Era," in M. Shin et al(eds.), *Partners in a Changing World*, Institute of East and West Studies, Yonsei University, December 1990, pp. 251-275.

and resulted in a revival of protectionism and prolonged slowdown of world economy.

The two oil crises were preceded by the following symptoms. Firstly, due to low prices which prevailed for several years, oil consumption increased continuously and the oil market was transformed into seller's market. Secondly, conservation measure lost merits and the stockpile level started to decrease. Thirdly, war between the Middle East countries or political upheaval in one of oil exporting countries reduce the oil supply unexpectedly and the panic-purchase of energy poor countries and increase in speculative demand resulted in shortage in the world oil market, leading to a rapid increase of crude oil price.

Recently, several well-known research institutes together with some individual oil specialists warned the increasing possibility of third oil crisis in the middle of 1990s. They pointed out the facts that the oil demand of developed countries started to increase again since the latter part of 1980s, while oil conservation efforts of these countries reached a limit. They are worried that non-OPEC countries do not have enough reserve to meet the increasing oil demand, and accordingly the OPEC countries would regain their lost market shares consolidating their market powers.

The third oil crisis hypothesis is based on the similarity of present oil market situation to those of the two previous crises. They predict that if unexpected events interrupt the smooth flow of oil supply in the world oil market, sudden surge of oil price cannot be escaped. There is no question that we should be alarmed by the changing pattern of oil consumption by developed as well as by developing countries in recent years. If the market turns into a seller's market, the price would increase to clear the market. But it seems too naive to believe that the present situation will lead to another oil crisis in the near future. The environment surrounding the world oil market has undergone a tremendous change during the 1980s. In the Middle East, extreme Islamic regime of Iran became much moderate after Khomeini's death, the Iran-Iraq war which continued for nearly a decade came to an end, and the antagonism between Israel and Arab countries is not so tense as before. Globally, Cold War diplomacy of superpowers gave way to East-West reconciliation policy encouraged by Gorbachev's Perestroika, and the successive democratization movement of the East European communist bloc is changing the principle of East-West confrontation into a new international order of mutual understanding and coexistence.

In the midst of prevailing sentiment of mutual cooperation in the international politics, OPEC countries began to realize that the unilateral pursuit of their own interest would be detrimental not only to importing countries but to themselves eventually. Instead of sticking to high crude oil price policy, they are aiming at promoting the export of refined oil products with higher values and are increasing the investment in refining industries and service sectors of oil importing countries to secure market and to reduce risk through business diversification. Especially, some Middle East OPEC countries began to pay attention to Asia-Pacific region as a place to expand their downstream investments. So far, OPEC invested to European and American oil industries and markets. Japan, Korea, and few other Asian countries are reducing government regulation toward petroleum industries and speeding up the liberalization policy, thus promoting modernization and vertical integration of domestic refining industries. Such a development would provide favorable environment to the investment of Persian Gulf OPEC countries.

Asia-Pacific Region has been the most vital in the world economy in recent years and the energy consumption of NIES as well as fast developing ASEAN countries has been increasing rapidly. Even Japan is showing a sign of changing from an energy miser to an extravagant energy user. As the Asia-Pacific region is expected to remain as a fast growing economy in the 1990s, present trend of increasing oil demand will last and the oil dependence on Middle East OPEC countries will increase.

According to a recent report of East-West Center, the volume of petroleum shipped from the Persian Gulf to Asian region would increase from 5.7 million barrels per day to 8.9 million barrels per day in ten years, while daily production of crude oil in the Region would decrease from 5.9 million barrels to 5.4 million barrels. One government official of the U.S. Department of Energy predicted that the oil dependence rate of Asia on Persian Gulf would increase from 67% in 1985 to 82% in 1995 and that it could increase to 90% in 2000.

Naturally, one of the most important tasks of energy cooperation among Asia-Pacific region countries will be to reduce vulnerability to increasing oil dependence on Persian Gulf OPEC countries. There are several ways to cope with this problem. One way is to form a regional energy agency through which the oil-importing countries can cooperate in purchasing oil from out-of-the region and share the burden of economic impact in case of emergency. Second way is to reduce dependence on oil by switching to alternative energy sources such as coal, natural gas, nuclear power, geothermal energy, and also through energy conservation. Third way is to resort to new international order of mutual dependence and coexistence. Persian Gulf countries are eager to modernize through industrialization. They need the expertise and investment of industrialized countries and ask for the participation of Asia-Pacific countries. The third way is positive and more conducive to the development of new international economic order while the first and second ways are relatively passive and traditional.

'Energy security through economic cooperation with Persian gulf countries' must be a very challenging task to study further. However, the present topic is energy cooperation in the Asia-Pacific region so I will discuss about traditional way of energy cooperation among Asia-Pacific countries in this paper.

II. Energy Supply and Demand in the Asia-Pacific Region

It is often said that the 21st century will be an era of Asia-Pacific region. Asia-Pacific region is emerging as potentially the most important economic bloc in the world. For this region to function as a center for world economic and industrial activities, proper solution of energy problem is crucially important. However, as the Asia-Pacific region is consisted of various countries diverse in land size, population, climate, ethnic group, economic development stage, and natural resource endowment, it will not be an easy task to develop a regional energy cooperation strategy that each and every country agrees.

To investigate the energy situation in the Asia-Pacific region, we should select countries to be included in the analysis. There are several researches being done on this topic and the countries included in the analysis are not the same.[1] In this paper, we will include 16 countries in the Asia-Pacific region and classify those countries into six subgroups as follows : Japan, East Asian NIES (Korea, Taiwan, Hong Kong), ASEAN (Thailand, Indonesia, Malaysia, Philippines, Singapore, Brunei), Oceania (Australia, New Zealand, Pacific Island States), U.S.A., Canada, and China.

Asia-Pacific region's primary energy consumption was 3,414.8 million tons of oil equivalent in 1987 and composed 44.8% of world total. United States alone was responsible for 54.6% of the region's total primary energy consumption. The share of each energy source in total primary energy consumption was 33.6% for coal,

---

1) The region which covers the Pacific Ocean and surrounding countries is called by many different names with slight changes in countries involved such as Pan-Pacific, Pacific Rim, Asia-Pacific, Western-Pacific, Pacific Asia, etc. The Asia-Pacific region described in this paper is mainly equal to the Western-Pacific Community (excluding North Korea) plus the US and Canada. See the following interesting article about four possible scenarios on trading blocs of the Asia-Pacific region. Kim Duk Choong, "The Pan-Pacific Card," *Far Eastern Economic Review*, 21 December 1989, pp. 60-61.

|Table 1| Primary Energy Consumption by Country/Region (1987)

Million TOE, (%)

	Coal	Petroleum	Natural gas	Nuclear	Hydro & others	Total
Japan	73.4	230.0	40.8	42.2	22.9	409.3
NIES	37.9	53.7	3.1	16.2	2.7	113.6
ASEAN	5.8	66.8	16.4	0.0	5.5	94.5
Oceania	37.3	35.3	16.4	0.0	8.8	97.8
U.S.A.	511.4	766.4	417.6	107.8	62.5	1,865.7
Canada	32.8	75.7	47.6	17.3	66.9	240.3
China	448.2	109.2	13.8	0.0	22.4	593.6
Asia-Pacific total	1,146.8 (33.6)	1,337.1 (39.2)	555.7 (16.3)	183.5 (5.4)	191.7 (5.6)	3,414.8 (100.0)
World total	2,248.8 (29.5)	2,968.9 (39.0)	1,549.8 (20.3)	388.5 (5.1)	461.7 (6.1)	7,617.7 (100.0)
Asia-Pacific /World	(51.0)	(45.0)	(35.9)	(47.2)	(41.5)	(44.8)

Source : Constructed based on Mitsuru Miyata, "Energy Demand and Supply Forecast for the Pan Pacific Region in Year 2000 and Tasks for Energy Cooperation," Japan Institute of Energy Economics, January 1990.

39.2% for petroleum, and 16.3% for natural gas. The share of coal in the region was higher than the world total. China received 75.5% of total primary energy from coal and the share of oil was only 18.4%. United States and China accounted for 83.7% of coal consumption in the region. As for oil consumption, United States and Japan respectively composed 57.3% and 17.2% of total oil consumption in region, which was 1,337.1 million tons in 1987.

Natural gas accounted for 16.3% of primary energy consumption in the region and United States, Japan and Canada shared 82.5% of total natural gas consumption.

Since the second oil crisis, world primary energy consumption hardly increased during 1979~1986 period, at the annual rate of 1.1%. But the consumption growth rate rose to 3.1% between 1986 and 1988. Especially Asian region recorded an annual growth rate of 11.6% during 1986~1988. According to the energy demand forecast made by the Japan Energy Economics Institute, Asia-Pacific region's primary energy consumption will increase at the annual rate of 2.4% and reach 4,881 million tons of oil equivalent in 2000, a 37% increase from the 1987 consumption of 3,568 million tons of oil equivalent. The consumption share of the region in world consumption of primary energy will remain at 47%. United States, the largest energy consuming country in the world, will increase primary energy consumption at 1.2% per annum and other developed countries in the region will register 2.0~2.3% consumption growth rate. As China and East Asian NIEs will continue to grow at higher rates than other countries in the region, energy consumption growth of these countries will remain high. China's energy consumption will grow at the annual rate of 4.1% and the East Asian NIEs are expected to increase their primary energy consumption at 5.4% per annum.

According to the forecast, oil demand in the Asia-Pacific region will grow only 24.1% from 1,471 million tons in 1987 to 1,758 tons in 2000 at the annual rate of 1.8%. However, it seems to be too low an estimate considering the high oil consumption growth recently experienced by Japan and other fast-growing Pacific Rim countries encouraged by low oil price and high economic growth. As per capita income grows in the region, demand for light oil products will grow faster than the residual oil and supply-demand imbalances among oil products will be intensified in the future.

Coal demand has been growing continuously in the region due to the increasing coal use in coal-fired thermal power plants and cement industry. It is expected that coal will remain as one of major energy sources in the Asia-Pacific region despite environmental concern over acid rain to meet growing energy demand.

Asia-Pacific region produced 38.3% of world primary energy in 1987 while consuming 44.8%. Thus, energy self-sufficiency rate was 86.4%, signifying that this region as a whole is energy-poor. Asia-Pacific region is relatively rich in coal and poor in oil. This region contributed 52.7% of world coal production but the share in world oil production was only 27.7%.

Asia-Pacific region produced 837 million tons of oil while it consumed 1,337 million tons in 1987, so the self-sufficiency rate of oil was 62.6%. However, required amount of coal and natural gas could be secured fully within the region.

Crude oil production in the Asia-Pacific region has grown 7.4% between 1981 and 1987. The output increase came from Malaysia, China, and Australia while Indonesia and Brunei cut the production during the period. In North America, Canada increased the oil production by 365,000 barrels per day but the production of the United States decreased by 275,000 barrels during the period.

Out of 836.5 million tons of oil produced in 1987, United States

|**Table 2**| Primary Energy Production by Country/Region (1987)

Million TOE, (%)

	Coal	Petroleum	Natural gas	Nuclear	Hydro & others	Total
Japan	8.1	0.7	2.3	42.2	22.9	76.2
NIES	12.1	0.1	1.0	16.2	2.8	32.2
ASEAN	4.2	101.8	52.2	0.0	5.6	163.8
Oceania	104.7	29.6	16.4	0.0	8.8	159.5
U.S.A.	563.5	475.5	397.7	107.8	58.9	1,601.4
Canada	38.7	92.4	70.7	17.3	70.7	289.8
China	453.7	136.4	13.8	0.0	22.4	626.3
Asia-Pacific total	1,185.0 (40.1)	836.5 (28.4)	554.1 (18.8)	183.5 (6.2)	192.1 (6.5)	2,949.2 (100.0)
World total	2,248.6 (29.2)	3,016.6 (39.2)	1.574.5 (20.5)	388.5 (5.1)	462.5 (6.0)	7,690.7 (100.0)
Asia-Pacific /World	(52.7)	(27.7)	(35.2)	(47.2)	(41.5)	(38.3)

Source : Same as table 1.

accounted for 47.6%, China 16.3%, Canada 11.0%, and ASEAN countries 12.2%, when consumption is compared with production, consumption exceeded production by 229.3 million tons in Japan, 53.6 million tons in East Asian NIEs, 5.7 million tons in Oceania, and 290.9 million tons in the United States. Surplus producers of oil in the region were ASEAN with 35 million tons, Canada with 16.7 million tons, and China with 27.2 million tons. Asia-Pacific region as a whole, consumption exceeded production by 500 million tons and 226 million tons were in short supply when North America was excluded. Surplus oil producers in ASEAN were Brunei with 6.4 million tons, Malaysia with 15.3 million tons, and Indonesia with 42.3 million tons.

According to 'the Asia-Pacific Petroleum Outlook' prepared by the East-West Center, five net oil exporters exported 1,874 million barrels while thirteen net oil importers imported 5,335 million barrels, resulting in a net import of 3,461 million barrels in 1985.[2] The share of Persian Gulf oil supply in total oil consumption of Asia-Pacific countries was 65% in 1985 and is expected to grow continuously reaching 85~90% in 2000.

Japan is the largest importer of natural gas in Asia and imported 38.5 million tons of oil equivalent and Korea imported 2.1 million tons of oil equivalent in 1987. Surplus producers were Indonesia with 19.5 million tons of oil equivalent, Malaysia with 8.3 million tons of oil equivalent, and Brunei with 8.0 million tons of oil equivalent. In North America, Canada could fill the amount that the United States need to import. Production of natural gas is expected to increase from 554.1 million tons of oil equivalent to 616.5 million tons of oil equivalent from 1987 to 2000, but the share in world total production will decrease from 35.2% to 26%.

Largest producer of coal in 1987 was the United States with 47.6% of Asia-Pacific total and China followed next with 38.3%. However, Australia had the largest surplus with 67.2 million tons

2) Five net oil exporters are China, Indonesia, Malaysia, Brunei, Burma and thirteen oil importers are Japan, South Korea, Taiwan, Hong Kong, Singapore, Philippines, Thailand, Australia, New Zealand, India, Pakistan, Bangladesh, and Sri Lanka. East-West Center includes some Southeast Asian countries and excludes North American countries in the Outlook.

of oil equivalent, the United States followed with 52.1 million tons of oil equivalent, Canada with 5.9 million tons of oil equivalent and China with 5.5 million tons of oil equivalent. Total coal surplus of these countries amounted to 130.7 million tons of oil equivalent. Japan was the largest net importer with 65.3 million tons of oil equivalent and East Asian NIEs imported 25.8 million tons of oil equivalent. Asia-Pacific region as a whole produced the surplus of 38 million tons of oil equivalent in 1987. Coal production in the Asia-Pacific region is expected to grow 45% between 1987 and 2000 and reaches 1,728.1 million tons of oil equivalent in 2000. United States and China will have a large increase in coal production with 200 million tons of oil equivalent and 250 million tons of oil equivalent respectively.

III. Structural Change in Korea's Energy Demand

Korea is poorly endowed with energy sources and only indigenous fossil fuel available is anthracite coal. To fuel the rapid industrialization, Korea increased the import of energy sources and accordingly Korea's energy dependence rate on imported sources increased continuously reaching 83.1% in 1988 from 8.6% in 1961. In 1987, Korea's energy import amounted to $5.5 billion, 14% of total import and 5% of GNP, of which $3.2 billion was spent for oil import and $0.8 billion for bituminous coal.

During the past three decades, Korea's primary energy consumption grew more than seven times and per capita energy

|Table 3| Composition of Primary Energy by Source in Korea

%, (1000 TOE)

	1962	1973	1979	1985	1988
Coal	36.8	30.2	27.4	38.8	32.8
Anthracite	35.7	28.5	20.8	21.5	15.8
Bituminous	1.2	1.7	6.6	17.3	17.1
Petroleum	9.8 (1,012)	53.8 (13,453)	62.8 (27,135)	48.5 (27,142)	47.4 (35,390)
LNG	–	–	–	–	3.6
Hydro	1.7	1.3	1.3	1.6	1.2
Nuclear	–	–	1.8	7.5	13.4
Firewood	51.7	14.7	6.7	3.6	1.6
Total (1,000 tons of oil equivalent)	100.0 (10,346)	100.0 (25,010)	100.0 (43,241)	100.0 (55,998)	100.0 (74,756)

Source : Ministry of Energy and Resources.

consumption increased five times. At the same time Korea's energy sector experienced a structural change in energy demand. To explain the structural change in Korea's energy consumption pattern, we will categorize 1962~present period into 1962~1979 (1962~1973, 1973~1979), 1979~1985, and 1985~1988. Until 1961, more than 90% of total energy consumption was met by indigenous energy sources such as anthracite coal, firewood, and hydropower. However coal and oil replaced firewood since the first five-year economic development plan started in 1962 and by 1970 oil became Korea's major energy source composing 47.2% of total primary energy consumption.

As mentioned earlier in this paper, the first oil crisis of 1973~74 severely damaged the economies of many developed countries. However, Korean economy quickly recovered from the impact of the oil shock and gained the momentum to continued economic growth realizing GNP growth rate of 13.4% in 1976. Despite the quadrupled crude oil price there was no structural change in the pattern of energy demand in Korea after the first oil crisis.[3)] During the 1973~79 period, oil consumption increased at the rate of 17.0% per annum and reached 27.1 million tons in 1979 accounting for 62.8% of total primary energy consumption. During the same period, coal consumption increased 57 percent but the share of coal dropped from 30.2% to 27.4%.

The second oil crisis of 1979~80 hit hardly the Korean economy which was still left vulnerable to outside shocks, and plunged it into deep recession. For the first time since the economic development plan started, Korea experienced a GNP growth rate of minus 4.8% and wholesale price index jumped nearly 40% in 1980. Since then Korea's GNP growth rate had been below 10% except 1983 until 1986 when the so-called three low symptoms helped the Korean economy recover from long recession. After the second oil crisis, Korean government mainly initiated by the Ministry of Energy and Resources established in 1978 had taken several measures to reduce vulnerability to imported oil.

These measures included maximum production of domestic anthracite coal, fuel switching from oil to bituminous coal in

3) See the following paper for the rigorous test of this hypothesis. Euisoon Shin, "The Impact of the First Oil Crisis on Energy Demand in Korea," *Energy Economics*, October 1982, pp. 259-268.

thermal power plants and cement industry, construction of nuclear power plants, and the import of LNG and LPG. Along with these measures, the Korean government encouraged rational use of energy through improved energy efficiency and conservation. These intensive efforts together with market response to high energy costs and economic recession resulted in a structural change in Korea's energy demand pattern. Firstly, overall energy consumption slowed down after the second oil crisis. Average annual growth rate of primary energy consumption dropped to 5.0% during the period of 1979 to 1985, from 12.1% of 1973~79 period. Secondly, oil consumption remained the same in absolute quantity during the six year period and the share of oil dropped to 48.5% in 1985, 14.3% point drop from 1979. Thirdly, coal consumption increased 83.4% during the period and accounted for 38.8% of total primary energy consumption in Korea.

Anthracite coal has been the principal energy source in the residential and commercial sector in Korea and accounted for 21.5% of total primary energy consumption in 1985. However, domestic coal reserves are limited in Korea and the quality is poor to compete with imported sources. Furthermore, oil, city gas, and electricity consumption has been growing much faster than anthracite coal in the residential and commercial sector, so the share of anthracite coal has been decreasing continuously. On the other hand, bituminous coal which is totally imported from overseas became one of major energy sources in Korea composing 17.3% of total primary energy consumption in 1985. Korea consumed 25.6 million metric tons of anthracite coal and 21.3 million metric tons of bituminous coal in

1988, taking 15.8% and 17.1% of total primary energy consumption respectively.

Fourthly, the share of nuclear energy increased rapidly since the second oil crisis and composed 7.5% in 1985 and 13.4% in 1988 of total primary energy consumption. In 1980, 77.3% of power generation was fueled by oil. However, oil was replaced by alternative energy sources since the second oil crisis and oil accounted for only 12.8% of fuel consumption for power generation in 1988, while nuclear energy supplied 47.5%, bituminous coal 19.1%, and LNG supplied 11.6% of fuel. The generation capacity of nine nuclear power plants at the end of 1989 was 7,616MW, 36.7% of total generation capacity in Korea.

1986 was a very meaningful year for Korea. Thanks to the low world oil price together with low world interest rate and high value of Japanese yen, Korea realized a trade surplus of $4.2 billion for the first time in the history of Korea and the GNP growth rate soared to 12.9%. For three consecutive years since 1986, Korea's GNP growth rate remained high around 12% and cumulative trade surplus reached $23 billion. In 1989, GNP growth rate dropped to 6.7% and the trade surplus decreased to $4.6 billion.

Average C&F import price of crude oil which was $27.73 per barrel in 1985 dropped to $15.10 per barrel in 1986. Through this oil price decrease, Korea could save $2.6 billion in 1986. In addition to this direct net gain, indirect benefit of oil price decrease to the Korean economy was enormous. However, oil consumption started to increase again from 1986 : 6.0% in 1986, 4.9% in 1987, and 19% in 1988. Even though GNP growth rate dropped to

6.7%, oil consumption increased 13.9% in 1989 and during the first quarter of 1990, it increased 21.2% compared to the same period of 1989.

During the four years from 1985 to 1989, oil consumption increased 50.8% from 189.2 million barrels to 285.3 million barrels at the rate of 12.6% per annum. The oil consumption growth rate since 1986 is comparable to pre-second oil crisis period and clearly different from the 1979~1985 period. Even if we allow for the unusually high economic growth, recent oil demand growth is so high that we might have to change the understanding that structural change took place in Korea's energy demand pattern since the second oil crisis.

By comparing the sectoral oil consumption pattern between 1985 and 1989, we can figure out the cause of rapid oil consumption growth. As Table 4 shows, transportation sector and residential and commercial sector recorded higher oil consumption growth rate than other sectors, with 86.2% and 88.9% respectively during four year period. Accordingly, those two sectors' share in total oil consumption also increased from 25.2% to 31.1% and from 13.6% to 17.2% respectively. These two sectors together accounted for two thirds of total oil consumption growth during the period. This fact shows us that oil demand grows steadily in non-industrial sectors as per capita income grows, so structural change into energy-saving industry is not enough to reduce overall dependence on oil.

Table 4 Petroleum Products Consumption by Sector

(1,000 barrel, %)

	1985	1989	1985~1989 change rate
Industrial	74,504 (39.4)	109,569 (38.4)	47.1
Transportation	47,670 (25.2)	88,774 (31.1)	86.2
Residential & Commercial	25,808 (13.6)	48,764 (17.2)	88.9
Electric Utilities	28,460 (15.1)	21,601 (7.5)	−24.1
Public & others	12,750 (6.7)	16,591 (5.8)	30.1
Total	189,192 (100.0)	285,299 (100.0)	50.8

Source : Korea Petroleum Development Corporation

IV. Energy Demand Outlook in Korea

Korea Energy Economics Institute forecasted the energy demand in Korea up to 2010 based on the following assumptions : (1) GNP will grow at the annual rate of 6.9% during 1991~2000 and 5.8% during 2001~2010. (2) Population will grow 0.9% per annum. (3) Oil price will rise at an average rate of 3.2% per annum. (4) The share of manufacturing sector will increase from 35.9% in 1987 to 48.0% in 2010 while the share of agriculture and fishery sector will decrease to 4.6% and service sector to 47.0% in 2010.[4)]

According to the projection, total primary energy consumption will grow at the average annual rate of 4.4% reaching 180.0 million

4) Korea Energy Economics Institute, *Sectoral Energy demand in the Republic of Korea : Analysis and Outlook*, August 1989.

tons of oil equivalent in 2010. Oil consumption is projected to grow at the annual rate of 4.3% during the period and the share of oil in total primary energy consumption will slightly decrease to 43.1% in 2010. It is expected that the transportation sector will grow at the rate of 6.0% and industrial sector will grow at 3.4%. Total oil consumption is expected to reach 476.5 million barrels in 2000 and 562.9 million barrels in 2010.

As already mentioned, demand for anthracite coal will steadily decrease reflecting consumer taste's change into high quality fuel such as electricity and town gas and to meet higher environmental standard. However, the role of bituminous coal in the industrial sector will increase steadily to meet the increasing demand by cement and steel industries and to fuel newly constructing bituminous coal power plants. Korea Energy Economics Institute projected that the share of anthracite coal in total primary energy consumption would decrease from 18.5% in 1987 to 5.7% in 2000 and the anthracite coal consumption would decrease from 26.3 million tons in 1987 to 17.9 million tons in 2000 and to 10.4 million tons in 2010. On the other hand, the share of bituminous coal is projected to increase to 22.8% in 2000 and 26.2% in 2010, and the consumption would increase to 47.8 million tons in 2000 and 71.6 million tons in 2010.

Since 1987, two million tons of LNG has been imported from Indonesia annually and mainly used for electricity generation. However, as the town gas distribution network is expanded, more LNG will be required for gasworks. LNG demand is expected to grow at an annual rate of 8.4% reaching 6.3 million tons in 2000

|Table 5| Projection of Primary Energy Consumption in Korea

(1,000 TOE, %)

	1987	1990	2000	2010	annual change rate
Oil	29,653 (44.0)	42,817 (49.6)	66,043 (47.7)	77,516 (43.1)	4.3
Bituminous	10,704 (15.9)	14,484 (16.6)	31,548 (22.8)	47,243 (26.2)	6.7
Anthracite	23,183 (18.5)	10,795 (12.5)	7,903 (5.7)	4,579 (2.5)	−6.8
New & Renewable	1,319 (2.0)	1,643 (1.9)	2,794 (2.0)	5,600 (3.1)	6.5
LNG	2,104 (3.1)	2,838 (3.3)	8,234 (6.0)	13,543 (7.5)	8.4
Nuclear	9,829 (14.6)	12,993 (15.0)	20,893 (15.1)	30,856 (17.1)	5.1
Hydro	1,336 (2.0)	833 (1.0)	1,290 (0.9)	677 (0.4)	−2.9
Total	67,423 (100.0)	86,403 (100.0)	138,333 (100.0)	180,015 (100.0)	4.4

Source : Korea Energy Economics Institute, *Sectoral Energy Demand in the Republic of Korea : Analysis and Outlook*, August 1989.

and 10.4 million tons in 2010.

As the economy grows, electricity consumption will increase to satisfy high living standards. According to the projection, electricity demand will grow at the annual rate of 6.0% and reach 244,582 GWH in 2010 from 64,169 GWH in 1987. To fulfill this demand growth, nuclear power generation will continue to grow. Besides nine operating nuclear power plants, five additional units with total generation capacity of 4,700 MW will be constructed by 2000. It is projected that nuclear energy will compose 47.4% of total power generation and 15.1% of total primary energy consumption in 2000.

V. Energy Cooperation in the Asia-Pacific Region

Asia-Pacific region consists of energy-abundant and energy-scarce countries in terms of indigenous energy resource endowments and of developed and developing countries in terms of economic development stage. Considering these characteristics, it is possible to classify the region into four groups as shown in Table 6 : energy-abundant developed countries ; energy-abundant developing countries ; energy-scarce developed countries ; energy-scarce developing countries.

As Asia-Pacific region is composed of these four groups of countries, it is not easy to develop common agenda and standards for energy cooperation which will give benefits to all the participating countries. Thus we need to delineate specific role that each group of countries should play to enhance economic and social development and stability of the region through energy cooperation.

Energy-scarce developed countries should take the leading role in creating the environment favorable to regional energy cooperation and contribute directly to solve impending problems at the same time. Japan set the directions and priorities of pacific energy cooper-ation based on "three major directions of cooperation" : Firstly, Japan should help developing countries solve their economic

Table 6 Typology of Primary Energy and Development by Country (1987)

Country	GDP per capita (US $)	Energy production(P) (million TOE)	Energy consumption(C) (million TOE)	P/C (%)	Group
Brunei	14,783	15.2	0.8	19	A
Indonesia	430	97.2	35.8	2.71	B
Malaysia	1,870	39.2	15.9	2.46	B
Australia	11,493	147.3	80.9	1.82	A
Canada	17,080	289.8	240.3	1.20	A
China	253	626.3	593.6	1.05	B
U.S.A.	18,200	1,601.4	1,865.7	0.86	C
New Zealand	8,185	11.9	14.0	0.85	C
Thailand	880	8.7	19.4	0.45	D
Korea	2,180	21.2	66.2	0.32	D
Taiwan	4,320	11.0	37.8	0.29	D
Philippines	550	3.4	13.9	0.24	D
Japan	13,180	76.2	409.3	0.18	C
Pacific Islands	-	0.3	2.9	0.10	D
Singapore	6,810	0.1	8.7	0.01	D
Hong Kong	8,250	0.0	9.6	0.0	C

Group A : energy abundant, developed (P/C>1, GDP per capita>$8,000)
Group B : energy abundant, developing (P/C>1, GDP per capita<$8,000)
Group C : energy scarce, developed (P/C<1, GDP per capita>$8,000)
Group D : energy scarce, developing (P/C<1, GDP per capita<$8,000)
Source : Constructed based on Mitsuru Miyata, op. cit. and CIA, *Handbook of Economic statistics*, 1988

and social construction through proper energy development and use. This objective includes measures such as the improvement of rural energy situations through conversion from non-commercial to commercial energy and the construction of an optimal supply system to better meet changing needs in urban and industrial areas. Increased use of LPG and town gas is a way to meet this end and the construction of subway networks and long-distance, high-speed mass transportation system will also help. Introduction of energy-saving equipments in industrial, transport, commercial and residential sectors as well as construction of storage facilities in preparation for emergency will be necessary. Also every effort should be made to develop increasing usage of available conventional energy sources and concurrently new and renewable alternative energy sources should be utilized. Japan predicted that electricity-related cooperation was and will be a high-priority energy cooperation agenda in the future. ODA funds will be used for this purpose. Secondly, Japan should help developing countries prepare and implement energy master plan which considers future as well as present energy situation and establish energy data base which stores well-classified information on economy and energy. This effort also includes technology transfer in the field of energy supply, energy conservation, and environmental preservation. Thirdly, Japan should promote international cooperation in attaining smooth energy flow. As energy and natural resource problems are common concerns of all the countries in this region, it will be necessary to organize regular meetings or even establish a new international organization which exclusively deals with energy and resource problems. Especially, to solve environmental problems like acid rain, multilateral cooperation among countries in the region is essentially important.

As a result of sharp decline of crude oil price in 1986, energy situation underwent rapid changes. Energy exporting countries are facing deep financial problems caused by decreased revenues from the energy export. However, as the energy consumption grows at a higher rate than expected before the fall of oil price, energy market will be reversed into a seller's market in the near future pushing up the crude oil price again. Energy-scarce countries, especially oil importing countries should develop adequate long-term energy mix which seriously considers this possibility, thus alleviating the risk of indulging in oil shortage situation again which might trigger another round of sharp oil price upsurge.

It is advisable for energy-poor countries to develop energy resources jointly by forming consortium and to secure stable supply of energy. Among various risks related to the natural resource development, especially marketing risk is important for coal and natural gas mainly because coal market is very competitive and there is a storage problem for both sources. Actual users of these energy sources can reduce the marketing risk and enhance the chance of success compared to the sole development by resource owners.

Timely and sufficient investments on the exploration and development of resources require smooth and accessible flow of funds. Economic cooperation in the energy sector takes various forms, including bilateral ODA (official development assistance), multilateral cooperation through international financial institutions such as the World Bank or ADB, and non-concessional private sector capital flow. Around 10% of ODA was for energy cooperation, and mainly used for the electrification of developing countries. Private funds are largely invested on overseas direct development of oil and gas projects followed by the development of coal, uranium, etc. Overseas direct investment is funded by the loans on commercial basis by export-import banks and other banking institutions.

Nemetz constructed a typology of energy and development in Pacific countries using commercial energy only. He describes the role that Canada can play for each group of countries :[5)]

(i) Canada can export energy for energy-poor but developed countries like Japan and pay for the imported goods from Japan.

(ii) Canada can facilitate the development and utilization of "appropriate" energy technology for energy-poor and less developed countries.

(iii) Canada can aid the development of indigenous energy sources through loan or transfer of advice, expertise and equipment for energy-rich developing countries such as China.

However, Canada can do more for energy scarce and developing countries like Korea than just transmitting "appropriate" energy technology. Two-way trade between Korea and Canada has increased at the annual rate of 30% between 1965 and 1985, and Canada became the fifth largest merchandise export market to Korea while Korea became the eighth largest export market to Canada in 1985. In 1986, Canada became Korea's fourth largest

---

5) Peter N. Nemetz, "Introduction and Overview," in Peter N. Nemetz, ed., *The Pacific Rim : Investment, Development and Trade*, University of British Columbia, 1987, p. 39.

export market and Korea became Canada's fifth largest export market in the world.

It is inspiring to see that the economic relation between two countries has been steadily growing. However, as pointed out by Okazaki and Lee in separate papers,[6] growing trade deficit to Canada arouse deep concern from Canadian side in recent years. Since Canada enjoyed a trade surplus of $87 million due to the sale of CANDU nuclear reactor to Korea, Canada's trade balance turned into a deficit and the size of the deficit has been growing. The continuing trade imbalance between Korea and Canada was believed to have been caused by different comparative advantages of the two countries.[7] As Canada is rich in natural resources, main items imported from Canada have been crude materials and fuels, followed by chemicals, food and tobacco, iron and steel, and nonferrous metals. On the other hand, major items Korea exported to Canada were skilled labor-intensive industry products such as textiles and clothing, and other light industry products. Okazaki complained that fully manufactured products composed 79.8% of Korea's export to Canada while crude materials and fuels composed more than half of

---

6) Abraham Okazaki, "Canada-Korea Economic Relations : A Canadian Perspective," in D. Kim and M. Shin eds., *Korea-Canada in Emerging Asia Pacific Community*, Institute of East and West Studies, Yonsei University, 1988, pp. 85-98.
Yongsun Lee, "Korea-Canada Trade Relations : A Korean Perspective," in D. Kim and B. L. Evans eds., *Korea and Canada : New Frontiers in the Asia-Pacific Era*, Institute of East and West Studies, Yonsei University, April 1989, pp. 195-214.

7) Seung-Soo Han, "Korea-Canada Economic Cooperation in the Regional and Global Perspective," in D. Kim and M. Shin eds., *Korea-Canada in Emerging Asia-Pacific Community*, Yonsei University, 1988, p. 76.

Canada's export and manufactured products took only 13.6% of export to Korea.[8)]

However, Canada is not only resource rich but also technologically advanced country. Lee pointed out that Canadian exporting industries have not tried hard to sell technology-intensive products which they might have comparative advantage in Korea.[9)] However, considering that the two countries have been increasing intra-industry trade in Asia-Pacific region recently, it is highly plausible to expect that Canada can capitalize her comparative advantage in technology-intensive products by promoting more intra-industry trade in Korea.

Another way for Canada to cut the trade deficit from Korea is to induce more investments on the direct development of natural resources in Canada. Canada is richly endowed with bituminous coal, petroleum, natural gas, and uranium which Korea imports 100% from abroad to satisfy domestic demand. Several Korean firms have already been investing on resource development in Canada, such as POSCO on Greenhills Coal Mine and Daewoo and KEPCO on uranium development projects.[10)] However, to meet the target of securing 20% of crude oil, 30% of bituminous coal, and 30% of uranium from overseas direct development, Korea needs to increase investment on resource development projects. According to a recent study performed by Korea Energy Economics Institute,

---

8) Okazaki, *op. cit.*, p. 93.

9) Lee, *op. cit.*, p. 205.

10) Euisoon Shin, *A Study on the Promotion of Overseas Resource Development* (in Korean), Korea Academic Research and Development Foundation, January 1988.

Canada was ranked the top out of 65 countries as the most suitable country for overseas direct development of natural resource and energy, considering resource endowments, investment environments, and political and economic stability.[11)]

References

East-West Center, *Asia-Pacific Petroleum Outlook*, 1988.

Han, Seung-Soo, "Korea-Canada Economic Cooperation in the Regional and Global Perspective," *Korea-Canada in Emerging Asia-Pacific Community*, eds. by Dalchoong Kim and Myungsoon Shin, Institute of East and West Studies, Yonsei University, 1988.

Japan Institute of Energy Economics, *Energy Cooperation in the Pacific Region Toward the 21st* Century, February 1987.

Kim, Dalchoong, and Euisoon Shin eds., *Energy Policies in Korea and Japan : Comparison and Search for Cooperation*, Yonsei University Press, December 1986.

Korea Energy Economic Institute, *A Study on Energy Supply and Demand in Pan-Pacific Region* (in Korean), May 1989.

______, *Sectoral Energy Demand in the Republic of Korea : Analysis and Outlook*, August 1989.

______, *Korea Energy Review Monthly*, January, 1990.

Lee, Young Sun, "Korea-Canada Trade Relations : A Korean Perspective,"

---

11) Sang-Kil Shin, "A Study on the Promotion of International Cooperation on Energy and Resource in Free Trade Era (in Korean)," Korea Energy Economics Institute, January 1990.

in Dalchoong Kim and Brian L. Evans eds., *Korea and Canada : New Frontiers in the Asia-Pacific Era*, pp. 195-214.

Ministry of Energy and Resources, *Yearbook of Energy Statistics*, 1988.

Miyata, Mitsuru, "Energy Demand and Supply Forecast for the Pan Pacific Region in Year 2000 and Tasks for Energy Cooperation," paper presented at the Fourth Symposium on Pacific Energy Cooperation, January 29-30, 1990, Tokyo, Japan.

Nemetz, Peter N., *The Pacific Rim : Investment, Development and Trade*, University of British Columbia Press, 1987.

Okazaki, Abraham, "Canada-Korea Economic Relations : A Canadian Perspective," Dalchoong Kim and Myungsoon Shin, (eds.) *Korea-Canada in Emerging Asia Pacific Community*, Institute of East and West Studies, Yonsei University, 1988, pp. 85-89.

Shin, Euisoon, "The Impact of the First Oil Crisis on Energy Demand in Korea," *Energy Economics*, October 1982, pp. 259-268.

______, *A Study on the Promotion of Overseas Resource Development* (in Korean), Korea Academic Research and Development Foundation, January 1988.

5. Northeast Asian Cooperation for Russian Energy Development*

I. Energy resources in Russia

Russia is richly endowed with energy resources. Russia composes approximately 50 percent of the CIS population, 75 percent of the CIS territory and produces 90 percent of oil and 80 percent of gas for the CIS. Proved gas reserve in the CIS is 45.3 trillion cubic meter and composes 38 percent of world total. Proved oil reserve is 57 billion barrels and ranks seventh in the world. Oil production of CIS peaked in 1987 with 12.5 million barrels per day but decreased to 10.3 million barrels per day in 1991, a 17.4 percent drop from the peak year. Gas production has increased at the rate of 7 percent in the 1980s but the trend is slowing down in the 1990s.

Oil export decreased considerably for the past three years, from

---

* "Northeast Asian Cooperation for Russian Energy Development," in Kap-Young Jeong(ed.), *Cooperation between Korea and Russia*, East and West Studies Series 25, Yonsei University, 1993, pp. 87-96.

205 million tons (4.1 million b/d) in 1988 to 156 million tons (3.2 million b/d) in 1990. The CIS exported 110.4 billion cubic meter of gas in 1990, which was 47.3 percent of world total gas export. Gas export to Western Europe was 65 billion cubic meter, of which Germany took 43 percent, Italy took 23 percent, and France took 17 percent.

|**Table 1**| CIS Position of Oil and Gas

	Production (1990)		Proved Reserve[1]	
	Oil	Gas	Oil	Gas
	million b/d (%)	billion m^3 [2] (%)	billion barrel (%)	trillion m^3 (%)
CIS	11.5 (19.1)	759 (37.7)	57.0 (5.7)	45.3 (37.9)
U.S.	7.2 (11.9)	492 (24.4)	26.1 (2.6)	4.7 (3.9)
S.A.	6.3 (10.4)	31 (1.5)	257.5 (25.8)	5.1 (4.3)
Venezuela	2.1 (3.5)	22 (1.1)	50.0 (5.0)	3.0 (2.5)
World	60.3 (100.0)	2014 (100.0)	999.1 (100.0)	119.4 (100.0)

[1] As of 1991. 1.
[2] Standard m^3
Source : BP, *BP Statistical Review of World Energy*, 1991. 6
IPE, *International Petroleum Encyclopedia* 1990, 1991
WGI, *World Gas Intelligence*, 1991. 4

Before the first oil crisis, energy contributed 20 percent of Soviet Russia's foreign currency earnings from merchandise export and 90 percent of this came from the sale of oil. Along with the increase in the price of oil, hard currency earnings from the sale of gas and oil also increased comprising more than 50 percent of merchandise export in 1988. Soviet Russia earned 12.8 billion dollars from the sale of energy in 1988, 76 percent of this was from oil, 20 percent was from gas, and 4 percent was from coal.

Since the first oil crisis, the western countries started to import energy from Russia to diversify their import source. Energy trade between Russia and the western countries increased steadily up to early 1980s. However, due to energy substitution and conservation policies adopted by the western countries since the second oil crisis, hard currency earnings from energy sale started to decrease. Russia initiated several cooperative programmes with the western countries to encourage energy export. One of them was the construction of gas pipelines from West Siberia to European importing countries.

For the past 20 years, the investment on the energy industry increased twice every ten years and composed a 40 percent of the total industrial investment. Despite this continued effort, the Russian energy industry is ailing seriously due to the depletion of oil reserves in areas close to the consumption centers and insufficient investment to replace outdated technology and equipments in the existing production fields. Additionally, unfavorable living conditions together with insufficient infrastructure in the remote area of East Siberia and the Far East makes it difficult for Russia to develop new energy sources in this area alone. Naturally Russia is eager to introduce foreign capital and technology to this area. However, following problems make it difficult for potential investors to invest on this risky business :

(1) Disputes among various government organizations, such as the one between the Russian Ministry for Fuel and Energy and the Russian National Oil and Gas Corporation.

(2) Intensified environmental regulation and the requirement of ecological examination before starting exploration and production of mineral resources. ·

(3) Insufficient legal and institutional environment for investment. EBRD (European Bank for Reconstruction and Development) which was founded to help economic transformation of former Soviet Union and the Eastern Bloc considers that this task should be solved first before considering investment on oil and gas development sector.

(4) Hyperinflation which increased development cost rapidly.

(5) Difficulty in selecting a contract partner. The Russian Federation as well as various republics and autonomous regional governments in Russia claim the right to a ct as legitimate counterparts. The ultimate solution on the ownership of resource rights will come only after the relation between Russian Federation and the regional government is clearly defined.

Russian government cannot solve all of these problems in a short period of time. However, all the possible measures should be taken to minimize the impact of these internal problems.

II. Asia-Pacific Energy Balance

Northeast Asian region which includes South and North Korea, the CIS, Japan, and China takes up 21.8% of the world in territory, 30.2% of world population, and 25.9% of world GNP as of 1989.

Intra-regional trade volume in 1990 was 63.1 billion dollars in export and 76.2 billion dollars in import. The share of intra-regional export among total export of these countries increased from 9.9% in 1980 to 12.2% in 1990 and the import share increased from 10.5% to 15.9% during the same period.

Intra-regional trade dependency of the CIS is the lowest among Northeast Asian countries. However the importance of Northeast Asia in the trade of the CIS has been gradually increasing. In 1980 intra-regional export was only 3.1% of total export but increased to 6.7% in 1990. Intra-regional import dependency also increased from 5.5% in 1980 to 11.6% in 1990. In 1990, the CIS recorded 6.8 billion dollars of intra-regional trade deficit.

In 1990, the share of each economic region out of world trade volume was 41.0% for EC ; 16.6% for NAFTA in export and 19.1% in import ; 15.5% for Northeast Asia in export and 13.9% in import ; and 4.2% for ASEAN in export and 4.7% in import. While the EC secured 60.5% of export and 57.9% of import within the region, Northeast Asia procured only 12.2% of export and 15.5% of import. This shows that intra-regional trade in the Northeast Asia is not as active as in other economic regions in the world.

Asia-Pacific region excluding Russia is rich in coal but relatively poor in gas and very poor in oil. In 1990, this region produced 6.6 million barrels per day of oil and consumed 13.6 million b/d, importing 7.0 million tons from outside of the region, mostly from the Middle East. It is expected that oil dependency to outside source will become even larger in the future. There are only few countries exporting oil in this region, namely Indonesia, Malaysia, Brunei, and China. Vietnam, Australia, and Papua New Guinia might join this group in the near future. However, the export of oil from China and Indonesia will decrease as these countries experience rapid economic growth.

The prospect with gas looks better compared to oil. It is expected that the gas consumption in this region will increase steadily mainly caused by Japan, South Korea, and Taiwan and will reach 75 million tons by 2010 which is double the consumption volume of 1990. However the increased demand will be adequately met through supply expansion from prospective gas fields in Australia, Indonesia, Alaska, and the Russian Far East.

III. Oil and gas development in the East Siberia and the Far East

Most of oil and gas production in Russia is concentrated in the West Siberia. And the onshore oil and gas fields in Sakhalin are depleting rapidly. So the Russian Far East such as Khabarovsk, Maritime Territories, and Sakhalin region will experience serious shortage of oil, gas, and electricity if proper offshore development of energy sources is not prompted.

There is a rich endowment of undeveloped energy source in the East Siberia and the Far East as shown in Table 2.

Several years ago, Russian Republic's Committee on Geology and Utilization of Energy and Mineral Resources together with the former Soviet Union's government agencies initiated the so-called Vostok Programme. Major part of this programme is to construct a gas pipeline system from Sakhalin and Yakutsk, through Khabarovsk, Vladivostok, North Korea, and South Korea to offshore Japan, which runs a distance of 6,280 km.

According to the Vostok Programme, the full name of which is "the Concept of Developing Yakutian and Sakhalin Gas and Mineral Resources of Eastern Siberia and the U.S.S.R. Far East", the Soviet Far East will produce about 33.5 million tons/year of gas by 2005 and 15.3 million tons/year will be exported to Korea and Japan.

It is not certain now whether this plan is still alive. What is certain is that if the Sakhalin tender goes to US-Japanese consortium without the participation of South Korea, Korean participation for the development of Russian Far East oil and gas will be delayed. On March 30, 1992, the Russian government formally awarded 3M (composed of McDermott, Marathon, and Mitsui) a contract to conduct a feasibility study for the development of oil and gas in areas of Sakhalin's offshore. Hyundai submitted a proposal for the Sakhalin tender but failed. In the meantime, a consortium of Samsung and Palmco submitted a proposal to construct offshore platforms and onshore pipelines, and build a gas liquefaction plant. The LNG plants would be owned by Palmco, while the other facilities would be owned by the Russians. In return, Plamco would be granted the export rights for LNG and condensate. Final decision on this proposal is still pending. Many other Korean companies are also interested in participating in

|Table 2| Oil and Gas Reserves in the East Siberia and the Far East

	Gas (billion m^3)	Oil & Condensate (million tons)
Yakutsk	1,333.4	239.3
Vilyui	521.5	20.2
Nepa Boyuba	811.9	219.1
Irkutsk	136.8	245.6
Sakhalin*	789.8	290.8
Piltun-Astokskoye	52.0	66.3
Lunskoye	391.0	32.0
Chaive & Odoptu	172.0	165.3
Total	2,660.0	775.7

* : According to Russia's report, reserves of oil, condensate, and gas in Sakhalin were much higher than Oil & Gas Journal's estimates (oil and condensate 0.7 billion tons, gas 1,000 billion m^3).
Source : Oil & Gas Journal, various issues

Russian Far East oil and gas development projects. Recently, a Korean consortium was set up for Vietnam offshore oil development.

In the long term perspective, the Sakhalin contract is the first step toward a full implementation of the Vostok programme. Even if the Sakhalin tender went to 3M, it does not mean that future development of Sakhalin oil and gas should be monopolized by 3M. Indeed, the cooperation of the Japanese and the Korean side is essential to expedite the development of oil and gas in this area. The two countries are heavily dependent on foreign energy sources and the stable supply of energy is essential for their sustained economic growth. Oil and gas developed in Russian Far East could

|Table 3| Gas Production and Supply Plan

Unit : million ton (billion m^3)

	1995	2000	2005	2010	2015
Production	2.3 (5.0)	25.9 (33.7)	33.5 (43.6)	36.9 (48)	36.9 (48)
Sakhalin	3.8 (5.0)	16.7 (21.7)	18.1 (23.6)	16.9 (22)	16.9 (22)
Yakutsk	-	9.2 (12.0)	15.4 (20)	20 (26)	20 (26)
On-site Consumption	0.1 (0.1)	2.9 (3.7)	3.8 (4.9)	4.1 (5.3)	4.1 (5.3)
Domestic Consumption	2.6 (3.4)	10 (13.0)	14.4 (18.7)	17.5 (22.7)	17.5 (22.7)
N. Korea	-	1.5 (2.0)	1.5 (2.0)	1.5 (2.0)	1.5 (2.0)
S. Korea	1.2 (1.5)	6.9 (9.0)	6.9 (9.0)	6.9 (9.0)	6.9 (9.0)
Japan	-	4.6 (6.0)	6.9 (9.0)	6.9 (9.0)	6.9 (9.0)

* : gas 1 ton = 1,300 m^3
Source : Vostok Programme

be a great relief for them.

In the Northeast Asia, the formation of an energy cooperation regime comparable to the European Energy Charter is necessary. Russia and China are endowed with huge amount of untapped reserves of oil and gas, but are stranded because of bottlenecks in capital, technology, and equipment necessary for the exploration and development of energy resources. Japan, Taiwan, and South Korea can provide necessary capital and equipments for this purpose and secure stable supply of oil and gas in return, thus mitigating the burden of heavy dependence on Middle East oil. The establishment of a "Northeast Asian Energy Charter" will enhance mutual benefits of participating countries and would mark the beginning of energy cooperation regime in Asia-Pacific region.

|Table 4| Uneven Distribution of Production Factors among Northeast Asian Countries

	Oil & Gas	Coal & Mineral	Labor	Capital	Technology	Management Know-how
Russia	VR	VR	VP	VP	S	S
China	R	VR	VR	VP	S	S
Taiwan	S	S	S	R	R	R
N.Korea	A	R	R	VP	VP	VP
S.Korea	A	S	S	R	R	R
Japan	VP	S	S	VR	VR	VR

Note : VR : Very Rich ; R : Rich ; S : Short ; VP : Very Poor ; A : Absent.
Source : Paik Keun-Wook, "Towards a Northeast Asian energy charter", *Energy Policy*, May 1992.

IV. Natural Resources Cooperation between Korea and Russia

The growth rate of trade between Korea and Russia has been slowing down since 1991. Main reasons for this are the Russia's restriction of natural resource export and the fluctuating exchange rate.

There are few development projects operated by Korean companies in Russia now. Hyundai's timber development project in the Far Eastern region of Svetlaya and Jindo's fur manufacturing joint venture are the larger ones. Besides the two ongoing projects, a number of initial negotiations are under way in the field of natural resource development including oil and gas. However, the slow participation of Korean firms in the development of the Russian Far East is below the expectation of both countries.

|Table 5| Trade between Korea and Russia

(Unit : million $, %)

	'87	'88	'89	'90	'91	'92.5
Korea's Export	67.2 (34.7)	111.6 (66.1)	207.7 (86.1)	519.1 (149.9)	625.1 (20.4)	204.8 (31.1)
Korea's Import	133.1 (108.3)	178.8 (34.3)	391.7 (119.1)	369.7 (−5.6)	577.3 (56.1)	228.1 (−16.6)
Total	200.4 (76.1)	290.4 (44.9)	599.4 (106.4)	888.8 (48.3)	1,202.4 (35.2)	432.91 (0.7)

Note : Figures in parentheses are the rate of percentage increase in comparison to the previous year.

According to a source, the average flow of new wells in the West Siberian oil fields declined from 160 tons per day in the 1975 to less than 23 and 14 tons respectively in 1989 and 1990. Consequently the former Soviet Union's crude oil production declined from 607.3 million tons in 1989, to 569.7 million tons in 1990 and 515 million tons in 1991. The production of natural gas also declined slightly in 1991. As the production of oil and gas from West Siberia slows down, Russia expects East Siberia and Far East to play a more positive role in the supply of oil and gas.

Running a business in the Far East is not an easy task because of the lack of infrastructure and severe weather. Basically the slow economic development of Far East coincides with the low productivity of this region. This region, so far, failed to attract foreign business. As of January 1, 1992, approximately 5,000 joint ventures were established, of which 2,000 were active. The Far East, despite its vast endowment of natural resources, has attracted only 128 joint ventures as of August 1, 1991, or about 2.6 percent of the total of such enterprises registered in the former Soviet Union. The joint venture enterprises engaged in natural resources exploitation constituted only a small share.

The investment environment in the Russian Far East is not attractive by any means. In fact there are many prospective rival resource frontiers in developing as well as in developed countries such as Australia and Canada. To expedite the investment of foreign enterprises in the Far East resource development, Russian government should prepare more favorable investment environment including proper institution building. Resource development investment in the Russian Far East requires huge amount of capital and risk taking which is too much for an individual company to assume. Naturally it will enhance the interest of Russia to encourage multi-national joint ventures to the extent possible.

V. Concluding Remarks

Russian economy is experiencing a rapid transition now. During this transitional period, the Korean government should support the efforts of the Korean enterprises for expanding business opportunities and operations in Russia. On the other hand, the Russian government should provide favorable environments for Korean firms to expedite their investments. As Russia is expected to emerge as a new economic power after the transition is completed, a long-lasting companionship based on mutual benefits should be established between the two countries.

Russia is rich in energy resources, but she has difficulty in mobilizing necessary capital funds to increase energy production. Japan, Korea, and Taiwan are all eager to secure a stable supply of energy and their economies are mostly dependent upon imported energy sources. China is rich in energy and mineral resources and could be a competitor to Russia in large scale energy exploration and development. In this context, it will be to the benefits of all the Northeast Asian countries to establish a Northeast Asian Energy Charter and to enhance potential gains from cooperation in energy development and trade.

6. Restructuring of the Korean Electric Power Industry*

I. Brief History of Electric Power Industry in Korea

Electricity was introduced to Korea in 1887. Eleven years later two Americans, H. Collbran and H.R. Bostwick established the Hansung Electric Company. Up to 1910 electric companies were established around three big cities, Seoul, Busan, and Incheon, but 60 to 70 electric companies existed throughout the country by the 1930s. During this period the Korean electric power industry was consisted of small companies with generation plants and regional distribution networks. All the electric companies were operated privately.

The private electric companies charged excessively high prices without considering public interest, which induced consumers' organized appeal for lower price and public management of electric

* "RESTRUCTURING OF THE KOREAN ELECTRIC POWER INDUSTRY," 22nd IAEE Annual International Conference Proceedings, Vol. 2, June 9-12, 1999. pp. 247-254.

utilities. The Japanese colonial government enacted the 'Chosun Electricity Enterprise Order' in 1932 and started to integrate the small distribution companies in the country. By 1942 distribution companies were integrated into four regional companies, two in the north and two in the south. In 1943 Japanese colonial government integrated and nationalized 9 companies in generation and transmission sectors into the Chosun Electric Co. Ltd.

In 1945 there were three electric companies in South Korea, one generation/transmission company and two distribution companies. These electric companies had been making ever-increasing losses because of low productivity, low capacity utilization and numerous free riders. The necessity to integrate the three ailing electric companies surfaced naturally as a way of reducing losses and to attain economy of scale. However, differing interests of the three companies delayed the integration process until 1961 when the three companies merged as the Korea Electric Co. Ltd.

As the Korean economy grew rapidly since 1960s, the electricity supply could not meet the demand. So the Korean government encouraged the private enterprises to participate in the construction of thermal power plants. But some of the participating companies either withdrew or sold their initial investments to the government as the electricity demand fell short of the original expectation. Only Kyungin Energy (later renamed Hanwha Energy) remained as a private power producer.

Korean Government established the Korea Electric Power Corporation (KEPCO) in 1982 as a statutory corporation after the acquisition of private minority shares in the Korea Electric Company.

KEPCO sold 21% of its stock to the public in 1989. As of July 1998, the Korean Government held 58.2% and domestic banks owned 15.6% of the stock. Private investors held 24.8% and the rest were held by KEPCO.

In March 1999, KEPCO sold 5% of its entire stock, which was owned by the Korean Government, at the New York Stock Exchange at 753.6 million dollars.[1] Thus the Government-owned stock decreased to 53.2%. According to 'the KEPCO Act', the government must retain an investment of no less than 51% in KEPCO. Foreign ownership of shares in KEPCO was restricted to 30%. However the decree in mid-1997 removed restrictions on foreign ownership of generation plants.

II. Overview of Electric Power Industry in Korea

1. KEPCO'S Capacity and Operation[2]

Electricity demand grew by more than 10% per year during the past decade. Peak demand in 1997 was 35,851 MW, with KEPCO's electricity sale of 201 TWh to 13.9 million customers. However the Korean economic crisis of late 1997 brought a sharp reversal in demand growth. Peak demand in 1998 fell by 8.1% compared to 1997.

---

1) Chosun Ilbo, 1999.3.26

2) This part was drawn from the Korea Electric Power Corporation(1998).

In December 1998, total generation capacity of South Korea reached 43,173 MW, 17th in the world. KEPCO holds 94.2% of domestic generation capacity with 244 generation units, and 30 units with the generating capacity of 16,750 MW are presently under construction. At the end of 1997, KEPCO had 427 transmission and distribution substations with total installed capacity of 106,835 MVA. Transmission line length amounted to 24,254 circuit-kilometers covering a route length of 13,039 kilometers.

|**Table 1**| Generation Capacity of Korea (December 1998)

(Unit : thousand kW)

Plant Type	Nuclear	Coal	LNG	Oil	Hydro	Total
Capacity	12,016	11,400	9,518	7,110	3,131	43,175
Share(%)	(27.8)	(26.4)	(22.0)	(16.5)	(7.3)	(100.0)

Source : Ministry of Commerce, Industry, and Energy (MOCIE)

KEPCO purchases power from a number of other generators whose aggregate installed capacity amounted to 2,499 MW in 1997. These include seven hydroelectric units of the Government-owned Korea Water Resources Management Corporation totaling 965 MW of capacity, several other small hydroelectric units with an aggregate capacity of 32 MW, and Hanwha Energy and privately owned cogenerators which sell surplus generation to KEPCO under short term arrangements. Power producers other than KEPCO accounted for 4.2% of total generation during 1997. KEPCO has also entered power purchase agreements (PPAs) with four new

Independent Power Producers (POS Energy, LG Energy, Hyundai Energy and Daegu Electric Power) representing around 3,100 MW of capacity which is due to commission between 2001 and 2005.

As of 1998, KEPCO's principal affiliates include a 40.5% interest in Korea Heavy Industries and Construction Corporation, a 35.5% interest in Korea Gas Corporation, and a 26.1% interest in Korea District Heating Corporation. KEPCO has a number of other interests in Korea and internationally.

2. Regulatory Framework

The Government regulates the electric power industry in three ways : entry regulation, price regulation, and management control.

KEPCO is a statutory judicial corporation established under the KEPCO Act. The KEPCO Act defines KEPCO's broad areas of operation. These include the development of electric power resources, the generation, transmission and distribution of electricity, related investments and research and development. KEPCO's license authorizes it to generate, transmit and distribute electricity. Although other companies hold licenses to generate power, KEPCO is presently the only organization licensed to transmit and distribute electricity. The Ministry of Commerce, Industry and Energy (MOCIE) administers the license. MOCIE has the authority to appoint senior KEPCO management and to approve applications for tariff changes (subject to final approval in the Cabinet meeting).

KEPCO's tariffs are regulated by the Government according to a formula based on allowable rate of return. The allowable rate of return is set by reference to KEPCO's anticipated cost of capital. KEPCO's tariff structure is organized by type of customers. Tariff rate also varies with factors such as supply voltage, season, time of day, and demand-side management measures. KEPCO's current tariffs are summarized in Table 2.

|Table 2| Electricity Tariff System in Korea

Tariff	Household	General	Education	Industry	Agriculture	Total
Won/kWh	100.95	102.96	85.76	54.49	42.60	72.79
(index)	(139)	(141)	(118)	(75)	(59)	(100)
Sales share	18.5%	19.8%	0.9%	57.9%	2.1%	100.0%

Source : Ministry of Commerce, Industry and Energy (MOCIE)

The household and general customers subsidize agricultural and industrial customers. KEPCO has been one of the most efficient electric companies in the world in terms of load factor, transmission and distribution losses, and blackout time. The electricity tariff was lower than that of 1981 despite the general price rise during the period and it is relatively cheaper compared to other countries as shown in Table 3.

|Table 3| Inter-Country Comparison of Electricity Tariffs

Country	Korea	Taiwan	Japan	U.K.	U.S.A.	France
Tariff (Won/kWh)	72.53	86.53	183.18	134.50	95.58	105.81
Index	100	119.3	252.5	185.4	131.8	145.9

Source : Ministry of Commerce, Industry and Energy (MOCIE)

KEPCO's operations are subject to a number of other laws and regulations, including the ones related to environmental protection and safety. The Government-Invested Enterprise Management Basic Act of 1983 (the GIE Act) defines the general relationship between the Government and companies such as KEPCO in which the Government holds an investment of at least 51% of stated capital. The GIE Act prescribes the requirements for corporation and management organization and defines the Government's obligations and supervisory role.

III. Electric Power Industry Restructuring Plan

1. Background of the Plan

For two years during the period of 1994 to 1996, KEPCO went over overall management diagnoses by a team of outside consultants. The consulting team advised to keep KEPCO as a public enterprise for a considerable period of time and to bring competition to generation and retail supply market through strong restructuring scheme. Following was the recommendation on restructuring timetable :

- Preparation Stage ('97-'98) : Formation of KEPCO restructuring committee
- First Stage ('99-'03) : Accounting separation of generation, transmission, and distribution sectors, and the establishment of

operation divisions

- Second Stage ('04–'08) : Separation of operation divisions as KEPCO subsidiary companies
- Third Stage ('09–'10) : Introduce power pool and wholesale competition
- Fourth Stage (After 2010) : Establish power pool system and consider privatization of subsidiary companies

The Ministry of Commerce, Industry and Energy (MOCIE) evaluated the recommendation of the consultant' report and concluded that KEPCO should carry out comprehensive managerial reforms before implementing the restructuring schedule of the Korean electric power industry. MOCIE questioned the U.K. – type power pool system as a final goal because the conditions facing Korea was quite different from those of U.K.

The Korean Government established 'the Electric Power Industry Restructuring Committee' in June 1997 to bring managerial reformation in KEPCO, to ease entry limitation in the electric power industry, and to come up with affordable restructuring plan. The Committee had monthly meetings and seminars to study a set of alternative plans prepared by a task force composed of staffs from the Government and KEPCO. After having a public forum in November 1998, the restructuring plan was finalized and reported to the president.

'The Electric Power Restructuring Plan' set the following objectives :

- to raise efficiency in electricity supply by introducing competition to the monopolistic electric power industry
- to provide cheap and stable supply of electricity in the long run
- to increase consumer benefit through expanded consumer choice

To achieve the objectives, the Plan recommended in the short-term the separation of generation sector into several generation companies and the sequential privatization of them to reduce generation costs and to improve efficiency. In the long-term transmission network will be open to private generators and the distribution sector will be segregated to bring retail as well as wholesale competition. To achieve the goal in a sequential manner, a timetable was set as shown in Table 4.

IV. Critical Evaluation of the Plan

When the Korean Government announced the finalized restructuring plan at the public hearing, majority of people accepted the necessity to bring structural reformation and competition to the monopolistic Korea Electric Power Corporation (KEPCO). However many raised questions to the way the Government prepared the restructuring plan and the selected restructuring model. The opposing side including the Korean National Electrical Workers Union questioned the rationale of the objectives based on the following reasoning :

Table 4 Timetable for the Restructuring of Korean Electric Power Industry

Phase 1 – Preparation	
January 1999– December 1999	• Institution building for the introduction of competition in generation · Legislation · Valuation and separation of KEPCO's assets · Establishment of generation subsidiaries (Gencos) · Development of generation pool
Phase 2 – Competition in Generation	
October 1999– December 2002	• Start competition in generation · Privatization and sale of Gencos · Competition among Gencos through price bidding • Establishment and privatization of distribution subsidiaries (Discos) • Establishment of an independent regulatory agency • Preparation of two-way price bidding • Allow direct power trade between Gencos and large buyers
Phase 3 – Wholesale Competition	
2003–2009	• Commence wholesale competition · Wholesale competition based on two-way price bidding between Gencos and Discos · Independent operation of distribution network and tariff system by Discos • Expansion of direct power trade
Phase 4 – Retail Competition	
After 2009	• Commence retail competition · Elimination of regional supply franchise through the opening of distribution network · Emergence of consumer cooperatives and power marketers · Establishment of consumer's sovereignty through extended Choice

Source : Ministry of Commerce, Industry and Energy (MOCIE)

Firstly, KEPCO has been one of the most efficient electric companies in the world in terms of load factor, transmission and distribution losses, and blackout time. As a public utility KEPCO minimized the profit and maintained low tariffs. It was made possible through continued technological development and managerial reformation.

Secondly, entry and exit costs of privatization, together with regulation cost and subsidy to remote areas would raise the electricity price significantly. So it is contradictory to the idea of bringing down price through privatization.

Thirdly, agriculture and fishing towns and remote areas will experience a sharp rise in electricity prices. General tax or subsidy to alleviate their burden will arouse opposition from other consumers.

Fourthly, it is too early to evaluate the success of U.K. privatization and restructuring experiences, so Korea should be cautious in introducing U.K. – type power pool system.

Fifthly, energy security is very important in Korea. In the U.K., the following conditions made it possible to implement comprehensive restructuring and privatization of electric power industry : Electricity demand reached the saturation point in the late 1980s ; U.K. has rich endowment of energy sources such as petroleum and natural gas, and the price of coal dropped significantly after the privatization of coal industry ; U.K. electric power network is connected to the European transmission system via EDF of France, thereby making it possible to import from other countries in case of emergency. Unlike U.K., Korea is energy–poor country with no connection to other countries' electricity network. And the electricity demand has been growing at the average annual rate of 10% for the past decade. Even if demand decreased temporarily due to the economic crisis in Korea and Asia, it will start to grow again once the economy is recovered. Contrary to the government's wishes, the privatization could bring instability to electricity supply system. Public enterprise might be more effective in providing stable supply of electricity in the long run.

Sixthly, KEPCO is enjoying the economy of scale and it is uncertain whether competition could bring efficiency.

V. Conclusion

De facto monopolist, KEPCO, has operated the electric power industry in Korea since 1961. Even if KEPCO is a vertically and horizontally integrated public enterprise, it performed quite efficiently providing stable supply of electricity at relatively low rate. However the fact that it has been a public enterprise as well as a monopolist instigated a constant restructuring request. While the restructuring discussion during the 1970s centered around the participation of private capital to alleviate the burden of the government to meet the fast growing electricity demand, the present restructuring discussion started to improve efficiency of KEPCO through the introduction of competition into the industry. International trend of deregulation, privatization, and restructuring in electric power industry from the late 1980s also stimulated the discussion.

The dilemma of Korea is not whether a competition should be introduced to the electric power industry but how fast and in what degree. The internal and external conditions facing Korea is not the same as those of U.K., U.S.A., Japan, or other countries which have undergone the restructuring process recently. First, Republic of Korea is an energy-poor country confronting the North Korea, so secure and stable supply of electricity is as important as achieving cost efficiency. Second, KEPCO performed quite well as a public enterprise and there is no guarantee that the privatization would bring improved efficiency and lower price. Third, it is not known whether the inefficiency of public enterprise comes from the excessive government regulation and bureaucratic management or the mere fact that the government is a majority shareholder. Considering all these facts, we come to the conclusion that the restructuring discussions so far in Korea missed the point and scratched the surface. To prescribe right drugs, correct diagnosis should precede. Nobody will take drugs willingly without knowing what his or her disease is. You cannot give drugs to healthy person just because other people take drugs.

There is no question that Korean electric power industry requires deregulation, privatization, and restructuring. However, it must be a dynamic process rather than a model setting and go for it approach. U.K. - type government initiated complete divestiture model is very risky in that it is economically irreversible once it is implemented. We need to follow the no-regret approach, which is based on accumulated experiences and real needs of the stakeholders. Divestiture and privatization of KEPCO per se do not automatically bring competition and efficiency to the Korean electric power industry. More in-depth analysis, which considers the internal and external conditions facing Korea, should be performed before implementing the restructuring plan.

References

Harvard Electric Policy Group, "Reshaping the Electric Industry - A Public Policy Debate", January 1999.

Joskow, Paul L., "Restructuring, Competition and Regulatory Reform in the U.S. Electricity Sector", *Journal of Economic Perspectives*, Vol.11, NO.3, Summer 1997, pp .119-138.

Korea Electric Power Corporation, "KEPCO-Directions for the Future", December 1998.

Ministry of commerce, Industry and Energy, "Chollyuk Sanop Kujo Kepyun Kibon Kewhek", January 1999.

Ministry of Trade, Commerce and Industry, *Hankuk Cholluk Kongsa Kyungyong Jindan Pyungka Bogoseo*, July 1996.

Shin, Eui-Soon and Byung-Jae Lim, *Chollyuk Sanop Kujo Chungchege Kwanhan Yonku*, Korea Energy Economics Institute, May 1992.

PART II

Water-Use Conflicts and Natural Resources

7. Application of Transaction Cost Economics to the Analysis of Water-Use Conflicts in Seoul Metropolitan Region*

I. Introduction

Concentration of population and industries in Seoul Metropolitan Region has given rise to an increasing scarcity of potable water source. The introduction of area-wide waterworks was mainly aimed at solving this problem. But the degradation of the raw water source has made people suspicious of tap water quality, and commercial water markets have provided an alternative to public waterworks.

While the 1970s and 1980s were a water supply expansion period in Seoul Metropolitan Region, the next decade will be a period when the demand for quality becomes the major concern. Thus, the water system of Seoul Metropolitan Region is transforming from an "expansion phase" to a "mature phase."

---

* "APPLICATION OF TRANSACTION COST ECONOMICS TO THE ANALYSIS OF WATER-USE CONFLICTS IN SEOUL METROPOLITAN REGION," *Regional Development Dialogue*, Vol. 12, No.4 (Winter 1991), pp. 21-37.

As neoclassical economics is based on market analysis, it fails to answer why some transactions take place in bilateral markets, others in competitive markets, and in some cases are internalized. According to Williamson,[1] transaction costs, both *ex ante* and *ex post*, which are the costs of running the economic system, constitute a major factor in institutional choice.

The objective of this article is to apply the transaction cost approach to the analysis of the water management system developed in the Seoul Metropolitan Region. The format of analysis is as follows : First, the water management system of the Seoul Metropolitan Region is introduced briefly and four stages of transactions are explained. Then in each stage, the different types of transactions are analyzed and potential conflicts identified. Then, various institutions developed for conflict resolution and transaction cost minimization are investigated. The last part contains summary and concluding remarks.

II. Water Management System in the Seoul Metropolitan Region

The Han River system is made up of the North Han, the South Han, and the Lower Han Rivers. The Soyanggang Multipurpose Dam was constructed on the North Han River and the Choogju

1) Oliver E. Williamson, *The Economics Institution of Capitalism* (New York : Free Press ; London : Collier Macmillan), 1985.

Multipurpose Dam on the South Han River. The North and the South Han Rivers coverage at the Paldang Reservoir and flows through the Seoul Metropolitan Region. The Seoul Metropolitan Region is composed of Seoul Special City, Incheon Directly-Governed City, and Kyunggi Province.

Along the water management system from multipurpose dam to final water users, there are four major points of transaction. Single or multiple sellers and buyers are at each transaction stage. Our major interest is to investigate what kind of governance structure was developed at each transaction stage and to explain the reason, where possible, in terms of transaction cost minimizing behavior.

The first transaction occurs between the Ministry of Construction, the constructor of multipurpose dams, and the parties who establish dam-use rights. The second takes place between dam-use rights holders and wholesalers. The third is between wholesaler and area-wide waterworks. In the final stage, local governments produce tap water and sell it to the final users through local waterworks. Figure 1 is a schematic diagram showing the four stages of transactions along the surface water management system.

1. Stage I : Construction of Multipurpose Dam and Cost Sharing

1) Financing of Construction Capital

A multipurpose dam is constructed by the Ministry of Construction to secure two or more kinds of benefit out of flood control, irrigation water supply, domestic/industrial water supply, and hydropower generation. According to the *Specific Multipurpose Dam*

|Figure 1| Surface Water Management System

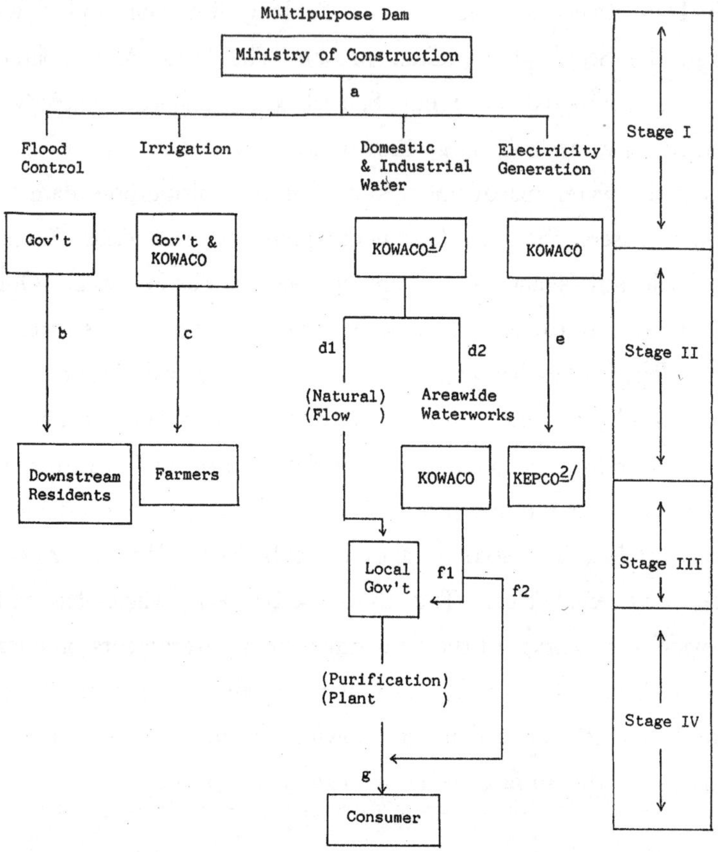

Notes : 1/ KOWACO -- Korea Water Resources Corporation
2/ KEPCO -- Korea Electric Power Corporation

Act (*SMDA*), the parties who establish dam-use rights should share the construction cost based on the benefits they receive.

The Choongju Multipurpose Dam was financed through various sources such as government funds, domestic and foreign loans, and

|Table 1| Financing of Construction Capital for Choongju Multipurpose Dam

Classification		Won (million)	Share (%)	Annual Interest Rate (%)
Domestic Fund	Government Fund	111,558.2	20.1	
	KOWACO Fund	179,962.7	32.4	
	Subtotal	291,520.9	52.5	
	Petroleum Business Fund	33,900.9	6.1	10
	KDB2/ Loan	8,670.9	1.6	10.5
	Subtotal	42,570.9	7.7	
	Total	334,091.8	60.2	
Foreign Fund	IBRD Loan	112,149.8	20.2	7
	OECF1/ Loan	58,368.6	10.5	3.5
	KDB Loan	50,437.1	9.1	flexible (10.5)
	Total	220,955.5	39.8	
Total		555,047.3	100.0	

Source : KOWACO, *Analysis of Waterworks and Sewerage Projects and Rate Structure Rationalization Plan* (1989) (in Korean).
Notes : 1/ OECF - Overseas Economic Cooperation Fund
2/ KDB - Korea Development Bank

internal funds of the Korea Water Resources Corporation (KOWACO), as shown in Table 1. KOWACO provided 32.4 per cent and the government financed 20.1 per cent. A loan from the World Bank and Japan Overseas Economic Cooperation Fund (OECF) supplied 20.2 per cent and 10.5 per cent, respectively. A loan from the Korea Development Bank (KDB) supplied another 10.7 per cent, and 6.1 per cent was borrowed from the Petroleum Business Fund.

2) Cost Sharing

Cost sharing is based on the expected benefit from the use of a dam. There are two kinds of costs to be allocated : Exclusive facility cost and common facility cost. First, the exclusive facility cost is attributed to each benefit and then facility costs common to all four purposes are allocated according to their expected benefits. Table 2 shows the final cost share schedule for the construction of Choongju Multipurpose Dam.

Among the four benefits, hydropower generation took the greatest share of total construction costs with 65.9 per cent. Next was flood control with 16.9 per cent, followed by domestic and industrial water supply with 14.4 per cent and irrigation with 2.9 per cent.

The cost sharing arrangement is internal as it.is made between the Ministry of Construction and the dam-use rights holders, who are the Ministry itself and the KOWACO, a government-invested organization.

3) Cost Recovery

The allocation of property rights for respective purpose is based on the *SMDA*, *River Act*, and *Farm Village Modernization Promotion Act*. For flood control, the government covers full costs and the dam-use right is assigned to the government (Ministry of Construction). For irrigation, 70 per cent is paid by the government and 30

|Table 2| Cost Share for the Construction of Choongju Multipurpose Dam

Classification \ Purpose	Flood Control	Irrigation	Domestic/ Industrial Water	Hydropower Generation	Total
Common Facility Cost Share (%)	20.4	3.5	17.4	58.7	100
Total Construction Cost Share (%)	16.8	2.9	14.4	65.9	100
Total Construction Cost (million won)	93,107	15,952	79,501	363,857	552,417

Source : KOWACO, *Analysis of Waterworks and Sewerage Projects and Rate Structure Rationalization Plan* (1989) (in Korean).

per cent is the responsibility of the KOWACO. For this purpose, dam-use rights are retained by the KOWACO. For domestic and industrial water supply, the KOWACO assumes the responsibility for construction costs and retains the dam-use right. The KOWACO also pays the full capital cost for electricity generation and retains the dam-use right.

4) Analysis

"The governance structure (e.g. competitive market, bilateral market, firm, or government) adopted will tend to be that which minimizes the sum of product costs and governance costs."[2] Asset specificity plays a crucial role in transaction cost economics. If the

2) James Nickum and K. William Easter, "The Application of Transaction Cost Economics to Asian-Pacific Metropolitan Water-Use Issues", *Regional Development Dialogue*, vol. 12, No. 4 (winter 1991), pp. 3-14.

transaction requires the use of fixed assets, the value of which is not easily transferred to other uses, the securing of "credible commitments" becomes particularly important and bilateral dependency prevails.

We find a case of credible commitment through the *ex ante* cost sharing arrangement in the construction of a multipurpose dam. Such nonstandard contracts are formulated to govern the transactions of service from a dam, which is a transaction-specific asset. The value of the dam also depends on the continuation of the present arrangements.

The costs of constructing a multipurpose dam are very high. If the constructor does not secure credible commitments from the users in advance, there is a risk that the construction costs cannot be fully recovered. This is one reason why such dams tend to be constructed by the state. As a way of preventing various kinds of *ex post* transaction cost, *ex ante* cost sharing and long-term contracts were developed for the construction of the multipurpose dam.

2. Stage II : Structural Change in Cost Recovery System

1) Contracting

The KOWACO, as the property-rights owner of dam water as well as administrator of the multipurpose dam, enters into water intake contracts directly with actual users and collects water fee based on the amount of water withdrawn. There are three types of transactions.

First, the KOWACO makes a contract with local governments

who take raw water from the Han River to treat and sell them through waterworks to end users. This contract entails a potential conflict between the KOWACO and the local governments because they have withdrawn raw water directly from the river long before the completion of the dam. If a dispute develops, the river management agency intervenes to determine the amount of water to which the local government has a vested right. However, not enough information is available on vested water-use rights. There is no separate water code in the Republic of Korea, and the provision on water-use rights specified in the *SMDA* is too ambiguous to be applied to conflict resolution.

Second, the KOWACO generates hydro-electricity and sells them to the Korea Electric Power Corporation (KEPCO), thereby recovering the construction and operation/maintenance costs of the multipurpose dam for electricity generation purposes.

Third, the KOWACO made irrigation water supply contracts with thirty-four different farmland improvement cooperatives. However, confronted by strong protests by farmers against the so-called irrigation water tax, the government decided not to collect fees. Consequently, the share of construction costs for irrigation will be paid entirely by the government.

2) Structural Change in Dam Water Rates

The water rate structure has undergone several changes since the completion of the Soyanggang Multipurpose Dam in 1973. Up to the end of the 1970s, the KOWACO operated at a loss because the demand for dam water was far below supply capacity and the users were reluctant to pay for river water which, historically, they had used free of charge.

From 1980 to 1984, dam-use rights holders made charge contracts with actual users based on the cost sharing principle to recover construction as well as maintenance and operation costs. However, the revised *SMDA* of May 1984 added a provision which allowed dam-use rights holders to collect a user's fee from actual and potential users of dam water. This transformed the water rate system from the previous cost sharing contract to a government-backed user's fee system, breaking the direct relationship between costs and benefits.

Another problem developed at the end of 1985 when water demand for the Soyanggang Multipurpose Dam reached full capacity and the Choongju Multipurpose Dam was completed. Due to the high construction cost of this dam, its water rate was set at 8.75 won/m^3, more than twice that of the Soyanggang Dam. Naturally, users were reluctant to enter into a contract with the Choongju Dam Authorities. To solve this problem of different prices for water from the same system, two types of unified rate structure were proposed – one within the same river system and the other nationwide. The government chose the latter option, sacrificing efficiency to solve a distributional problem, thereby reducing conflict.

In December 1986, the government approved a unified national rate of 5.94 won/m^3 for domestic and industrial water. If local governments were to be responsible for constructing a multipurpose dam, the relative scarcity of water would be revealed by different water rates charged by local governments and more efficient allocation through water transfer, for example, could be secured.

Multipurpose dam is constructed through an *ex ante* cost sharing contract between the constructor and dam-use rights establishers. An *ex ante* cost sharing contract and the allocation of dam-use rights are ways to secure credible commitments. The essence of this system can be preserved only if the holder of a dam-use right can transfer costs to water users. However, confronted by protests and boycotts from dam water users, the KOWACO was forced to rely on a fee-paying system rather than on the cost sharing contracts, as initially planned. Even after the change in cost recovery methods, the conflict between the KOWACO and dam water users persisted.

To minimize *ex post* transaction costs, such as the cost of resolving legal conflicts over vested water-use rights and costs involved in fee-setting or fee-collection procedures, the KOWACO developed an alternative way to sell dam water. The idea was that rather than depending on fluctuating demand by uncertain users, the KOWACO would set up reliable bilateral contracts with customers to sell them water through exclusive water pipelines. Through the development of a bilateral market as a substitute for cost-sharing contracts, the KOWACO could avoid various problems in selling dam water. The first stage of this system is the transaction of dam water between the KOWACO and the area-wide waterworks which purchase dam water from the KOWACO and sell them to local governments through pipelines. The operator of the area-wide waterworks is the KOWACO itself, so the transaction between the KOWACO and the area-wide waterworks is internalized and the transaction costs incurred due to opportunism and bounded rationality are avoided.

3. Stage III : Area-wide Waterworks

1) Rationale of Area-wide Waterworks

The establishment of area-wide waterworks is a way to reduce the transaction costs involved in selling dam water to actual users. This is because the internalization of transactions and the imposition of bilateral dependency through specific assets greatly reduce transaction costs.

However, the construction of area-wide waterworks is a public project so that if it does not satisfy the public, it cannot be implemented. The following are reasons presented by the advocates of area-wide waterworks :

(a) Local governments face growing difficulties in securing sufficient raw water of potable quality to use for local waterworks. In particular, the Seoul Metropolitan Region should construct new water intake stations upstream to secure better quality raw water.

(b) Area-wide waterworks can provide good quality raw water at lower cost than several small scale water transmitting pipelines, thanks to planned investment and economies of scale.

(c) Water transfers among the network of area-wide waterworks are possible and water will be allocated more efficiently throughout the nation.

(d) The national unified rate structure will mitigate different tap water rates among local governments.

(e) If each local government constructs its own raw water transportation pipelines to the water source, conflict will arise between upstream and downstream users and between large and small cities.

In summary, the construction of area-wide waterworks not only reduces the transaction cost of the KOWACO in selling dam water, but also is a way of securing better quality raw water at low cost. However, because of the unique character of bilateral dependency and the KOWACO's role as a sole supplier, unequal transaction might take place. Therefore, the water rate structure of area-wide waterworks needs to be studied to investigate the real reason for the development of the system.

2) Rate Structure

The KOWACO sells raw and purified water to local governments through area-wide waterworks. The monthly charge is based on the following formula. The rate structure is shown in Table 3. Monthly charge=(basic use rate × monthly contracted amount)+(measured use rate × monthly actual used amount)+(excess use rate × quantity exceeding contracted amount).

The area-wide waterworks charge system is analogous to an average cost pricing scheme where the basic use charge covers average fixed costs and the measured use charge covers average variable costs. The excess use charge is a kind of penalty charged

|Table 3| Raw and Purified Water Rate in 1990

(Unit : won / m^3)

	Basic Use Rate	Measured Use Rate	Excess Use Rate
Raw Water	21.55	16.48	69.14
Purified water	67.49	9.65	92.04

Source : KOWACO, *Analysis of Waterworks and Sewerage Projects and Rate Structure Rationalization Plan* (1989) (in Korean)

for the quantity in excess of the initially contracted amount. Overuse by one user means that some other users might not receive what they initially contracted for.

The KOWACO requests a revision of the water rate structure when necessary. The Ministry of Construction is authorized to approve the revision after consultation with the Economic Planning Board. This rate-making system of area-wide waterworks is analogous to that of local waterworks.

Table 4 shows the composition of raw water sources for waterworks in Seoul Metropolitan Region. In 1988, the City of Seoul secured 66 per cent of its raw water from the Lower Han River. The remaining 34 per cent was supplied by the metropolitan area-wide waterworks. In the City of Incheon which is located by the Yellow Sea, 76 per cent came from the Paldang Reservoir through metropolitan area-wide waterworks and the rest was pumped from the Lower Han River. Kyunggi Province consists of many cities and towns located far from the Han River, so it depends in area-wide waterworks for 75 per cent of its raw water.

|Table 4| Seoul Metropolitan Region Waterworks Capacity by Raw Water Source in 1988

(Unit : 1,000 m^3/day)

Area	Water Purification Plant	Capacity	Raw Water Source			
			Surface Water	Area-wide waterworks	Riverbed	Ground-Water
Seoul	9	4,970 (100)	3,290 (66)	1,680 (34)		
Incheon	2	1,060 (100)	250 (24)	810 (76)		
Kyunggi-do	54	1,331 (100)	101 (7.5)	993 (75)	216 (16.2)	21 (1.3)
Total	65	7,361 (100)	3,641 (49.5)	3,483 (47.3)	216 (3)	21 (0.2)

Source : E. Shin, "Water Use Conflicts in the Seoul Metropolitan Region," mimeo, 1989.
Note : Figures in parentheses are percentages.

4. Stage IV : Public Water Supply in the City of Seoul

1) Water Supply and Demand in Seoul

Water demand in Seoul has been growing continuously due to population growth and improved living standards. In 1989, 4.97 million m^3 per day were supplied to Seoul. Out of 10.6 million residents, 99.3 per cent received water service, with per capita daily supply of 427 liters.

There are nine water purification plants in Seoul. As noted above, out of a total daily capacity of 4.97million m^3, 66 per cent of raw

|Table 5| Water Purification Capacities in the City of Seoul in 1989

(Unit : 1,000 m^3/day)

Purification Plant	Capacities by Raw Water Source		
	Paldang Reservoir (Areawide Waterworks)	Han River (Surface Flow)	Total
Paldang	1,000	-	1,000
Amsa	-	1,000	1,000
Kuui	-	1,130	1,130
Ttukdo	-	500	500
Bokwangdong	-	300	300
Noryangjin	160	140	300
Sonyu	180	220	400
Youngdungpo	240	-	240
Kimpo	100	-	100
Total	1,680	3,290	4,970

Source : Seoul Waterworks Authority.

water is taken from the surface flow of the Lower Han River and the rest is delivered from the Paldang Reservoir through metropolitan area-wide waterworks. Seoul pays a fee to the KOWACO for the raw water taken from the Lower Han River and for the raw and purified water delivered through pipelines (see Table 5).

2) Water Rate Structure in Seoul

As local waterworks are operated by local governments, water rate structures vary. Table 6 shows the water rate structure in Seoul, where water users are classified into nine categories. The monthly water bill is composed of a basic charge and an additional

|Table 6| Water Rate Structure in Seoul (1990)

Classification	Type of Industry	Number of Taps	Basic Rates		Additional Rates	
			Usage Volume	Value	Usage Volume	Unit cost/m³ (won)
First Class	Commercial	95,334	30	8,270	31-200 201-300 301+	410 550 700
Second Class	Commercial	60,558	20	2,100	301+	260
Third Class	Household	1,238,186	10	600	11-30 31-50 51+	79 174 230
Fourth Class	Luxury public baths	77	500	273,000	501+	880
Fifth Class	Public baths	2,117	500	54,000	501+	140
Sixth Class	Public institutions	4,501	170 won per m^3			
Seventh Class	Public waterworks	671	100	5,000	101+	50
Eighth Class	Temporary supply	295	410 won per m^3			

Source : Seoul Waterworks Authority.

charge. As shown in Table 6, first class commercial users pay 4.6 times as much as households for the first $10m^3$. Households consume almost 90 per cent of total supply but contribute only 35 per cent of total revenue, thus they are highly subsidized.

Presently, the water rate is lower than production costs in Seoul, so the waterworks authority borrows approximately 80 billion won every year. Local loans are spent on construction of additional

Figure 2 Patterns of Tap Water Drinking Habits

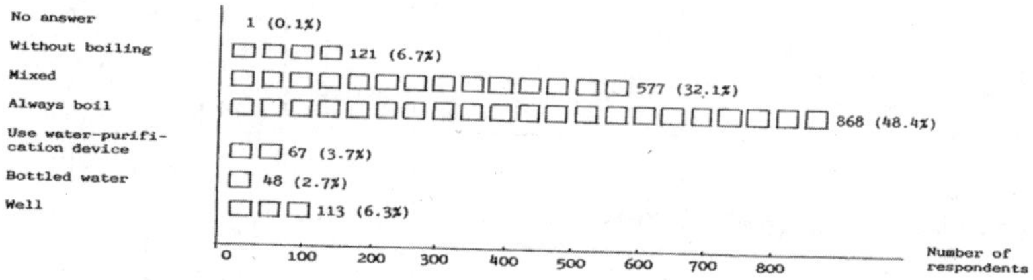

Source : Office of the Environment, *A Survey on People's Opinion for Environmental Preservation* (1987).

purification plants and on the improvement of water quality through rehabilitation of old pipes.

3) Growing Distrust in Tap Water Quality

According to a survey conducted by the Office of the Environment in 1987,[3)] 48.4 per cent of respondents said they boil tap water before drinking, 32.1 per cent of respondents said they drink sometimes without boiling and sometimes after boiling, and 6.7 per cent said they always drink without boiling (see Figure 2).

By income level, the poorest are most likely to take their drinking water from wells. As expected, the highest income group has a dominant share in the category of using a water purification device at home. By region, residents of cities and industrial complexes prefer drinking after boiling, while people living in farming or fishing villages often drink tap water without boiling.

The Waterworks Association conducted a separate survey in 1989

3) Office of the Environment, *A Survey of People's Opinion Concerning Environmental Preservation* (1987) (in Korean).

|Table 7| National Survey on Water Quality by the Waterworks Association

Survey Contents	Evaluation	
Sanitary Condition	Bad : 78.7%	Average : 12.5%
	Good : 3.4%	Others : 5.4%
Uncomfortable Experiences	Rust : 34.4%	Sediment : 34.4%
	Odour : 17.8%	Combined : 13.4%
Causes of Unsatisfactory Water Service	Polluted raw water :	42.2%
	Old facilities :	23.5%
	Insufficient purification :	23.5%
	Others :	13.3%
Tap Water Drinking Habits	Boil :	79.9%
	Water purification device :	7.7%
	Natural water :	6.6%
	Tap water, as is :	5.8%

Source : Waterworks Association (1989).

on people's attitudes towards local waterworks, covering 2,500 households in fourteen cities. The survey results, presented in Table 7, show that 78.7 per cent of people thought that the sanitary condition of tap water was bad, and most respondents had negative experiences with water such as a high rust content, sediment, or disagreeable odor. As the main cause, 42.2 per cent of people indicated a polluted raw water source while the rest mentioned old facilities or insufficient purification.

Consequently, 79.9 per cent responded that they always, or at least sometimes, boil tap water before drinking. This result is very close to the one obtained from the survey by the Office of the

Environment.

III. Water Crisis and the Growing Private Water Market

1. Development of a Natural Water Market in the Republic of Korea

The *Food Sanitation Law* prohibits the sale of natural water to Koreans living in the Republic of Korea. However, the Ministry of Health can authorize the establishment of a natural water company on condition that the product be either exported or sold only to foreigners in the Republic of Korea.

Fourteen natural water companies produced 109,900 tons of natural water and earned 20 billion won in 1989. More than 95 per cent of these earnings were from sales in the domestic market. The sales volume has been growing at an explosive rate since 1986 but the per capita consumption is still very small compared to the developed nations shown in Table 8. The low per capita consumption of natural water in Japan might be the result of a difference in life-style between East and West, because of water quality differences, or simply because the Japanese have great confidence in the government water supply.

Natural water is sold in 18.9 liters, 1.8 liters, and 0.9 liters bottles directly to large-scale consumers or is delivered to households through sales agents. Seoul takes 90 per cent of its sales volume through agents. Principal consumers are households, which consume

|Table 8| Private Water Market

	Total (1,000 kilo liter)			Per capita (liter)		
	1985	1986	1987	1985	1986	1987
Republic of Korea	-	-	36.7	-	-	0.9
Japan	82.4	82.5	89.6	0.7	0.7	0.7
USA	4,743	5,203	5,566	19.6	21.5	23
Germany (West)	3,520	4,087	4,148	57.7	67	68
France	3,373	4,009	4,396	61	72.5	79.5
Italy	3,375	3,774	4,180	59.1	66.1	73.2
Belgium	569	628	680	57.5	63.4	68.7
Switzerland	325	339	360	50.8	53	56.2

Source : Anonymous Company.

87 per cent, with the remainder consumed by the business sector.

Up to 1986, foreign residents and the upper-income groups were major customers. However, the demand for bottled natural water has extended to the middle-income groups during the past five years. Now each household consumes four 18.9 liters bottles a month, on average.

Table 9 shows that agents' margins from the sale of bottled water are quite high, more than 30 per cent. The price per ton is 184,210 won in the case of the 18.9 liters bottle. As the Seoul resident pays 600 won for up to 30 tons of city water, average price of city water per ton is 20 won. Thus, the price of bottled water is 9,210 times more expensive than tap water. This is an indication that people are willing to pay much more to get better quality drinking water.

|Table 9| Prices and Selling Agents' Margins

	Consumer Price (won)	Agent Price (won)	Margin (%)
18.9 liters 1/Box	3,500	2,100	40.0
1.8 liters 12/Box	6,000	4,000	33.3
0.9 liters 15/Box	6,000	4,000	33.3

Source : Natural Water Manufacturers' Association

2. Conflicts between the Government and Natural Water Producers

In 1990, eleven of fourteen natural water companies were charged with breaking the *Food Sanitation Law*'s prohibition on the sales of natural water to Koreans. One company was ordered to suspend business for five months. That company later filed an administrative appeal to the Seoul High Court of Justice for the removal of the suspension order.

The Ministry of Health has fined those natural water companies which violate the law more than three times and has strengthened the penalty after learning that sales of natural water to domestic consumers are still increasing.

The government and producers have different opinions on the issue of legitimating natural water sales to domestic consumers. The government worries that the legitimation of domestic natural water will increase people's distrust in public water and will trigger a protest from the low-income groups which cannot afford to buy better quality bottled water. Additionally, the government worries that mushrooming natural water production could deplete groundwater sources, against which there is no present legal constraints. On the other hand, producers assert that people should have the freedom to choose better quality water and that it is unfair to differentiate domestic customers from foreigners. They also insist that the legitimation of the natural water market is a good way to improve efficiency through open competition. But more than anything else, they contend that the natural water market can serve as a complement to the existing public waterworks.

3. Analysis

Deteriorating water quality and the growing distrust of public waterworks recently became an important social issue in the Republic of Korea, especially in the summer of 1989 when it nearly developed into a water crisis. People questioned whether there might be harmful new chemicals which are not included in evaluating the quality of tap water and whether installed water purification plants are adequate to treat these harmful materials. They also wondered whether purified water could be polluted en route to households due to rusted or leaking pipelines and unsanitary water tanks.

According to tests performed by the City of Seoul and other research institutions, the quality of tap water is safe for drinking. But most people do not believe these results. The problem is how to assure people that the quality of tap water is truly safe. This dilemma, which cannot be solved through neoclassical marginal analysis, may be amenable to a transaction cost approach.

A waterworks system operates through fixed asset and bilateral dependency. The supplier uses a metering device to measure the quantity consumed and can secure a steady demand. The supplier does not have to incur high *ex post* costs to monitor water theft even though water loss in the process of transportation is quite high due to deteriorating pipelines and mismanagement.

However, a large degree of bounded rationality is involved in city waterworks transactions. As pointed out by Williamson,[4] "given bounded rationality, all complex contracts are unavoidably incomplete." The monthly rate is charged according to volume used but the quality dimension is not included in the contract.

As there are no clear provisions on the quality of tap water sold and no compensation or penalty is guaranteed in case of violation, consumers must depend on their own information sources to judge the quality of water. However, it is costly to test the water quality of all users and because there are many ways for the water to be polluted, it is impossible to find evidence to charge the waterworks authority with intentional quality deterioration. Instead, people resort to the available risk minimizing options of boiling water, utilizing private water purification devices, or purchasing natural water, depending on their income levels.

4) 4 Oliver E. Williamson, "Operationalizing the New Industrial Economics : The Transaction Cost Economics Perspective" (1989), mimeo.

IV. Concluding Remarks

This investigation of the stages of transactions in the Seoul water management system and of the current controversy over bottled water shows that, at the very least, framing the problems in a Williamsonian transaction cost framework yields important insights into water-use conflicts. For example, it allows us to look inside an organization such as the KOWACO to see how it arranges transfers of water, and to understand better the logic of internalization. It also shows how vested rights and the political process can increase transaction costs of new development, in particular through the avoidance of cost sharing by riverine cities and agriculture.

The controversy over drinking water can also be looked at through a transactional approach. Credibility is important in maintaining a bilateral relationship. The state's loss of credibility in the quality of its water supply, whether deserved or not, has led consumers to expand their sources, even at high cost. Attempts by the state to use the police to impose high transaction costs on alternative transactions appear to be less successful.

Clearly, there is much work to be done before the transaction cost approach becomes fully operational in policy applications. Nonetheless, the results obtained here are encouraging for continued efforts to that end.

References

Industrial Site Development Corporation, *A Study on the Allocation of Property Rights of Choongju Multipurpose Dam and Management Plan* (in Korean), 1985.

Korea Water Resources Corporation, *Analysis of Waterworks and Sewerage Projects and Rate Structure Rationalization Plan* (in Korean), 1989.

Ministry of Construction, *Waterworks*, 1989.

Seoul Metropolitan Government Waterworks Headquarters, *'90 Waterworks in Seoul*, 1990.

Shin, Euisoon, "Water Use Conflicts in the Seoul Metropolitan Region," mimeo, 1990.

Williamson, Oliver E., *Economic Organization*, New York University Press, 1986.

______ "Transaction Cost Economics : The Governance of Law and Economics," 1979.

8. Water-Use Conflicts in the Seoul Metropolitan Region*

I. Introduction

Seoul has been the capital of Korea for the past 600 years. The population of Seoul reached 1 million in the 1940s and was 2.4 million in 1960. Since then, it has grown more than twice as fast as that of South Korea as a whole, partly because of rapid industrialization. By 1989, the population of Seoul exceeded 10 million, or 24 percent of the total population of South Korea.

The Han River, one of four large rivers in South Korea, flows through the Seoul Metropolitan Region. Until the early 1970s, the Han River provided sufficient clean water for farms and households in the river basin. However, rapid industrialization and urbanization in the region increased water use in the domestic, commercial, and industrial sectors, causing major problems.

---

* "Water Use Conflicts in the Seoul Metropolitan Region," in James E. Nickum and K. William Easter(eds.), *Metropolitan Water Use Conflict in Asia and the Pacific*, Westview Press, 1994, pp.113-129.

First, as the increasing demand could not be satisfied with the natural flow of the Han River, multipurpose dams were constructed to increase the potable water supply. These facilities are expected to meet water demand in the Seoul Metropolitan Region until the year 2000. Most multipurpose dam sites have already been developed, however, and even if groundwater can help alleviate upcoming water shortages, its effect will be minimal. That means water resource management in the region should include demand restriction as well as supply expansion in the future.

Second, people and industries along the Han River and its tributaries have discharged sewage and wastewaters beyond the river's self-purification capacity, polluting the river. As a result, Seoul was obliged to purchase more raw water from the Paldang Reservoir, which is located upstream on the Lower Han River. The water quality of the Paldang Reservoir also has been deteriorating recently. The reservoir may become unsuitable as a source of city water unless proper measures are taken soon.

This paper first explains the water demand and supply management in the region, focusing on how the increasing water shortage problem has been resolved. It then investigates the present status of Han River pollution and efforts taken by the government to alleviate the causes and effects of water pollution. Thereupon it analyzes the water-related government organizations and institutional arrangements established for managing water resources in Korea. A summary concludes the analysis.

II. Water Demand and Supply Management

1. Water Demand and Supply in Korea

Average annual precipitation in Korea is 1,159 mm, which is 1.5 times the world average of 730mm. However, annual per capita volume of water from precipitation is only 10 percent of the world average because of high population density. The total volume of water available in 1987 was about 114 billion m^3. Of this, 42 percent was lost through seepage and evaporation, and the remaining 66.2 billion m^3 flowed into the rivers. However, 40.5 billion m^3 was concentrated during the flood season and only 25.7 billion m^3 constituted normal flow. The surface water actually used was 16.7 billion m^3, only 15 percent of total volume. In addition to the use of surface flow, 6.5 billion m^3 was recovered through dams and 1.6 billion m^3 was recovered from the groundwater. As a whole, 24.8 billion m^3, or 22 percent of total water volume from precipitation, was actually used in 1987 (Ministry of Construction, 1988).

Table 1 shows water demand and supply trends in Korea. Water demand includes domestic, industrial, and agricultural sectors and the volume required to maintain river flow throughout the year. Total water demand has increased 26.7 percent from 1981 to 1986 and is expected to increase at a slightly lower rate in the future. In 1981, the agricultural sector accounted for more than one-half of total water consumption, and the domestic and industrial sectors used 21 percent. During the past 10 years, the agricultural share

|Table 1| Water Demand and Supply in Korea (million m^3/year)

Sector	1981	1986	1991	2001
Total demand	20,327	25,760	31,770	37,710
Domestic	2,503	4,260	5,669	7,443
Industrial	1,778	2,127	2,906	4,130
Agricultural	10,684	11,804	13,482	15,794
Maintenance	5,362	7,569	9,713	10,343
Total supply	18,979	23,685	30,211	38,503
River flow	14,319	16,359	18,265	21,404
Groundwater	1,164	1,513	1,744	2,025
Reservoir	3,496	5,813	10,202	15,074
Final balance	−1,348	−2,075	−1,559	793

Source : Ministry of Construction, 1987b.

decreased relative to the domestic and industrial sectors. Water demand in the domestic sector increased 70 percent from 1981 to 1986. The industrial sector is expected to experience the highest demand growth in the 1990s.

In 1981, 19 billion m^3 of water was supplied, but 1,348 million m^3 more was required to satisfy total demand. River flow provided 75 percent of total water supply ; reservoirs, 18.4 percent ; and groundwater, only 6.1 percent. As normal river flow carries only 22 percent of the total water resource, there is a limit to dependence on natural flow as a source of water. It is projected that increasing water demand will mostly be met by constructing new multipurpose dams. Reservoirs will provide nearly 40 percent of total supply by 2001, and the contribution of river flow will decrease from 75 to 56 per cent. Groundwater will remain a minor source, as there are

|**Figure 1**| Water and Sewerage Treatment Plants in the Seoul Metropolitan Region

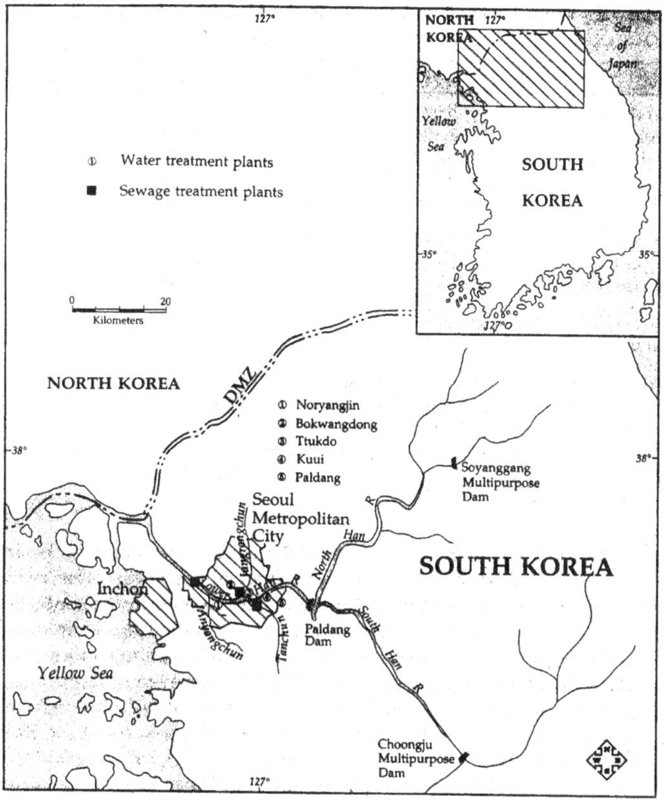

no large aquifers in South Korea.

2. Water Use in the Han River Basin

The Han River system is composed of the North Han, the South Han, and the Lower Han Rivers (see Figure 1). It is 470 km long and the basin area is 26,219 km^2, covering one-third of South

Korea. Total volume of water carried annually in the Han River is 32.2 billion m^3, or 28.2 percent of the national total. The North and the South Han Rivers originate from the mountainous area in the eastern part of the Korean peninsula and converge at Yangsuri, forming the Lower Han River. The Lower Han River flows through the fertile Kyunggi Plane and the Seoul Metropolitan Region, then into the Yellow Sea.

Until the early 1970s, the Han River could satisfy water demand in the river basin with natural river flow, even during the dry season. Irrigation was the major use. However, rapid industrialization and concentration of population in the Seoul Metropolitan Region quickly increased water demand, and natural flow was no longer sufficient. To meet the increasing water demand in the Seoul Metropolitan Region, the Soyanggang Multipurpose Dam was constructed on the North Han River (1967-1973), and the Choongju Multipurpose Dam on the South Han River (1980-1985) with a capacity of 1,213 and 3,380 million m^3, respectively. In addition to these, there are six more dams on the Han River, mainly for electric power generation. Paldang Dam, which is located where the North and the South Han Rivers converge, functions as a reservoir of raw water for the Metropolitan Region Area-wide Waterworks.

Table 2 shows the water demand and supply trends and projections for the Han River basin. There are several differences between the water demand patterns of the Han River and the nation as a whole. First, the share of maintenance water in the Han River is nearly one-half of total demand, while it is less than 30

|Table 2| Water Demand and Supply in the Han River Basin (million m^3/year)

Sector	1981	1986	1991	2001
Total demand	5,091	7,745	8,724	9,916
Domestic	1,304	2,035	2,511	2,894
Industrial	468	492	517	570
Agricultural	1,111	1,276	1,439	1,722
Maintenance	2,208	3,942	4,257	4,730
Total supply	5,248	9,432	9,696	11,357
River flow	3,814	4,538	4,746	5,040
Groundwater	221	301	351	385
Reservoir	1,213[a]	4,593[b]	4,599[c]	5,932[d]
Final balance	157	1,687	972	1,441

[a] Water supply from Soyanggang Reservoir.

[b] Water supply from Choongju Reservoir (3,380 million m^3).

[c] Includes Kwangdong Reservoir (6 million m^3).

[d] Includes Hangcheon Reservoir (1,333 million m^3).

Source : Ministry of Construction, 1980.

percent in other rivers. This is because the Han River has large reservoirs, formed after eight dams were constructed. Second, the share of agricultural demand in the Han River basin is less than 20 percent, compared to more than 40 percent in other river basins. This is because most large farmlands are located in the southern part of the Korean peninsula. Third, water supply in the Han River basin depends heavily on multipurpose dams, which will contribute more than one-half of total water supply by 2001. Table 3 lists seven multipurpose dams in Korea with a total annual water supply

|Table 3| Multipurpose Dams in Korea

Dam	Feature		Total Capacity (million m^3)	Benefit		
	Height (m)	Length (m)		Flood Control (million m^3)	Water Supply (million m^3/year)	Electricity (million kwh/year)
Total			9,040	1,530	8,300	1,808
Soyanggang	123	530	2,900	500	1,213	353
Andong	83	612	1,248	110	926	158
Namgang	21	975	136	43	134	43
Sumjingang	64	344	466	27	350	160
Daechung	72	495	1,490	250	1,649	250
Choongju	97.5	447	2,750	600	3,380	844
Nakdongang Estuary	-	2,400	50	-	648	-

Source : Ministry of Construction 1988.

capacity of 8,300 million m^3 ; Soyanggang and Choongju dams on the Han River account for 55.3 percent of this figure.

Within the Han River system, the South Han River basin uses more than 50 percent of the total agricultural water, and the Lower Han River basin consumes another 30 percent. More than 80 percent of residential and industrial water demand is concentrated on the Lower Han River, which flows through Seoul. To discourage further concentration and to satisfy water demand, the Revised Second Comprehensive National Land Development Plan (1987-1991) calls for relocation of population and industries in the Seoul Metropolitan Region. The region was classified into five areas : Seoul and its suburbs are classified as a "Move-Encouraging Area," where the establishment of new resident-increasing facilities such as universities are prohibited, but the transfer of existing facilities is encouraged. The plan classifies the Upper Han River basin as "Nature-Preservation Area," where the establishment of environmentally damaging industries is prohibited and various restrictions are put on the activities of existing businesses, to preserve the water source of the Seoul Metropolitan Region.

3. Water Supply through Area-wide Waterworks

Increasing demand for water in and around Seoul can no longer be satisfied by the waterworks of local governments. Since the rivers near big cities are polluted and new sources of clean water are hard to find, each city seeks water from more distant rivers. However, such developments could be costly and inefficient, as they might result in overlapping investments and externality problems. It is more efficient for a specific water supply authority to construct area-wide waterworks and to distribute the raw water to nearby cities and towns.

The waterworks system in Korea is divided into area-wide waterworks and local waterworks. Area-wide waterworks are constructed by the Ministry of Construction and managed by the Korea Water Resources Corporation, a government corporation. Local waterworks are constructed and managed by local governments. Area-wide waterworks supply water to about one-half of total benefited population in Korea, mostly city residents.

The Korea Water Resources Corporation sells raw water and

treated water to the water authorities of local governments through area-wide waterworks. The water fee charged by the corporation includes a basic-use fee and a measured-use fee. The basic-use fee is set by dividing total fixed cost by initially contracted quantity of water. The measured-use fee is equal to the average variable cost, which is total variable cost divided by total water actually supplied. Thus, the rate structure of area-wide waterworks is close to the average cost-pricing scheme, which sets price just high enough to cover supply cost, including a normal rate of return on invested capital. In addition to the basic-and measure-use fees, an excess-use fee can be added when necessary for efficient distribution of water. Water fee revisions are made by the Ministry of Construction, upon the request of the Korea Water Resources Corporation, in consultation with the Economic Planning Board. Currently, the Korea Water Resources Corporation charges 38.03 won per ton of raw water and 77.14 won per ton of treated water uniformly to all users of area-wide waterworks.

As of 1988, total capacity of area-wide waterworks in Korea was 3.05 million m^3/day, with an additional capacity of 2.06 million m^3/day under construction. The Metropolitan Region Area-wide Waterworks project was started in 1973, and stages 1 and 2 were completed by 1981. Stages 1 and 2 area-wide waterworks have a total capacity of 2.6 million m^3/day and supply good quality water from the Paldang Reservoir to eight cities including Seoul and Incheon in the Seoul Metropolitan Region. Stage 3 started in 1984 and was completed in 1988. It supplies 1.3 million m^3/day to twenty-five cities. Stage 4 started in 1989 to supply an additional

1.5 million m^3/day to twenty-nine cities.

Table 4 shows the raw water sources for the Seoul Metropolitan Region. In 1988 Seoul received 66 percent of its raw water from the Lower Han River and bought 34 percent from the Paldang Reservoir through the Metropolitan Region Area-wide Waterworks. In Incheon, 76 percent of raw water came from the Paldang Reservoir, and 24 percent was pumped from the Lower Han River. In Kyunggi Province, 75 percent of raw water came mainly from the Paldang Reservoir, 16.2 percent from the riverbed in the Han River tributaries, and only 7.5 percent from the surface flow of the Han River or its tributaries. The main flow of the Lower Han River still makes up more than one-half of the total raw water supply to Seoul and Incheon. However, cities and towns in the Kyunggi Province receive and use only a small amount of raw water from the surface flow, since the Han River is far away and its tributaries are too polluted. All raw water transmitted from the Paldang Reservoir to Seoul, Incheon, and Kyunggi Province is supplied by the Korea Water Resources Corporation through the Metropolitan Region Area-wide Waterworks.

4. City Water Supply in the Seoul Metropolitan Region

According to the Sixth Five-Year Economic and Social Development Plan (1987-1991), the nation is divided into four extensive economic regions along four large rivers in South Korea. One of them is the Seoul Metropolitan Region, which receives water from the Han River. This region includes Seoul Special city, Incheon

Directly Governed city, and Kyunggi Province. The Seoul Metropolitan Region accounts for 39 percent of the South Korean population and produces 40 percent of total national output. Thus, the importance of the Han River to the Korean people and economy is enormous.

|Table 4| Seoul Metropolitan Region Waterworks Capacity by Raw Water Source (1988) (1,000 m^3/day)

Area	Water Plants	Capacity	Raw Water Source			
			River Flow	Paldang		Ground water
				Riverbed	Reservoir	
Seoul	9	4,970 (100%)	3,290 (66%)		1,680 (34%)	
Incheon	2	1,060 (100%)	250 (24%)		810 (76%)	
Kyunggi Province	54	1,331 (100%)	101 (7.5%)	216 (16.2%)	993 (75%)	21 (1.3%)
Total	65	7,361 (100%)	3,641 (49.5%)	216 (3%)	3,483 (47.3%)	21 (0.2%)

Source : Ministry of Construction, 1987b.

The concentration of population and improved living standards brought a rapid increase in the demand for city water in Korea. In 1986, 68 percent of the people in South Korea received city water, with a daily per capita supply of 295 liters. Water services in Seoul are far better than the national average (see Table 5). In 1986, 98 percent of Seoul residents received city water, with a daily per

|Table 5| City Water Supply in the Seoul Metropolitan Region(1986)

Area	Total Population(A)	Serviced Population(B)	(B)/(A) (%)	Daily Total (1000m^3)	Daily Per Capita (ℓ)
Seoul	9,798,542	9,573,167	98	3,729	390
Incheon	1,441,131	1,376,280	95	454	329
Kyunggi Province	3,965,854	2,848,700	72	610	214

Source : Ministry of construction 1987a.

capita supply of 390 liters. Ninety-five percent of Incheon residents received an average daily supply of 329 liters per capita. However, only 72 percent of the people living in Kyunggi Province were serviced, with an average daily supply of 214 liters, which is only 55 percent of the level of Seoul. This inequality of water supply between big cities and small-to-medium towns is one of the problems that must be solved.

Another problem is the high loss ratio that occurs during city water transmission. Transmission losses range from 23 to 47 percent in the Seoul Metropolitan Region. The high delivery losses are primarily caused by aged waterworks pipes. In the network of 17,185 km of pipe, only 65.1 percent is less than 10 years old, 27.6 percent is 11 to 20 years old, and 7.3 percent is more than 20 years old. Besides causing water losses, old pipes increase the risk of water contamination during its delivery to the final users.

Since local waterworks are operated by separate local governments, rate structures for city water vary throughout the country. Also, different rates are charged for different usage classes. City water fees for industrial and commercial uses are generally higher than for domestic use fees. Since a uniform or progressive rate structure, combined with basic fees, is employed within the same usage class, large water users pay relatively more than small users. Seoul uses nine categories, including domestic, commercial, industrial, and public. Table 6 shows the water rate structure for domestic water use in Seoul and Kyunggi Province. Basically, the city water fee is the sum of the basic fee and an additional progressive fee. The basic fee for Seoul is 600 won for the first 10 tons, and an additional charge is based on consumption. Seoul's domestic water fee is one of the lowest in the country and some cities charge about five times as much.

Commercial water users in Seoul, including manufacturing and service industries, pay 4.6 times more for the basic fees and 5 times more for the additional fees than do domestic users. In this category the basic fee is 8,270 won up to the first 30 tons, and the additional fees are 410 won/ton for 31 to 200 tons, 550 won/ton for 201 to 300 tons, and 700 won/ton over 300 tons of city water used.

|Table 6| City Water Rate Structures for Domestic Customers in Seoul and Kyunggi Province

Region	Basic Charge (won/10 tons)	Additional Charge (won/ton)		
		11-30 t	31-50 t	Over 51 t
Seoul	600	79	174	230
Kyunggi Province	560-1,190	80-150	100-190	140-270

Source : Korea Research Institute for Human Settlements 1987.

|Table 7| Quality of Lower Han River at Water Intake Stations (1986)

(mg/ℓ)

Intake Station	BOD	COD	DO
Paldang	1.4	2.1	10.9
Kuui	1.7	3.3	10.1
Ttukdo	2.5	4.0	9.9
Bokwangdong	3.0	4.1	9.5
Noryangjin	4.1	4.7	8.5
Sonyu	4.2	5.3	7.6

Source : Office of Environment 1987.

III. Deteriorating Water Quality

1. Han River Pollution and Restoration Efforts

As mentioned, the discharge of urban and industrial wastes exceeds the river's self-purification capacity and has polluted the Lower Han River. Table 7 shows the water quality of the Lower Han in 1986. One can see that the water quality worsens as the river flows downstream. Of the six intake stations along the Lower Han River, Paldang, Kuui, and Ttukdo passed the water quality standard of class 2 (suitable for swimming) as specified in the Environmental Preservation Law. All other stations passed the class 3 standard (industrial grade), which was set as a minimum for water to waterworks (see Figure 2). The trend of 1980-1986 shown in Figure 2 indicates that the quality of the Lower Han River has improved since 1985. The completion of the Han River Com-

|**Figure 2**| Water Quality Trend in the Lower Han River

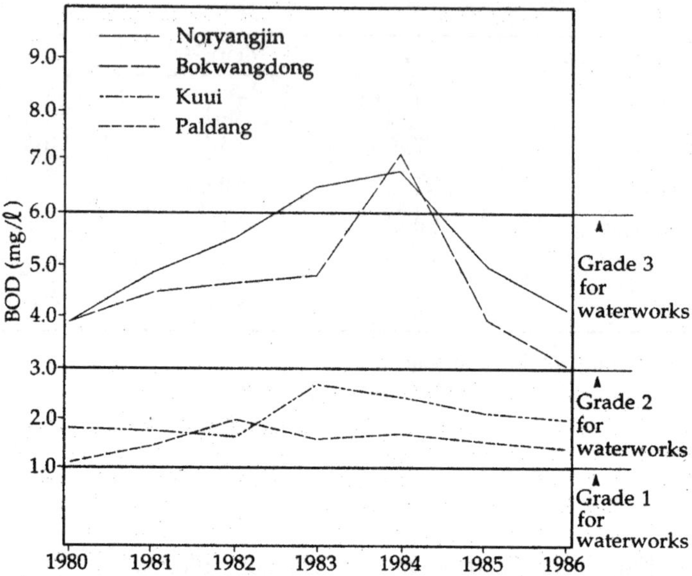

Source : Office of Environment, 1987

prehensive Development Project is credited for improving the quality of water flowing from the tributaries along the Lower Han River.

The Han River Comprehensive Development Project was started in 1982 to improve the quality and appearance of the Han River before the 1988 Seoul Olympics. This scheme included three basic and two accompanying projects. The basic projects were to maintain the average depth of waterway at 2.5m, to provide high-water parks along the river, and to expand the freeway from Kimpo Airport to Olympic Town. The two accompanying projects were the major contributors to quality improvement of the Han River. First, a sewer pipe system, which runs 53.8 km along the river, was constructed to collect domestic and industrial wastewaters from the city and to deliver them to sewage treatment plants, thus preventing untreated waters from flowing directly into the river. Second, three new sewage treatment plants were constructed to treat the polluted waters from three tributaries – the Jungrangchun, Tanchun, and Anyangchun rivers (see Figure 1). After this project was completed, the sewage treatment capacity of Seoul increased from 360,000 to 3,060,000 tons/day.

Although the Han River Comprehensive Development project improved the Lower Han River water quality, upstream water quality has continued to deteriorate, and the level of sewage treatment is not yet satisfactory. A recent survey conducted by the Korea Water Resources Corporation revealed that BOD levels in the Paldang Reservoir increased from 1.4 mg/ℓ in 1986 to 2.4 mg/ℓ in 1988. This is a serious threat to the residents of the Seoul Metropolitan Region, because the reservoir supplies 34 percent of raw water to Seoul and nearly 75 percent to other cities and towns in the region. The main cause of pollution is inflow of wastewater from residential areas, industrial plants, and animal farms upstream from Paldang Reservoir.

The Ministry of Construction states that 19 million tons of sewage is produced daily throughout the nation, of which only 26 percent is treated and the rest is discharged into rivers untreated. Even Seoul did not have any sewage treatment plants until 1979, and the present capacity handles only 82.3 percent of sewage generated. Also, the treatment level is insufficient. The Anyang and Nanji

|Table 8| Water Treatment Capacities in Seoul City (1988)

($1000m^3$/day)

Plant	Capacity by Raw Water Source		Total
	Paldang Reservoir	Lower Han River	
Paldang	1,000	-	1,000
Amsa	-	1,000	1,000
Kuui	-	1,130	1,130
Ttukdo	-	500	500
Bokwangdong	-	300	300
Noryangjin	160	140	300
Sonyu	180	220	400
Yongdungpo	240	-	240
Kimpo	100	-	100
Total	1,680 (34%)	3,290 (66%)	4,970 (100%)

Source : Ministry of Construction 1987a.

plants treat badly polluted wastewaters only partially, thus discharging water that is still polluted far beyond the wastewater effluent standards.

Seoul started to charge sewerage user fees in 1983, based on a "beneficiary pays principle." It is charged to all city water users, in addition to the city water fee. Users of groundwater and surface and industrial water are also charged the sewerage user fee separately. The fee is charged according to six categories of usage, and a progressive rate structure is employed to encourage water conservation.

2. Han River Pollution and Increasing Water Cost

Nine water purification plants along the Lower Han River supply water to Seoul. Of the total capacity of 4.97 million m^3, 66 percent is taken from the Lower Han River and 34 percent from the Paldang Reservoir (see Table 8). Seoul takes 660,000 m^3/day from the Lower Han River below Jungrangchun, where the water is the most severely polluted.

There is a positive correlation between the water quality and water treatment costs. One study compared the unit operating costs of two water purification plants located on the Lower Han River for 9 months in 1982. The Paldang plant receives water from the Paldang Reservoir, and the Bokwangdong plant takes raw water from the Lower Han River (see Figure 1). Table 9 indicates that the unit chemical cost of the Bokwangdong water purification plant is more than seven times higher than the Paldang plant. Unit energy and labor costs have no direct relation to the quality of raw water. Chemical treatment cost was 72 percent of total operating cost in the Bokwangdong plant, and only 32 percent at the Paldang plant. Unit operating cost of the former was more than three times higher than the latter.

Seoul has three options now to secure raw water for municipal waterworks : (1) continue taking raw water from the polluted area and pay higher treatment costs ; (2) construct new water intake facilities upstream where water quality is better ; or (3) purchase more from the area-wide waterworks, which supplies good quality raw water. In any case, Seoul must pay more to get the same

|Table 9| Operating Costs at Paldang and Bokwangdong Water Purification Plants

(won/m^3)

Item	Paldang	Bokwangdong
Chemical cost	0.957	7.411
Electricity	0.277	0.277
Labor cost	1.773	2.605
Total	3.007	10.293

Source : Office of Environment, 1983.

quantity and quality of water than before, because of river pollution.

IV. Water Organization and Institutional Arrangements

1. Organizations and Legal System

Water resource management can be classified into four categories : water resource development, river management, water resource use, and water quality control. Since several government organizations are involved in water resource management at different stages, overlapping investments and conflicts of interest among them are possible, causing efficiency losses and difficulties in achieving welfare maximization.

First, in water resource development, the Ministry of Construction is responsible for constructing multipurpose dams. The Ministry of

Agriculture, Forestry, and Fishery has jurisdiction over the construction of irrigation dams, and the Ministry of Energy and Resources oversees the construction of hydropower plants. Laws related to these activities are the Specific Multipurpose Dam Law, the River Law, the Electricity Business Law, and the Public Enterprise Law. Groundwater is developed by specific users such as local governments for domestic use, private persons for commercial or industrial uses, and the Agricultural Development Corporation for agricultural use.

Second, directly-controlled rivers in Korea are managed by the Ministry of Construction, whereas local rivers are managed by local governments such as cities or provinces based on the River Law.

Third, the national water use plan is the responsibility of the Ministry of Construction. The Korea Water Resources Corporation constructs and operates area-wide waterworks and industrial waterways, and local governments oversee local waterworks and supply city water to the final users. The Economic Planning Board (EPB) approves proposed waterworks plans following investment priorities, and evaluates and approves waterworks fees requested by the Ministry of Construction. City water fees are calculated by respective local governments based on total cost, including production cost and the rate of return on invested capital, which is about 7 percent in Korea. Local governments consult with the Economic Planning Board(EPB) when changing city water fees based on city ordinance, because the EPB supervises public utility fees.

Fourth, water quality control is mainly supervised by the Office of Environment, which was established in 1980 and expanded to the ministerial level in 1990. Although overall environmental policy is formulated by the Ministry of Environment based on the Environmental Preservation Law, several organizations are involved at the implementation stage. Based on the Sewerage Act, construction and management of sewerage systems are the responsibility of the Ministry of Construction. The Ministry builds sewerage systems in industrial complexes directly and supports construction costs to local governments – 30 to 50 percent of construction costs for large cities and 70 percent for small-to-medium cities. However, Seoul constructs and manages its sewerage system independently, and the Ministry of Environment supervises night soil and wastewater treatment plants.

The water quality standards set by the Environmental Preservation Law state that the biochemical oxygen demand (BOD) should be below 6 mg/ℓ to qualify as raw water for waterworks, and below 10 mg/ℓ for industrial use (see Table 10). No section of the Lower Han River satisfies the water quality standard for grade 1 raw water for waterworks. Some of the water treatment plants barely pass the standard for grade 3 raw water sources, a warning that the river flow might not be available for future use in the waterworks. BOD levels of some tributaries in Seoul, such as the Chunggyechun and Anyangchun, exceeded 100 mg/ℓ before they improved slightly in 1985.

2. Cost Allocation of Multipurpose Dams

The Korea Water Resources Corporation was established in 1967 based on the Water Resource Development Corporation Law to

|Table 10| Water Quality Standards (Rivers)

Class	Purpose	Standard				
		Hydrogen Ion(pH)	BOD (mg/ℓ)	SS (mg/ℓ)	DO (mg/ℓ)	Coliform (MPN[a] /100mℓ)
I	Water supply (grade1) ; Natural environment preservation	6.5-8.5	<1	<25	>7.5	<50
II	Water supply (grade 2) ; Fishery (grade 1) ; Swimming	6.5-8.5	<3	<25	>5	<1,000
III	Water supply(grade 3) ; Fishery (grade 2) ; Industrial use (grade 1)	6.5-8.5	<6	<25	>5	<5,000
IV	Industrial use (grade 2) ; Agriculture use	6.0-8.5	<8	<100	>2	-
V	Industrial use (grade 3) ; Living environment preservation	6.0-8.5	<10	No floating wastes	>2	-

[a] MPN= most probable number
Source : Ministry of Environment, 1991.

implement the activities specified in the Specific Multipurpose Dam Law and the Water Resource Development Law promulgated in 1966. Based on the Ten-Year Water Resource Development Plan initiated in 1966, the Soyanggang Multipurpose Dam was constructed for flood control, electricity generation, and water supply mainly for the Seoul Metropolitan Region. The Choongju Multipurpose Dam on the South Han River served the same purposes, plus supplying irrigation water. The two dams doubled the capacity of potable water supply from the Han River.

The Korea Water Resources Corporation assumed the responsibility for metropolitan waterworks facilities in 1981 from the Ministry of Construction and started to supply raw water, as well as purified water, to Seoul and other cities in the Seoul Metropolitan Region. To recover costs to continue multipurpose dam construction, the Water Resources Corporation allocates costs to the beneficiaries by the benefits they are expected to receive.

Table 11 shows the cost allocation schemes for the two multipurpose dams on the Han River. More than one-half of the net construction cost of both dams is allocated to the Korea Electric Power Corporation. Domestic and industrial users bear 22 percent of the costs of the Soyanggang Dam and 14 percent of the Choonggju Dam. The remaining construction costs are allocated to the beneficiaries of flood control and irrigation water.

Although the capacities of Soyanggang and Choongju dams are nearly the same (2,900 and 2,750 million m^3, respectively), the

|Table 11| Cost Allocation of Multipurpose Dams (million won)

Benefits	Soyanggang Dam		Choongju Dam	
Flood control	5,468	(19.0%)	93.107	(16.9%)
Domestic and industrial water	6,287	(21.8%)	79.501	(14.4%)
Irrigation	-		15,952	(2.9%)
Electricity generation	17,083	(59.2%)	363.857	(65.8%)
Net construction cost	28,838	(100.0%)	552,417	(100.0%)
Unclassified	3,247		2,630	
Total construction cost	32,085		555,047	

Source : Korea Water Resources Corporation, 1987.

construction cost of Choongju Dam was seventeen times higher than that of Soyanggang Dam. Rapidly rising construction cost and lack of proper dam sites make it difficult to construct additional multi-purpose dams on the Han River. As an alternative, construction of small dams or water transfer from other rivers can be considered. But eventually demand-side management through introduction of water-recycling systems, new water-pricing schemes and transfer of water between sectors should be seriously considered to cope with water shortage in the Seoul Metropolitan Region.

V. Summary

To meet rapidly increasing demand for water in the Seoul Metropolitan Region, the Soyanggang and the Choongju multipurpose dams were constructed, and area-wide waterworks were developed. This kind of supply-side management delayed water shortages in the region. However, rapidly rising construction costs and lack of suitable dam sites make it increasingly difficult to construct additional multipurpose dams on the Han River.

In addition to the absolute limit in the water supply, potable water is increasingly hard to get. The quality of the Lower Han River has been deteriorated because of urban and industrial wastes from the Seoul Metropolitan Region. The Paldang Reservoir which supplies 34 percent of raw water to Seoul and 75 percent to other areas in the Kyunggi Province was polluted by the inflow of waste waters from farms and towns upstream.

The diminishing potable water supply in the Seoul Metropolitan Region will increase conflicts among water users in the Lower Han River basin. Conventional water-supply management is still effective and necessary, but not sufficient. To cope with the upcoming water shortage, more efficient ways of allocating scarce water resource should be developed. Since different government agencies are involved in various stages of water resource management, overlapping investments or conflict of interests sometimes cause efficiency loss and government failure. A comprehensive water resource management system, which considers water development, water use, and water quality preservation at the same time, should be developed and existing institutions should be properly reorganized. Eventually demand-side management through water conservation, introduction of marginal cost pricing, and transfer of water use between sectors should be adopted.

References

(All references are government documents in the Korean language and printed by the Korean government in Seoul, Korea.)

Korea Research Institute for Human Settlements, *Waterworks Rate Structure Rationalization Plan*, 1987.

Korea Water Resources Corporation, *Long-Term Development Strategy to the Year 2000*, 1987.

Ministry of Construction, *Long-Term Comprehensive Water Resource*

Development Base Plan (1981-2001), 1980.

Ministry of Construction, *Revised Plan of the Second Comprehensive National Land Development Plan (1987-1991)*, 1987a.

Ministry of Construction, *Waterworks*, 1987b.

Ministry of Construction, *Annual Report on National Land Use*, 1988.

Ministry of Environment, *Korea Environmental Yearbook 1991*, 1991.

Office of Environment, *Comprehensive Han River Basin Environmental Preservation Plan : Report on Water Quality, Vols.1-4*, 1983.

Office of Environment, *Environmental Pollution Survey (1980-1986)*, 1987.

9. Natural Resources and Environmental Management in South Korea*

I. Introduction

South Korea, Japan, China, Mongolia and the Russian Far East are located within a short distance to each other in the Northeast Asia (NEA). They have different levels of economic development and different endowment of natural resources. Japan is one of the most developed countries with abundant capital and high technology but meager natural resources. South Korea is deficient in natural resources but is preparing to join the group of the developed countries with a valuable experience of successful economic development and highly educated human resources. Although the other three countries are endowed with rich natural resources such as minerals, crude oil and forests, they suffer from a lack of capital, technology and guideline for economic development. There-

* "Natural Resources and Environmental Management in South Korea," in Alexander Sheingauz and Hiroya Ono(eds.), *Natural Resources and Environment in Northeast Asia : Status and Challenges*, Sasakawa Peace Foundation, November 1995, pp. 79-94.

fore, in terms of production complementarity, there seem to be great potential mutual benefits if they develop closer economic relations. Though until recently, there were not many economic transactions among them except between South Korea and Japan, it will grow explosively in the near future.

Since environmental disruption has regional and global impacts, it is urgently required that these countries in the Far East Asia should cooperate to preserve the sound environment in the region. In this context, this paper is prepared to provide an overview about natural resources and environmental states in South Korea. This paper is organized as follows. The first section surveys the reserves, demand and supply of natural resources, and trades of primary sector products with foreign countries. The next section describes the environmental protection efforts and the following section discusses the preservation of natural ecosystem in South Korea. The final section concludes the paper.

II. Natural Resources

1. Geography and Land Resources

South Korea is largely mountainous, with small valleys and narrow coastal plains. The Taebeck Mountains, forming the backbone of the peninsula, run in a north–south direction along the eastern coastline. Several mountain ranges, extended from this backbone, oriented in a northeast–southwest direction. Principal rivers, such as the Han River, the Kum River, and the Nakdong River, have their origins in the Taebaek Mountains, and they flow between the ranges. There are comparatively extensive lowlands along the lower parts of the three rivers. Geologically, the Korean peninsula consists in large part of Precambrian rocks such as granite and gneiss, from which most soils derive. Sandy and brown colored soils are common and they are generally well leached and have little humus content.

South Korea has a moderate continental type of climate with cold winter and hot summer. The summer monsoon brings about 1,000 to 1,400 millimeters of average annual precipitation. The area of South Korea is 99,291 square kilometers. Among them forest area was 65.1 percent, farmland 21.1 percent and urban, settlement, industrial and other categories accounted for the remaining 13.8 percent in 1991. With growing urbanization and industrialization farmland and forest gradually decreased by 5.9 and 1.5 percent, respectively, in 1991 compared with those of 1973. In mid-1992, South Korea had a population of 43,663,000 and a density of 440 persons per square kilometer.

2. Agricultural Resources

Less than one-fourth of South Korea's area is cultivated for rice, barley, wheat, soybeans and other crops. Rice is the most important crop, constituting about two fifth of all farm products in value and accounting for 85.9 percent of the total grain production in 1992. Due to the efficient control of disease and insects, the improvement of soil fertility, water management, and the development and use of high-yielding varieties of rice, South Korea achieved self-sufficiency in rice in 1980s. Wheat and barley are also major food crops in South Korea. Although extensive research has been undertaken on ways to increase their productivity in order to meet the demands of a growing population, wheat and barley production have continued to decrease. This was mainly due to their low profitability for farmers and to the labor and technical constraints of double-cropping on rice paddy lands. While barley is approximately self-sufficient, wheat is not. Consumption of milled wheat has increased due to a shift towards western-style tastes and most of the milled wheat is imported from overseas.

Soybeans are one of the most important staple food crops in South Korea and are mainly used for soy paste, soy sauce and bean sprouts. In 1992, 176.0 thousand tons were produced, which were only 11.7 per cent of the total consumption. Among important grains, most consumption of wheat, soybean, and corn are supplied by imports from overseas (Table 1). Total grain production is expected to show a slight decline due to a decrease in cultivated acreage despite significant strides in the development of agricultural technology.

South Korea has favorable conditions for fruit production with its four distinct seasons, large fluctuations of temperature, and adequate precipitation. Many kinds of fruits : apples, pears, peaches, mandarin oranges, grapes and sweet persimmons are produced. Among them apples and pears are two of South Korea's major agricultural export products, which are known to foreigners for their sweet taste and flavor. Total fruit production was 2,090 thousand tons in 1992 and

|Table 1| Production, Consumption and Import of Major Agricultural Products in South Korea (thousand tons)

Year	Rice	Wheat and Barley	Corn	Soybean	Potatoes
Production					
1987	5,493	521	127	204	258
1990	5,606	417	120	233	209
1992	5,331	315	92	176	243
Consumption					
1987	5,617	4,660	4,654	1,225	302
1990	5,445	2,432	6,425	1,254	274
1992	5,526	4,886	6,209	1,503	237
Import					
1987	0	4,224	4,792	1,131	0
1990	0	2,303	6,198	1,092	12
1992	0	3,990	6,386	1,304	9

Note : Rice year is from Nov. 1 of the preceding year to Oct. 31 of that year.
Source : Ministry of Agriculture, Forest and Fisheries

is expected to increase in the near future.

At the same time, meat output has risen annually on a wave of consumer demand. In 1992, total meat output was 933 million tons, a 15.9 percent increase over the previous year. Consumption of meat products has increased along with the rise in national income and changes in dietary patterns. In 1993, meat consumption was 1,087 million tons and increased by 163 percent from 1987. Beef consumption in particular showed explosive growth since 1989. Consequently, beef imports increased to the peak, 142,845 tons in 1991 and dropped to 99,000 tons in 1993. Consumption of milk,

|Table 2| Consumption, Imports and Exports of Major Livestock Products in South Korea

Year	Beef	Pork	Chicken	All meat	Egg	Milk
Total consumption						(thousand tons)
1987	151.9	372.6	140.7	665.2	361.5	1424.8
1990	177.0	504.8	171.7	853.5	393.3	1879.0
1993	233.0	613.2	240.8	1087.0	445.5	1983.7
Consumption per capita						(kilograms)
1987	3.6	8.9	3.3	15.8	8.6	34.3
1990	4.1	11.8	4.0	19.9	9.2	43.8
1993	5.3	13.9	5.5	24.7	10.1	45.1
Imports						(thousand tons)
1988	14.2	0	0	14.2	0	0
1990	84.0	2.6	0	86.6	0	0
1993	99.0	0	0	99.0	139.7	0
Exports						(thousand tons)
1988	0	7.9	0	7.9	0	0
1990	0	5.8	0	5.8	0	0
1993	0	11.3	0	11.3	0	0

Source : Ministry of Agriculture, Forest and Fisheries

egg, chicken and pork also has increased annually but are approximately self-supplied (Table 2). Especially pork has been oversupplied and is exported every year. In 1993, imports and exports of agricultural products were 6,773 million dollars and 863 million dollars, respectively.

Although the government has implemented several medium and long-term rural restructuring policy packages to tackle agricultural problems that have arisen during the fast economic growth period, the farm population and the proportion of national income from agriculture are gradually decreasing and imports of agricultural products are expected to increase.

3. Forestry Resources

In South Korea, forests cover about 65 percent of the total land area. However, forest land per capita is only 0.2 hectares, which is merely one-quarter of the world average. The total stock volume stood at 284 million cubic meters and the average stock volume per hectare was estimated at 40 cubic meters in 1993 which was about the half of the world average (Table 3). The typical type of forest in South Korea is the coniferous forest which constitutes about 46 percent of the total forest while deciduous, mixed forests and other forests constitute 21, 30 and 3 per cent, respectively. In order to enhance forest resources, forests are managed through the government's long-term forest management plan which includes developing forest roads, improving self-sufficiency of timber and achieving a balance between conservation and development of forest resources (Table 4).

However, despite the large proportion of forest area to total land area and government efforts to increase self-sufficiency of timber, most of the wood industries in South Korea have relied largely on foreign raw materials. Of the wood used in South Korea in 1992, for example, 88 percent was imported from overseas. Thus a stable supply of raw materials has been quite important. The major

|Table 3| Forest Area in South Korea

Year	Forest Area (thousand hectare)			Forest Growing Stock (1,000m^3)		
	National Forest	Civil Forest	Total	National Forest	Civil Forest	Total
1987	1,320	5,160	6,499	75,500	125,302	200,802
1990	1,346	5,114	6,476	85,160	163,266	248,426
1993	1,382	5,077	6,460	94,207	189,622	283,829

Source : Ministry of Agriculture, Forest and Fisheries

|Table 4| Production of Forest Products in South Korea (thousand tons)

Year	Uncultivated Fruit				Mushroom	Fuel
	Sub-total	Including				
		Chestnut	Jujube	Acorn		
1987	66.9	57.0	4.6	2.3	2.2	2968
1990	95.8	85.0	6.0	1.7	3.0	1401
1993	93.1	81.0	7.0	1.7	3.1	488

Source : Ministry of Agriculture, Forest and Fisheries

imported products have traditionally been logs, bamboo, and rosin. Logs have been the largest import item and the total amount of imports of forest products was about 2 billion dollars. Forest products that were exported consisted primarily of plywood, wood products, wall paper, chestnut and mushrooms. The total value of exports of forestry was 0.6 billion dollars in 1992. Recently the quantity of chestnuts and mushrooms being exported has rapidly increased.

4. Fishery Resources

Because fish is a major part of the Korean diet, the fishing industry has been very important to the Korean people. In 1992, about half of South Korea's animal protein was supplied by fishery products and the total of 3,289 thousand tons of fishery products was produced (Table 5). Until the early 1960s, the Korean fishing industry was limited to coastal fishing. However, with the development of aqua culture and of the deep-sea fishing industry in the 1970s, the structure of the Korean fishery industry has been diversified, and South Korea is now one of the major fishing nations in the world.

|**Table 5**| Fish Catches by Fishery Section in South Korea (thousand tons)

Product	1987	1990	1992
Marine fisheries :			
Distant water fisheries	882.7	925.3	1,023.9
Adjacent water fisheries	1,526.0	1,542.0	1,295.4
Shallow-sea culture	866.1	772.8	935.5
Subtotal	3,274.8	3,240.1	3,254.8
Inland water fisheries :			
Fishing	47.6	18.6	14.2
Culture	9.5	15.8	20.0
Subtotal	57.1	34.4	34.2
Total	3,331.9	3,274.5	3,289.0

Source : Ministry of Agriculture, Forest and Fisheries

South Korea's peripheral waters contain a mixture of warm and cold waters, thereby giving South Korea's fishery industry a comparative advantage in fisheries production and in the variety of available fish species. In 1992, catches from adjacent water fisheries totaled 1.3 million tons, and 39.4 percent of the total catch. Distant water catches was about 1 million tons and consisted of Alaska Pollack, squid and tuna in 1992. However, the South Korean fishing industry now faces serious problems because of the introduction of 200-mile Exclusive Economic Zones by many coastal nations compounded with intensified fishing regulations for resource management, the financial burden of fishing permit fees, the decline of fishing resources and increased labor costs. Thus imports of fishery products have been accelerated since early 1980s, and the total amount of imports in 1992 was 10 times higher than that of the early 1980s, amounting about a half billion dollars. But almost half of total imports consist of raw materials for re-export.

The export of fisheries products has increased since 1962, but it represented only 2.3 percent of total national exports or about 1.5 billion dollars in 1992. Export items include tuna (33%), live and fresh fish (23%), frozen products (11%), seaweed and pickled products (10%), and other miscellaneous products (23%).

5. Mineral Resources

Although mineral resources in South Korea are generally meager, exploration reports show that the country's reserves of some metallic and most non-metallic mineral resources are relatively plentiful. In particular, tungsten, ore reserve is known as one of the most abundant in the world. In addition, good supplies of non-metallic minerals such as limestone, talc, pyrophyllite, kaolin and silica stone, categorized as essential raw materials, are all available (Table 6).

|Table 6| Reserves of Mineral Resources in South Korea (1993)

Resource	Grade (%)	Total Reserve	Recoverable Reserve
Gold (ton)	99.9	113	54
Silver (ton)	99.9	2,947	1,561
Copper ore (1,000 ton)	50	3,470	1,798
Zinc ore (1,000 ton)	50	5,750	2,979
Iron ore (1,000 ton)	60	99,222	40,314
Tungsten ore (1,000 ton)	70	459	211
Titanium ore (1,000 ton)	50	1,535	1,229
Limestone (million ton)	–	35,830	15,116
Silica stone (million ton)	–	1,969	1,043
Talc (million ton)	–	43	20
Pyrophyllite (million ton)	–	101	42
Kaolin (million ton)	–	240	117
Feldspar (million ton)	–	47	28
Diatomaceous earth (million ton)	–	8	5
Silica sand (million ton)	–	123	45

Source : Ministry of Trade, Industry and Resource

Until the mid-1960s, approximately 60 percent of all mineral resources produced in South Korea were exported and the remainder was consumed at home. But with rapid industrialization, the demand for minerals started to grow and since 1985, it increased by an annual rate of 14.1 percent (17.1 percent for metallic mineral

Table 7 Production and Consumption in Major Mineral Products of South Korea

Product	Production			Consumption		
	1987	1990	1992	1987	1990	1992
Gold (ton)	8	21	23	11	27	32
Silver (ton)	209	238	333	115	269	400
Copper ore (thousand ton)	661	196	0	558	381	245
Zinc ore (thousand ton)	47	46	44	444	533	529
Iron ore (million ton)	0.5	0.3	0.2	17.7	21.4	32.4
Tungsten ore (thousand ton)	4	2	0.4	4	5	3
Titanium ore (thousand ton)	109	350	348	130	250	408
Limestone (million ton)	41.7	49	65	41.3	48.6	65.2
Silica stone (thousand ton)	1,235	1,452	1,870	1,182	1,459	1,788
Talc (thousand ton)	161	182	150	186	238	347
Pyrophyllite (thousand ton)	691	658	603	456	426	373
Kaolin (thousand ton)	630	1,447	1,856	725	1,502	1,883
Feldspar (thousand ton)	180	237	282	157	212	278
Diatomaceous earth (thousand ton)	65	55	77	63	66	89
Silica sand (thousand ton)	1,350	1,408	1,266	1,599	1,921	1,958

Source : Ministry of Trade, Industry and Resource

and 10.9 percent for non-metallic mineral) and the rate of self-sufficiency decreased to 28.3 percent (3.1 percent for metallic mineral and 66.7 percent for non-metallic mineral) in 1991 (Table 7). Thus a large portion of metallic and non-metallic mineral resources has been imported.

In addition, the imports of major minerals such as iron ore, copper ore, zinc ore and silica sand, from 1987 to 1992 are expected to increase continuously. Due to increase in production and relatively abundant reserves of non-metallic minerals, limestone, silica stone, pyrophyllite, feldspar, kaolin are approximately self-sufficient, and limestone, pyrophyllite and kaolin are exported. The total values of mineral imports and exports were 3,570 million dollars and 396 million dollars, respectively, in 1993.

6. Fresh Water Resources

South Korea had an average rainfall of 1,274 millimeters in 1992 or 126.7 billion tons of rainfall in a year. Among them 45 percent were lost by evaporation and 55 percent of total rainfall or 69.7 billion tons flew to rivers or into ground. This amount is 1.3 times more than the world average, but the fresh water per capita in a year was about 3,000 tons which was only 1/11 of the world average. The rainfall in South Korea fluctuates from season to season. About 70 percent of the annual rainfall comes during June through September and winter months normally receive less than 10 percent of total annual precipitation. Thus it is necessary to build dams and reservoirs to accumulate, collect and conserve surface water in South Korea.

In 1992, the demand for water was 28.2 billion tons and consisted of agricultural water (53.1%), domestic water (17.8%), industrial water (9.1%) and maintenance water (20.0%), while the supply of water was 31 billion tons which came from river (53.2%), ground water (6.1%) and reservoir (39.7%) (Table 8). Although the supply exceeds the demand now, the demand for fresh water is expected to increase continuously and long term water supply plan

|Table 8| Status of Water Resources in South Korea

Index	Unit	1990	1991	1992
Average annual precipitation	mm	1,159	1,274	1,274
Total volume of water resource	100 million m^3	1,140	1,267	1,267
Total flow	100 million m^3	662	697	697
-flood period	100 million m^3	405	467	467
-normal period	100 million m^3	257	230	230
Loss	100 million m^3	478	570	570
Total demand	million m^3/year	294	271	282
Domestic water	million m^3/year	51	47	49
Industrial water	million m^3/year	26	25	25
Agricultural water	million m^3/year	128	150	151
Maintenance water	million m^3/year	89	50	57
Total supply	million m^3/year	276	295	309
River	million m^3/year	175	158	164
Groundwater	million m^3/year	16	18	19
Reservoir	million m^3/year	85	115	126
Total excess or deficiency	million m^3/year	-18	+18	+27

Source : Ministry of Construction

is needed. According to the long term plan of government for water supply, the demand for water will increase to 33 billion tons in 2001, to 37.1 billion tons in 2011 and increases in demand will be supplied by developing ground water and reservoir. Total reserve of ground water and the recoverable ground water in South Korea are estimated to be 22.8 billion tons and 16 billion tons, respectively, in a year. Only 15 percent of total recoverable ground water was used.

7. Energy Resources

South Korea's indigenous energy resources are anthracite coal and hydro power. In 1993, the total production of energy was 21,027, 000 TOE (tons of oil equivalent) and the composition was coal (20%), hydro (7%), nuclear (69%), and others (4%). It was only 17 percent of the total primary energy consumption in South Korea (Table 9).

|**Table 9**| Production and Consumption of Energy by Source in South Korea

(thousand TOE(tons of oil equivalent))

Year	Coal	Petroleum	LNG	Hydro	Nuclear	Others	Total
Production							
1987	11,166	-	-	1,336	9,829	1,319	23,649
1990	7,748	-	-	1,590	13,222	797	23,356
1993	4,249	-	-	1,502	14,535	742	21,027
Consumption							
1987	23,639	29,653	2,104	1,336	9,829	1,319	67,878
1990	24,385	50,175	3,023	1,590	13,222	797	93,192
1993	25,882	78,495	5,723	1,502	14,535	742	126,879

Source : Ministry of Trade, Industry and Resource

Anthracite coal is South Korea's major coal resource and as no liquid energy resources such as crude oil have been discovered and hydro energy resources are poor, it has been the country's major energy resource as well. The coal mining industry made great progress since 1960 but began to decline rapidly due to a drop in oil price and changes of energy consumption pattern since the

|Table 10| South Korea's Demand and Supply of Coal (thousand tons)

Year	Anthracite			Bituminous	
	Production	Imports	Consumption	Imports	Consumption
1987	24,274	3,491	27,086	17,834	16,218
1990	17,217	1,121	21,529	22,848	21,876
1993	9,435	124	10,157	35,157	31,518

Source : Ministry of Trade, Industry and Resource

second half of the 1980s (Table 10). As a result, the share of domestic coal production in total energy consumption dropped to 5.2 percent in 1993 from 21.9 percent in 1985. The proved reserves of anthracite coal was 1,585 million tons and the recoverable reserves was 754 million tons in 1988. It is expected to be exhausted in 30 years. As domestic coal production failed to meet the increasing energy consumption, the government switched from coal to petroleum as the major energy source after 1967. As a result, petroleum constituted 61 percent of total primary energy consumption in 1993 from 40.1 percent in 1969.

As South Korea does not have any domestic source of oil, all the oil had been imported, mostly from the Middle East. The import values of crude oil and petroleum reached 9.3 billion dollars and 3.1 billion dollars, respectively, and the total import bill for energy resources was 14.9 billion dollars in 1993. The self-sufficiency rate of energy resource was only 11.6 percent in 1990, and continued to decrease. Thus the government has adopted various policies for maximum utilization of domestic energy sources and for the reduction of dependency on imported oil on a long-term basis, such as substituting non-petroleum energy for petroleum energy and promoting the installation of nuclear power plants and coal-fired plants. In spite of remarkable achievements in the construction of nuclear, hydroelectric, and coal fired power plants and the introduction of liquefied natural gas since 1986, it is expected that South Korea will rely upon petroleum as its major source of energy throughout the 1990s.

8. Recreation and Tourism Resources

South Korea has three major categories of recreation and tourism resources including historical and cultural sites, national parks and water recreation resources. It has 20 national parks which are known for beautiful natural scenes. Among them, Mt. Seorak is considered one of the world's most spectacular and Mt. Halla, a volcanic cone which was active by 1007, is the most favorite place for a wedding trip in South Korea. Another important source of tourism is water recreation resources including beaches with fine sand as well as clean water for swimming and sunbathing, which are found everywhere along the shore of the east, south and west seas.

The tourist industry in South Korea has grown rapidly in recent years, spurred by the Seoul Olympic in 1988. As South Korea moves to expand its contacts and relationships with all parts of the world, more growth of tourist industry is foreseen. The number of foreign visitors increased from 84 thousands in 1967 to 3 millions in 1992 and among them, 57.6 percent were tourists. The number of hotel rooms also increased 35 times, from 1,244 in 1963 to 43,401 in 1992. Looking to a continuing expansion of tourism, there have been a number of plans and programs to develop and enlarge tourism resources and facilities in such areas as hotel accommodations, land, sea and air transportation, tourist services, national parks, museums, golf courses, and casinos.

II. Environmental Protection

During the last three decades, South Korea achieved rapid economic development through industrialization. All the national resources were mobilized for this purpose. As a result, the environment was deteriorated, causing serious social problems in the 1970s. In the 1980s, the living standards of people rose with economic growth and the needs for environmental protection became more urgent. A new article proclaiming the people's environmental rights was included in the national constitution in 1980 along with the establishment of the Environment Administration. In the fifth five-year economic development plan which started in 1982, the policy of balance and harmony between economic development and environmental conservation was adopted and various environmental programs and projects were undertaken.

While stimulating environmental awareness through public relations activities, the government implemented policies for the improvement of air quality in municipal areas, the improvement of water quality in rivers and lakes, and the proper disposal of industrial and municipal wastes. Thus a number of mid-term and long-term programs were launched including the production of low pollution cars and unleaded motor fuel, the construction of desulphurization facilities by major oil refineries, and the preparation of large scale landfill sites for wastes from metropolitan areas. As the people achieve higher living standards with economic growth, the need for a better environment has increased dramatically. In 1990, with the establishment of the Ministry of Environment, the government formulated a five-year environmental improvement plan which aims at environmentally sound and sustainable development, and planned to invest 15.6 billion dollars for environmental protection from 1992 to 1996.

1. Air Pollution

Although the air quality of South Korea has been improving recently, it is still worse than those of developed countries (Table 11). In order to improve air quality, the government reduced the legal sulfur content of Bunker-C oil to 1.0 per cent and of diesel oil to 0.2 per cent in metropolitan area from July 1993. In accordance with this new policy, major oil refineries set up plans to construct desulphurization facilities by the year 1995. And the natural gas, which was used by major power plants and consumers in Seoul and several cities since 1988, will be supplied to all major cities throughout the country by the year 2000. Also the government will strengthen emission standards up to the level of developed countries by the end of 1999.

|Table 11| Air Quality by Major Cities in South Korea (1992)

Substance	Seoul	Busan	Daegu	Gwangju	Ulsan
SO_2 (ppm)	0.035	0.033	0.040	0.017	0.031
TSP (microgram/m^3)	97	113	119	104	102
NO_2 (ppm)	0.031	0.023	0.03	0.012	0.026
Acid Rain (pH)	5.3	5.2	5.6	5.7	5.5

Source : Ministry of Environment, Air Quality Management Bureau

2. Water Pollution

In South Korea, sewerage, waste water discharge of industry and livestock farming, pesticides and chemical fertilizers used by farmers are major sources to water pollution. Especially, the waste water discharges of livestock farming households and small firms have become big problems because of difficulties to detect them. In 1992, the volume of sewerage was about 12 million tons in a day and only 39 percent of them were purified. And the volume of waste water discharge was about 2 million tons in a day and some portion of them, which was generally discharged by small firms, was not purified. Table 12 shows that despite of government and public activities to make rivers clean, water qualities of major rivers became worse except the Han River.

Recently the reinforced activities of the people, industries and government bodies have got under way to restore the water quality of all rivers, numbering about 4 thousands throughout the country. Regional and local governments were given specific functions to carry out these programs. In line with this program, 195 watersheds

|Table 12| Water Quality of South Korea's Major River Systems (1991)

River System	pH	BOD	COD
Han River			
upper stream :			
North Han River, Cheong Pyong	7.8	1.7	2.3
South Han River, Yang Pyong	7.8	2.1	3.2
middle stream, Kuui	7.7	1.9	2.9
downstream, Noryangjin	7.6	3.9	5.0
Nakdong River			
upper stream, Andong Dam	7.5	1.1	2.4
middle stream, Hapchon	7.8	4.1	6.6
downstream, Gupo	7.6	3.7	6.5
Yeongsan River			
upper stream, Damyang	7.3	1.1	2.6
middle stream, Gwangju	7.4	2.8	4.6
downstream, Muan	7.5	1.5	4.3
Kum River			
upper stream, Okchon	7.0	1.6	1.6
middle stream, Gongju	7.1	3.1	3.0
downstream, Ganggyong	7.2	4.9	5.0

Source : Ministry of Environment, Water Quality Management Bureau

were classified for the application of different water quality standards. And special measures were prepared for dealing with severely polluted streams flowing through municipal or industrial areas to restore them in a short period of time.

3. Waste Management

With economic growth, the generation of solid wastes has increased rapidly (Table 13). Solid wastes were mainly disposed of through landfill in South Korea. But as landfills have not been managed properly and have polluted the vicinities, the objections of neighborhood residents became strong. To cope with this situation, the government set new goals in waste management such as minimizing volume, providing for safe treatment, recycling wastes to the extent possible and managing landfill properly. Along with this effort, the government has been constructing plants for night soil treatment and hazardous industrial wastes, as well as a major coastal landfill site for Seoul, and introduced waste volume charge system from January 1995.

III. Preservation of Natural Ecosystem

South Korea's rapid urbanization, industrialization and development of natural resources have deteriorated its natural environment, and the ecosystem of its nature has been threatened. The forest area steadily decreased until 1990 and land, rivers and lakes have been polluted with various waste discharges and hazardous chemicals. In order to maintain benign cycles of ecological equilibrium as well as to provide high quality of life, a balance between conservation and development of natural resources are urgently required and the protection of natural environment has become one of the most

|Table 13| Generation of Industrial Solid Waste in South Korea

(thousand tons per year)

Waste	1987	1990
Specified		
Specified hazard	38	82
Waste oil	117	190
Waste and synthetic resin	136	302
Waste acid and alkali	258	394
Sub-total	549	968
General		
Organic	2,845	6,324
Inorganic	11,317	14,123
Sub-total	14,162	21,447
Total	14,711	22,415

Source : Ministry of Environment, Water Quality Management Bureau

pressing tasks of the government in South Korea.

For the purpose of effectively preserving South Korea's natural environment, the government has set up nature reserves and classified them into six categories such as natural environment area, natural ecosystem protection area, natural parks, natural monuments, forest reserve area and sanctuary area. The natural environment area has been designated for the purpose of preserving natural scenes, water resources, ecosystems and cultural assets. They continuously increased to 8,671 square kilometers in 1992 of which 6,369 square kilometers are land and 2,302 square kilometers are ocean (Table 14). The government has also designated natural ecosystem protection areas to protect the valuable ecosystems and habitats for wildlife and they reached 69.4 square kilometers by 1992.

|Table 14| Designation of Land Use Purpose in South Korea

(square kilometers)

Category	1988	1990	1992
Land			
Urban	12,804	2,882	13,455
Settlement	867	809	629
Farmland	24,376	24,210	25,929
Forest	46,343	46,169	50,467
Industrial	54	53	75
Natural environment	4,840	5,422	6,369
Recreation	148	158	183
Fishery	554	547	518
Development promotion	2,458	2,348	1,462
Reservation	24	5	0
Sub-total	-	92,602	99,291
Ocean			
Urban	39	176	220
Natural environment	628	751	2,302
Fishery	2,782	2,688	920
Sub-total	-	3,594	4,450
Area of announcement	92,467	96,169	103,740

Source : Ministry of Construction

There were 66 natural parks including 20 national parks, 20 provincial parks and 26 district parks, and they covered 7,445 square kilometers in 1992. They play important roles in conservation of ecosystem and providing public recreational areas. The government has also designated 275 natural monuments which occupies 700.9 square kilometers for the purpose of preservation of endangered or rare species in wildlife. In a highly populated country like South Korea, forest is main stabilizer of the ecosystem and serves many functions such as providing habitats for wildlife, cleaning air pollution and providing oxygen, as well as providing recreational areas and other functions. It is indispensable for the maintenance of a high quality of life.

In order to effectively preserve and manage the forests, the government divided the forests into reserve and semi-reserve forests. Reserve forests are managed for the purposes of land conservation, timber production, and scientific research, historic and cultural preservation and for other public benefits. They covered 49,328 square kilometers or 76 percent of total forests area in 1992. In addition, government also has designated 507 sanctuaries for the purpose of preservation of important wildlife. They occupied 113,190 hectares in 1992.

IV. Conclusion

Natural resources in South Korea are generally meager. In 1993, South Korea imported 22,720 million dollars of primary sector products while exported 3,211 million dollars of primary sectors products (Table 15). Among the import bill, 12,721 million dollars were spent for minerals and crude oil imports. And about half of the export value was from fishery products. Thus, a stable supply

|Table 15| South Korea's Exports and Imports of Primary Sector (1993)

(million dollars)

Items	Exports	Imports
All sectors	82,236	83,800
Primary sector		
Agriculture	863	6,773
Forestry	455	2,682
Fishery	1,497	544
Mineral/Energy	396	13,433
including :		
nonmetal	-	456
iron ore	-	888
copper ore	-	341
zinc ore	-	103
manganese ore	-	49
coal/cokes	-	1,733
crude oil	-	9,151
Total of primary sector	3,211	22,720

Source : Bank of Korea

of raw materials has been very important for a steady economic growth in South Korea and much effort has been made to diversify sources of raw materials imports and develop natural resources overseas. It will be very beneficial to South Korea if she can supply capital and technology to China, Mongolia and Russian Far East and gets raw materials such as minerals, crude oil, natural gas and forestry materials.

With rapid industrialization, South Korea has suffered the deterioration of environment. Since 1980, South Korea has made significant effort to improve her environmental state and preserve natural ecosystem. But the environment has not been improved much and South Korea still suffers from serious environmental problems. Due to global effect of environmental disruption, it is required to have collective environmental improvement efforts among the countries in the Northeast Asia.

PART III

Environmental Policy and Environmental Cooperation

10. Economic Instruments for Environmental Protection in Korea*

I. Introduction

This paper analyzes the economic instruments introduced in Korea to deal with environmental pollution problems. As in other developing countries, Korea relied heavily on command and control (CAC) measures rather than on market-based instruments (MBI) until recently. In fact most of the major economic instruments have been introduced since 1990 when the former Office of Environment was elevated to cabinet ministerial level. On efficiency grounds, MBI is preferred to CAC and growing number of countries are advocating the economic instruments. However, economic instruments are not panacea per se. As MBI itself suffers from various shortcomings, the user countries should be well aware of those

* "ECONOMIC INSTRUMENTS FOR ENVIRONMENTAL PROTECTION IN KOREA," a paper prepared for 'OECD/UNEP Workshop on the Application of Economic Instruments for Environmental Management', Economics Division, OECD Environment Directorate, May 1994.

problems. Korea has several years of learning experience with economic instruments. During the experimental stage, the government identifies problems and takes necessary steps to alleviate adverse effects. Based on the Korean experience, this paper derives some lessons and suggests policy recommendations.

II. Environmental Policy in Korea

1. Evolution of Environmental Policy Instruments in Korea

1) Before 1980

In 1963, the Public Nuisance Control Law was enacted in Korea. However the enactment ordinance was established in November 1969, and the pollution problems such as air and water pollution caused by rapid industrialization and urbanization were not considered seriously.

In 1977 the Environmental Conservation Law was enacted together with the Marine Pollution Prevention Law to positively deal with the intensifying pollution problems. In 1979, the Synthetic Resin Wastes Treatment Business Law was enacted to deal with the soil pollution problems caused by the disposal of synthetic resin wastes from industrial and agricultural activities. The Environmental Conservation Law was quite different from the Public Nuisance Control Law which was a kind of sanitary law. The Environmental Conservation Law had the article on environmental standards, implementation of environmental impact assessment, designation of areas which need special measures, and the polluter pays principle. However, necessary institutions were not there yet and the application of the Law was very limited because the government's top policy priority was laid on faster economic growth.

2) 1980-1989

Twenty years of successful economic growth in Korea changed people's concern from just increasing the size of economy toward better quality of life and the approach to deal with the environmental problems became more positive. In January 1980, the Office of Environment was established and the revised constitution proclaimed the environmental right as a basic right of people. In the fifth economic and social development plan (1982-1987), main goal of the environmental conservation plan was the harmony of economic growth and environmental conservation.

In the revised Environmental Conservation Law of December 1981, new environmental institutions were introduced such as the environmental impact assessment system, effluent charge system, and the establishment of the environmental pollution control fund to relieve the victims of the environmental pollution and to provide long-term loan at low interest rates for the investment of pollution control facilities.

3) 1990-Present

In January 1990, the Office of Environment was expanded to the cabinet ministerial level and was renamed the Ministry of Environment. In August 1990, the environmental legislation of Korea changed fundamentally and the Environmental Conservation Law was replaced by 6 new individual laws such as the Basic Environmental Policy Law, the Environmental Dispute Settlement Law, the Air Quality Preservation Law, the Water Quality Preservation Law, the Noise and Vibration Control Law, and the Toxic Chemicals Control Law.

In 1991, the Ministry of Environment drafted the Comprehensive Medium-term Environmental Improvement Plan to connect the investment on environmental quality improvement to the five-year economic and social development plan. In the 1990s, new economic instruments were introduced to secure necessary funds for environmental improvement investment. Those systems are the Environmental Improvement Charge System, the Deposit-Refund System for the Collection and Treatment of Wastes, and the Environmental Labelling. To promote the reuse of wastes, the Waste Management Fund was established and the Waste Disposal Charge System was introduced to deal with the wastes which do not fit to the deposit-refund system.

2. Environmental Legislation

Present environmental legislation underwent three stages of evolution. First stage was the single law system with the Public Nuisance Control Law. With the introduction of the Environmental Conservation Law in 1978, the system transformed into a mixed system. In 1991, the Environmental Conservation Law was repealed and replaced by 6 substituting laws changing the system to a multiple-law system like most of developed countries. Following is the major environmental legislation of Korea.

(1) Basic Environmental Policy Law
(2) Environmental Dispute Settlement Law
(3) Air Quality Preservation Law
(4) Noise and Vibration Control Law
(5) Water Quality Preservation Law
(6) Toxic Chemical Control Law
(7) Marine Pollution Prevention Law
(8) Waste Management Law
(9) Law Related to the Promotion of Resource Saving and Reutilization
(10) Law Related to the Transboundary Movement of Wastes and Their Disposal
(11) Law Related to the Treatment of Sewage, Night-soil and Livestock Wastewater
(12) Special Law on the Punishment of Environmental Crime
(13) Natural Environment Conservation Law
(14) Law Related to the Environmental Improvement Charges
(15) Synthetic Resin Wastes Disposal Business Law
(16) Environmental Management Corporation Law

III. Economic Instruments for Environmental Protection in Korea

1. Air and Water Pollution Control

1) Effluent Charge System

A. Purpose

This system is designed to give incentives for polluters to control the emission of pollutants within the limit of the effluent standard by charging effluent fees to the generators of pollutants emitted over the standard.

B. Operation of the Effluent Charge System

This system was introduced in September 1983 to expedite the implementation of legal order to properly control the emission of pollutants by the offenders of the effluent standard. It was common for the operators to emit pollutants even after they were ordered to control the emission or to relocate to other places. This system was first implemented in September 1,1983 and revised in 1987 and in 1991.

There are 25 object pollutants–15 water pollutants and 10 air pollutants. Effluent charge is composed of base charge and treatment charge. Base charge is levied to the offenders each time they are detected and classified into five categories from 500,000 won to 4 million won according to the total volume of emission. Treatment charge is charged to the pollutants above the standard and calculated by multiplying the excess amount of pollutants by unit charge rate and several kinds of coefficients which have the characteristics of penalty such as the excess rate over the standard, regional coefficient, year coefficient, and the violation frequency coefficient. If the operator self-reports malfunctioning of discharge or control facilities, base charge is exempted.

The treatment charge is calculated based not on the volume of discharge but based on the concentration of effluent or emission. Unit charge rate for each type of pollutants are specified separately. Excess rate coefficient is calculated as the rate of excess concentration divided by standard concentration of designated pollutants and is applied progressively. Regional coefficient is determined based on the environmental quality required in the region. For example, residential area has high regional coefficient. Year coefficient is to consider inflation rate and the violation frequency rate is to heavily penalize frequent violators.

Collected effluent charge is accumulated in the Environmental Pollution Control Fund. The fund is used for national pollution control project such as the construction and operation of industrial complex waste water treatment plant and for the loan to the construction of pollution control plants.

C. Problems

The effluent charge system in Korea is operated as a non-compliance charge system. It is applied only to the manufacturing plants which discharge air or water pollutants above the effluent/emission standards. If the violating firm is not detected, they

|Table 1| Computation of Treatment Charges in Effluent Charge System

Field	Pollutant	Computation
Air Quality	Sulphur oxides Fluoride compounds Dust Odor Hydrochloride Chloride Hydrocyanide Ammonia Hydrosulphide Carbon disulphide	Unit charge of each pollutant is multiplied by following coefficients : regional coefficient, year coefficient, violation frequency coefficient, etc.
Water Quality	BOD or COD Suspended solids Cadmium and its compounds Cyanocompounds Organo phosphorus compounds Lead and its compounds Chromium(+6) and its compounds Arsenic and its compounds Mercury and its compounds PCB Copper and its compound Chromium and its compounds Phenols Tetrachloroethylene Trichloroethylene	Computation index of 1992 : 2.7186

Source : Ministry of Environment, *Environment White Paper 1992*.

|Table 2| Annual Collection of Effluent Charge (million won)

	Total	'83-'89	'88	'89	'90	'91	'92
Amount	69,029	8,109	8,595	9,586	10,167	22,193	10,379
Cases	22,234	6,700	2,526	2,865	3,229	3,815	3,099

Source : Ministry of Environment, 'Environment White Paper '92', 1993.

don't have to pay the charge. Furthermore, as the treatment charge is calculated based on the concentration of pollutants, firms intentionally dilute the waste water during inspection. Therefore the present system does not provide incentives to polluters to reduce the amount of pollutants or to develop technology to reduce pollution. It is not reliable revenue source either because it is applied only to the manufacturing industry and the discharge of pollutants within the effluent/emission standards is free. The present charge rate is very low and the number of pollutants to inspect is too much compared to other countries which adopted the effluent charge system.

D. Remedies for the Improvement of the System

The effluent charge system is a cost-effective way of reducing the discharge of pollutants if it is applied properly. However even in developed countries the system is mainly operated as a means of raising revenues for environmental protection. In Korea, it does not give polluters incentives to voluntarily reduce pollution and it does not function as a dependable revenue source either. So it should be properly reformulated to fulfill at least one of its original function. First, treatment charge should be based on total quantity as well as on the concentration of pollutants discharged. Second, the charge rate should be raised to give economic incentives to polluters to voluntarily reduce the discharge of pollutants. Third, the system should be extended to all polluters who generate pollutants during their economic activities. As the effluent charge system is applied only to the manufacturing plants, the pollutants discharged in the process of distributing and consuming the products or services were excluded. To extend 'the polluter pays principle' to distribution and service industry, the environmental improvement charge system was introduced and began operation from 1993.

2) Environment Improvement Charge System

A. Purpose

The Environment Improvement Charge Law was enacted in December 1991 to institutionalize the preparation of comprehensive environmental improvement plan on a government-wide base and to secure necessary investment funds for the implementation of the plan. Based on the Law, the minister of the Ministry of Environment should set up a medium-term comprehensive environmental improvement plan every five year to implement environmental improvement investment in a comprehensive and systematic way. The plan should be revised if the economic and social conditions change. When the attainment of environmental standard is infeasible, the government can run environmental pollution control businesses with the cost-sharing of polluters.

|Table 3| Objects and Computation of Charges in Environment Improvement Charge System

Objects	Computation Equation	Assesment of Unit Charge
1. Facilities : buildings with roof, walls and pillars, which has total floor space more than 1,000m^2	Charge for air pollution = quantity of fuel used × unit charge × fuel coefficient × regional coefficient	Based on the cost to treat pollutants from fuels-standard amount : 20 Won (Cost to treat SOx emitted from 1 liter of diesel)
	Charge for water pollution = quantity of water use × unit charge × pollution coefficient × regional coefficient	Based on the cost to build a wastewater disposal facility-standard amount : 120 Won (average facility cost per 1 ton of waste water treatment)
2. Motor vehicles : diesel vehicles registered by Vehicle Management Law	Charge for water vehicles = unit charge × pollution coefficient × run-time coefficient × region coefficient	Based on the price of catalytic converter (minimum : 300 thousand won) - standard amount : 8,100 won / 6 month /vehicle

Source : Ministry of Environment, "Explanation of Environmental Improvement Charge System", 1993.

B. Operation of the Environmental Improvement Charge System

This system was implemented from July 1992. Environmental improvement charge is levied to the owners of buildings and automobiles which emit considerable amount of pollutants and cause environmental pollution. The charge is levied based on the quantity of fuel and water used in case of facilities, and on the quantity of exhaust gas in case of vehicle.

It is charged twice a year to buildings over $160m^3$ in case of restaurants, hotels, hospitals, indoor pools, and special private schools based on the quantity of fuel and water used. In March 1994, 42.3 billion won was charged to 42 thousand buildings and diesel cars as a charge for the second half of 1993. 22.3 billion won was charged to buildings.

C. Exemptions

As the environmental improvement charge is targeted to the owners of facilities or automobiles which become direct cause of environmental pollution in their distribution or consumption activities, structures such as factories, warehouses, energy-related facilities, parking lots, etc are exempted from the charge. Religious and education facilities, national hospitals, and social welfare facilities, and so on are also exempted. Among automobiles, government-owned cars, ambulances, garbage collection cars, private school cars, small freight cars, line buses and line freight cars, express buses, and some of tourist buses are exempted. It is planned to apply the charge to small freight cars, line buses, line freight cars, express cars, and tourist cars from 1996.

D. Problems

The most serious problem with the present system is that there are too many exemptions. Presently, the environmental improvement charge is levied only to diesel cars and to distribution and consumption facilities. It is not levied to manufacturing facilities which emit air and water pollutants. Manufacturing facilities are the object of the effluent charge system which is charged to the pollutants over the effluent/emission standards. Thus the heavily-polluting manufacturing facilities do not have to pay the charge if they restrict the discharge of pollutants within the limit of the standard. The fact that the manufacturing facilities are treated favorably compared to distribution and service sectors is unfair because the manufacturing sectors are more responsible to environmental pollution in general.

E. Remedies for the Improvement of the System

In 1993, out of 52 thousand manufacturing facilities which emitted air and water pollutants, 3.1 thousand facilities payed the effluent charge. Total amount of effluent charge collected was 12.7 billion won which was much smaller than the half-year revenue from the environmental improvement charge. As such, most of the manufacturing facilities do not pay the effluent charge and they are also exempted from the environmental improvement charge as it is targeted to only distribution and consumption facilities. The fairness of the system was questioned and the Ministry of Environment plans to revise the Environmental Improvement Charge Law to include manufacturing facilities as objects of the system. In that case the present effluent charge in the manufacturing sector should be renamed a noncompliance penalty and the total volume as well as concentration-based effluent charge should be newly introduced.

2. Solid Waste Management

1) Waste Management Policy in Korea

Korea began to deal with the waste problem with the introduction of Garbage Cleaning Law in 1961. In 1986, the Waste Management Law was enacted separately to systematically deal with the waste management. Before 1986, the role of government in waste management was limited to collection and landfill of garbage. In March 1991 and December 1992, the Waste Management Law was revised comprehensively. In the revised Law, wastes are classified into general wastes and special wastes. General wastes are composed of household wastes and nontoxic industrial wastes while special wastes are comprised of harmful and toxic wastes. General wastes are managed by local governments and the special wastes are managed by the central government.

To expedite the reduction of waste generation and the reuse of wastes, the Resource Saving and Reutilization Promotion Law was enacted separately from the Waste Management Law in December 1992. The Resource Saving and Reutilization Promotion Law includes provisions such as the deposit-refund and charge systems for collection and treatment of wastes, the fostering of recycling industry, and the regulations on compulsory promotion of resource conservation and reuse applied to specific types of industry and products. In addition to this, the Law on Transboundary Movement of Wastes and Their Disposal was enacted in December 1992 to incorporate the idea of Barsel Convention on transboundary transfer of wastes to domestic legal system.

Current waste management system in Korea consists of a deposit-refund system, charge system, mandatory treatment of wastes by emitters under certain conditions, financial assistance to firms in waste management business, and the regulations enforced by penalties in case of violation. Mandatory treatment of wastes covers all firms emitting toxic wastes and the firms which generate more than a certain amount of wastes specified by law, which is currently 300 kilo gram per day. The law also requires the emitters of toxic wastes to build landfill sites or contract firms specializing in waste treatment. Violators of mandatory treatment are penalized through imprisonment of up to two years or a fine of up to 10 million won. However, the mandatory treatment system is not effective as the implementation of the regulation requires large administration cost such as monitoring, measuring, and legal costs. In addition to this, the present penalty is not strong enough to give up illegal dumping of wastes. The disposal of general wastes are the responsibilities of administrators of each city, county, and ward.

2) Plastic Waste Charge System

According to the Plastic Waste Disposal Law which was enacted in 1979, manufacturers or importers of plastic resin should pay plastic waste charge based on the presidential decree to cover the collection and disposal costs of plastic wastes. Korea Resource Recycling Corporation was established in 1980 to collect and treat the waste plastic resin. The recycling ratio was estimated to have been around 22%. Beginning from January 1994, the Plastic Waste Charge System was abolished and merged in the Waste Disposal

Charge System.

3) Glass Bottle Deposit System

According to the Liquor Tax Law and the Food Hygiene Law, the Glass Bottle Deposit System is applied to reusable liquor and soft drink bottles. This system was applied to liquor bottles from 1985 and to soft drink bottles from 1988. Thanks to the introduction of the system, beer bottle collection rate increased from 85% in 1984 to 93% in 1990.

|Table 4| Items and Rates for Bottle Deposit System

Item	Range	Deposit Rate
Bottle of liquors	below 500ml	less than 35 won
	500 - 1 liter	less than 50 won
	over 1 liter	over 100 won
Bottle of soft drink	190ml - 300ml	40 won
	300ml - 640ml	50 won
	640ml - 1 liter	60 won
	over 1 liter	80 won

Source : Ministry of Environment, *Environment White Paper 1991*, 1992.

4) Waste Disposal Deposit-Refund System

A. Purpose

According to the article 18 of the Resource Saving and Reutilization Promotion Law, the minister of the Ministry of Environment can assign to the producers or importers of commodities or containers annual costs necessary to collect and treat the wastes which are designated as such and are easy to collect and reuse. When the operators collect and treat the wastes in proper ways the deposit is refunded to them. However the application can be exempted in case the related operator's association collects and treats the wastes with their own funds.

B. Operation of the Waste Disposal Deposit-Refund System

Commodities which become the objects of the deposit-refund system are the ones which generate toxic wastes, nontoxic but which generate much wastes after use, bulky or heavy commodities which require much treatment costs, non-degradable material or commodities, household's harmful commodities which should not be mixed with general wastes, and the commodities the recovery of resources and energy from which is fairly easy and economical.

The deposit-refund system covers five categories of items as shown in <Table 5>. Manufacturers of the products covered by the system are required to deposit specified amount for each unit sold. The deposits are reimbursed to the manufacturers when they collect and treat the wastes from the products they sold.

When the deposit-refund system was first introduced in 1992, 28 billion won was deposited and 53.3 million won was refunded, with the refund ratio of mere 1.9 %. In 1993,27.8 billion won was deposited and 2.23 billion won, 7.8 percent of it was refunded. Out of one hundred firms deposited the most, only 30 firms have records of collecting wastes and being refunded. Items which have relatively good records of collecting wastes were tire with 41.7%, lubricants with 30.7%, and batteries with 53.3 %.

Table 5 Items and Rates of Deposit-Refund System

Item	Classification & Size	Deposit Rate
1. Food/Beverage/ Liquors	A. Paper Pack	
	- below 250ml	0.2 won per unit
	- over 250ml	0.4 won per unit
	B. Metal Can	
	- Push-in Tab	2 won per unit
	- Removable Tab	4 won per unit
	C. Glass Bottle	
	- below 150ml(medicine)	1.5 won per unit
	- below 350ml	2 won per unit
	- over 350ml	3 won per unit
	D. PET Bottle	
	- below 500ml	3 won per unit
	- 500ml - 1,500ml	5 won per unit
	- over 1,500ml	7 won per unit
2. Battery	A. Mercury Battery	100 won per unit
	B. Oxidized Silver Cell	50 won per unit
3. Tire	A. Large Size	400 won per unit
	B. Middle or Small Size	100 won per unit
	C. Bicycle	40 won per unit
4. Lubricating Oil	Lubricating Oil	20 won per liter
5. Electric Home Appliance	A. TV	30 won per kg
	B. Washing Machine	30 won per kg
	C. Air Conditioner	30 won per kg

Source : Ministry of Environment, 'Environment White Paper '92', 1993.

C. Commodities Exempted from the Application

a) The case in which the collection, treatment, and reuse are already implemented on the basis of other laws or existing system. Examples are the used car collection based on the Automobile Management Law and the glass bottle collection based on the Bottle Deposit System. Pesticide bottles are collected and treated by the Korea Resource Recycling Corporation.

b) The case which might impose burdens to farmers such as tires for agricultural machines.

c) Export items.

d) Relatively harmless products such as non-mercury batteries.

D. Problems

This system was designed to reduce the generation of wastes from the source and to recycle wastes. However, following problems are encountered in the process of applying this system :

a) Improper items

Some of the designated items are hard to treat and reuse under the present technical and economic situations or it is difficult to establish collection and treatment systems of producers and importers.

b) Low deposit fee

Deposit fee was reduced in the process of political bargaining between the administration and the congress. As a result, current deposit-refund system fails to give enough economic incentives to the producers of designated items to voluntarily collect and treat the wastes. The amounts deposited are generally smaller than the costs of collecting and treating the wastes. For example, producers of lubricating oil for automobiles deposit 4000 won per drum for 65% of lubricating oil they sell. The treatment cost for a drum of used lubricant is 7000 won, thus the manufacturers lose 3000 won per every drum of used lubricant they collect and treat. The deposit-refund system did not work as a mechanism to integrate production and cleaning of generated wastes. Rather the system was used as an additional means of raising revenue by the government.

c) Minor role of NGO

Deposited money is refunded only to the producers and importers who made the deposit when the collection and treatment is completed either by themselves or by their contractors. However this constraint can form an entry barrier in the waste treatment business and discourage the development of waste treatment technology because they will be reimbursed only the amount the depositors deposited.

E. Remedies for the Improvement of the System

For the present deposit-refund system to work efficiently, it should be changed as follows :

a) Among the original items included in the deposit-refund system, items which are hard to reuse such as cosmetics, pesticides, butane gas container, and containers of toxic materials were transferred to objects of the newly established Waste Disposal Charge System. Polyethylene (PET) bottles and air conditioner which need the collection and treatment and are easy to reuse are included as new objects of the deposit-refund system in 1992. New objects should be added to the system if necessary.

b) Deposit rate should be raised gradually considering actual collection, transportation, and treatment costs. In addition to the efforts by the producers and importers, the Korea Resource Recycling Corporation should play a more active role together with the participation of schools and private collectors.

c) The reimbursement of deposit should not be restricted to the original depositors because it will prevent the development and free competition in the waste treatment business. As the individual waste collection and treatment agents are small and weak compared to the manufacturers, they have limited access to the necessary financial sources even when they have a good prospect. By this reason, some kinds of loan guarantees and tax credits might be required to promote the business and encourage the development of technology.

d) Product and process innovation by manufacturers to the direction of reducing waste generation and raising the resource reuse ratio should also be promoted as a prevention measure.

5) Waste Disposal Charge System

According to the article 19 of the Resource Saving and Reutilization Promotion Law, the minister of the Ministry of Environment can charge the costs necessary for proper treatment of wastes to producers or importers of products, materials, and containers which can cause problems in waste treatment or difficult to reuse, or contain harmful or toxic materials, to curtail generation of wastes and to prevent wasteful use of resources.

The waste disposal charge system was implemented from 1994 in

Table 6 Items and Rates of Waste Disposal Charge System

Item	Classification & Size	Rate & Amount
1. Insecticides, Butane gas, Toxic substances	- Insecticide / Toxic Substances container : below 500ml over 500ml - Butane gas container	 5 won/unit 11 won/unit 6 won/unit
2. Cosmetics	- Glass bottle : below 100ml over 100ml - Metal container spray type others	 2 won/unit 3 won/unit 6 won/unit 4 won/unit
3. Confectionery	- Composite materials container more than 3 more than 4	 5 won/unit 10 won/unit
4. Batteries	- Lithium battery, Nickel/Cadmium battery, Manganese battery, Alkaline Manganese battery	1.5 won/unit
5. Antifreezing solution		20 won/liter
6. Fluorescent		5 won/unit
7. Chewing gum		0.25% of sale price
8. Paper diaper		1 won/unit
9. Plastic resin		0.7 % of sale price

Source : Ministry of Environment, 1993.

addition to the existing deposit-refund system to deal with such items which can cause serious waste problems after their use or which the government should collect and treat as it is improper for private firms to run the business. However, it is not clear under what circumstances government can outperform private firms.

Collected revenue from the system will be deposited in the Waste Management Fund and will be used to support construction of waste treatment facilities, to promote the research and technology development of waste reduction and reuse, and to support local governments for their efforts to collect wastes and to subsidize reuse costs.

6) Volume Charge in Garbage Collection

In Korea, the generation of general wastes increased at the annual rate of 7 to 10 percent during the past five years, reaching 92 thousand tons a day in 1991. Daily waste generation per person was 2.3 kilo gram which was twice the volume in developed countries. Most of the general wastes collected are landfilled and the incineration rate is only 1.6%.(Environment White Paper, '92)

The garbage collection fee in Korea has been fixed regardless of volume or weights and is determined by city ordinance. In Seoul city, the fixed garbage collection fee is levied differently to residence group, large business group, and general business group. The residential group is classified into 8 classes based on the size of house and property tax. As the fee is fixed regardless of waste volume discharged, there is no incentive to reduce the discharge of wastes and to recycle reusable resources. And the more, the fee rate is unrealistically low and fails to cover the necessary cost to manage the wastes. In case of Seoul city, the garbage collection fee covers less than one fourth of costs incurred to collect and treat the wastes. As the garbage collection fee is so low, most of the citizens in Seoul pay extra tipping to the garbage collector.

To give economic incentive to the reduction of waste disposal and to increase the resource reuse ratio, a new system of volume charge was introduced to 31 pilot cities, counties, and wards from April 1,1994. The volume charge system will be applied throughout the nation from January 1 next year.

New system levies garbage collection fee based on volume of garbage discharged. In Busan city, 3 official garbage bags which can contain 60 liters of garbage is distributed basically to each citizen a month. A 20 liter bag costs 280 won. If people needs more bags in addition to the distributed ones, they can buy them separately. If people use unauthorized garbage bag or throw wastes illegally, they will be fined from 50 thousand won to 1 million won. Since the pilot volume charge system was introduced, one third of garbage disposal was reported to have been reduced. It is expected that the volume charge will reduce unnecessary bags and wrappings in the grocery and department stores. It will also accelerate the introduction of refill products system.

3. Environmental Labelling

Since 1980, people paid closer attention to the improvement of environmental quality and the investment on environment has increased considerably. However, most of the measures taken were based on regulation and penalty to large manufacturing firms and citizen's participation was very limited. In 1991, one electronic firm in the vicinity of Nakdong River accidently discharged phenol into the river and polluted the water source for tap water for many days. This caused great inconveniences to the people of Taegu city with 2 million people and aroused citizen's movement to boycott the products produced by the polluting firm. Government took this opportunity to introduce the environmental labelling system which informed the consumers about environmental friendliness of products.

The environmental label is attached to green commodities which are resource and energy saving and produce less pollutants in the process of production, consumption, and disposal. This system is operated under the auspices of citizen's organization to promote voluntary interaction between producers and consumers. Selection of object commodities and related rules are decided by the 15 membered environmental label committee.

If selected as an environmental label commodity, the producer should share the operating cost of the system. In 1992, four types of commodities such as sprays which do not use CFCs, recycled papers, and recycled plastic products were awarded environmental label. Eight items are added in 1993 and 124 products from 54 firms are sold with the environmental label in the market as of March 1993.

IV. Revenue Sources for Environmental Protection

1. Revenue Sources

Revenue sources for central government's investment for environmental protection are as follows : general budget account, special budget account, and some funds. General account is operated through tax revenue and used for the provision of basic government service such as national defence, security, and education. In 1993, total amount of central government's budget related to environmental protection was 896 billion won, 0.32 % of GNP. Of these, budget for the ministry of environment was 90.3 billion won which was 0.24 % of central government's general budget account. Other ministries such as the Ministry of Construction secured 391.2 billion won for environmental protection.

There is a special account which is separated from the general account and used for special purpose. Transfer payment to local governments is one of them. In 1993, 222.5 billion won, which was 15.1 % of total transfer payment to local government was used for the construction of waste water and night soil treatment plants and for the cleaning of polluted river. Besides government's budget, there are funds operated by the Ministry of the Environment. They are the Environmental Pollution Control Fund and the Waste Management fund. They amounted to 192.2 billion won in 1993.

2. Comprehensive Medium-term Plan

Korean government set up 'Comprehensive Medium-term Plan for Environmental Quality Improvement' for the period of 1992 and 1996. During the period, 12 trillion and 191.7 billion won, which is equivalent to one third of Korea's annual general budget account will be invested by public and private sectors for environmental quality improvement. During the new five-year social and economic plan of 1993-97, 7 trillion and 900 billion won is required for public sector's environmental investment. However only 5 trillion and 400 billion won is expected to be secured and the remaining 2 trillion and 500 billion won must be supplied from other sources. Existing charges such as waste treatment deposit, effluent charge, and environmental improvement charges are already tied to specific purposes and the revenue from the charges are not big enough to fill the gap. So the Ministry of Environment plans to secure necessary investment funds from following sources :

a) The introduction of special-purposed environmental tax and product charge to heavily-polluting products is being considered to strengthen the application of polluter pays principle. In addition to this, present effluent charge system which is a non-compliance charge imposed on the excessive emission over the regulatory standards is under review for the transformation into a Pigouvian tax type charge system which is applied to total amount of pollutants emitted.

b) Public loan from the international agencies such as the World

Bank will be promoted.

c) Environment bonds will be issued to recruit small scale funds under 100 billion won and "the Environment Bond Purchase Campaign" will be promoted in cooperation with mass media.

d) Issuance of foreign bonds and borrowing will be promoted to secure foreign capital necessary for the implementation of environmental investment projects such as the construction of environmental infrastructure.

e) To increase the share of user charge in waste disposal cost, garbage collection fee will be raised gradually.

f) To integrate funding sources for environmental investment, the Ministry of Environment plans to introduce special budget account for environmental protection which is earmarked to expenditures on the protection of the environment. The revenue sources of the account will be environment-related transfer payment from the existing special budget account for transfer payment to local governments, all the environment-related charges, and the new possible sources such as the environment tax, bond issue, and foreign loans.

g) As the government does not have enough money to invest on the provision of environmental infrastructure, participation of private sector will be encouraged. Presently the investment on environmental infrastructure is very poor. For example, by the end of 1992 the wastewater treatment rate in Korea was only 37% while it was more than 90 % in U. K. and Germany. By 1997, the rate will be raised to 73 %. Government will also intensify financial loan and tax break to firms investing on the construction of pollution control facilities.

3. Environmental Pollution Control Fund

1) Objective

Environmental pollution control fund system was initiated from September 1983 to raise necessary funds for environmental pollution control projects and to accelerate investment on pollution control facilities by lending funds to the operator at a long-term and low interest rates. The fund is made of effluent charge, endowments from government or non-governmental sources, interests from the operation of the funds, and other income from the Environmental Management Corporation. From 1993, the environmental quality improvement charge is included as a new source.

2) Operation of the fund

The environmental pollution control fund is managed and operated by the Environmental Management Corporation which was founded in 1987. Following are the major activities of the Corporation :

a) Run the environmental pollution control business
- Construction and operation of waste landfill facility
- Construction and operation of industrial wastes treatment facility
- Construction and operation of industrial complex wastewater treatment facility

- Management of pollution control facility on a consignment base
- Commissioning of night soil and waste treatment facilities
- Technical support to the constructors of pollution control facilities and industrial waste treatment facilities
- Public education and information dissemination on environmental pollution control
- Business activities related to pollution control

b) Loan to the construction of pollution control facility
c) Development of pollution control facility
d) Technical support to design, construction, and management of control facility
e) Relief to the damage caused by environmental pollution

3) Fund Management

For the past 9 years from 1984 to 1992, 155.6 billion won was raised, of which 80.4 billion won was government endowment and 43.7 billion won was from the effluent charge , and 31.5 billion won was interest income. In 1992, 36.4 billion won was lent out to 320 firms, about 100 million won per case.

The loan from the environmental pollution control fund takes up 10 % of total investment for the construction of pollution control facility. As the raised fund was not enough to meet the increasing demand for the loan, the Environmental Management Corporation secured additional fund from the Korea Industrial Bank and the Bank for Small and Medium Firms. It is expected that newly established 'Environmental Improvement Charge' will channel more than 100 billion won to the Fund and the usage of the fund will be extended to new areas such as the upbringing of environmental industry, support to environmental technology development, and the construction of waste water purification facilities.

4. Waste Management Fund

Waste management fund is made of waste collection and treatment deposits, loans, fund operating revenues, government endowments, and revenues from the sale of wastes. The fund is used for the purchase and stockpile of recycled wastes, refund of the deposit, support to the waste reuse business, establishment and support to the waste treatment facilities, waste reuse research and technology development, and so on.

V. Energy Tax System in Korea

There is no tax system in Korea such as carbon tax which intends to reduce CO^2 emission. The energy tax system in Korea is composed of import tariff, value added tax, and special consumption tax as shown in Table 7. As the special consumption tax rate is high for gasoline and low for diesel oil, the energy price structure is distorted among petroleum products In fact, this special tax structure is adverse to the protection of air quality from energy consumption because tax rate for diesel oil which emits more pollutants than gasoline is lower and there had been subsidy for coal producers until recently. This distorted tax structure made diesel oil relatively cheaper in Korea compared to other countries. The price of gasoline per liter was 610 won in Korea while it was 915 won in Japan and 497 won in Taiwan in 1993. However, the price of diesel oil was cheaper in Korea compared to both Japan and Taiwan. It was 210 won in Korea while it was 472 won in Japan and 366 won in Taiwan. In general, the price of petroleum products in Korea is lower than most of IEA member countries except U. S. and the price of diesel oil was even cheaper than the U.S.

Korean government adopted low energy pricing policy in the 1980s to control domestic price level and to support manufacturers and households. Especially mass media and politicians were very sensitive to any attempt to raise energy prices. As a result, industrial structure of Korea remained energy-intensive and the energy consumers did not feel economic incentive to conserve energy in spite of government's continued campaign for energy conservation. As a result, energy consumption grew faster than the GNP growth rate since late 1980s. In 1992 energy consumption increased 12.5% while GNP grew only 4.7%, thus the energy/GNP elasticity was 2.66. In the same year, energy/GNP elasticity was 0.84 for Japan, 0.86 for U.S. and 0.46 for U.K.

Recently, there was a strong effort to introduce environment tax in Korea by NGO's and the Ministry of Environment. However, the priority was set on the improvement of social overhead capital and the special consumption tax to gasoline was earmarked to the investment on social overhead capital. The Ministry of Environment plans to revise the Basic Environmental Policy Act to include provisions which will be a legal base to introduce carbon tax or pollution tax. However, it will be difficult for the time being to introduce carbon tax on petroleum products separately from the special consumption tax as strong opposition is expected from energy consumers.

Price ceiling regulation has been applied to petroleum products in Korea. Beginning from February 1994, a new pricing scheme was introduced in which external factors such as world crude oil price change or foreign exchange rate fluctuation are evaluated every month and the price of petroleum products are adjusted monthly. This pricing scheme is considered as an interim measure toward full liberalization of petroleum products market.

|Table 7| Energy Tax System in Korea

Classification	Petroleum products	Coal
Import tariff	1 %	-
Value added tax	10 %	10 %
Special Consumption Tax	Gasoline 190% Diesel oil 25% Kerosene 10% LPG 10% LNG 10%	
Subsidy ('91 standard)		Price subsidy 9843 won per ton Production subsidy 286 won per ton

VI. Lessons

Korea failed to pay serious attention to environmental problems until the beginning of 1990s. Influenced by the United Nations Conference on Environment and Development in Rio and thanks to the increasing per capita income, people began to realize the importance of environment in their life. Thus the quality of life became one of top priority in national policy making. Until 1980, Korea depended upon direct regulation to control environmental pollution as in other countries. The only economic instrument applied in environmental policy was the effluent charge system introduced in 1983.

The effluent charge system in Korea was operated as a non-compliance charge system and the primary purpose was to discourage polluters to discharge wastes beyond effluent/emission standards. It was a complementing instrument to direct control rather than a substitute for it. Korea learned some lessons from more than 10 years' experience with the modified effluent charge system in Korea.

First, when introducing an economic instrument for pollution control, use it as a complement to existing direct control methods. Don't try to replace direct control with the market-based policy instruments. Make it work first by alleviating barriers, then remedy the problems encountered later. It is impossible to find theoretically optimal level of pollution in developing countries. Government does not have necessary information on the environmental damage from the pollution and the pollution control costs. With insufficient information, the government should not be too ambitious to attain optimal level of pollution through economic instruments. As a main instrument to discourage pollution, emission standard and other types of direct regulation should be applied first, and then supplement them with economic instruments.

Second, the charge rate should not be high at the initial stage. The most significant barrier to the introduction of a charge system is financial burdens to industries and their concerted opposition. So the charge rate should start from low level and be raised on a trial and error base. If the polluters do not respond to the charge, the rate can be raised gradually. In this way, the opposition and lobbying efforts from industries can be mitigated.

In Korea the effluent charge system was introduced as a penalty to the violators of regulatory standard and the charge rate was low. However, several problems were encountered in implementing the modified effluent charge system. First problem was that the charge system did not give significant incentive to reduce pollution. Polluters feared to be detected of violating direct control and be given penalties such as relocation, shut down or imprisonment. But they did not worry about paying the non- compliance charge when detected. Second problem was administrative problems. The effectiveness of compliance monitoring is critical to the prevention of illegal discharges. Polluters often times keep the effluent standard through cheating and bribing. As the effluent standard and charge computation was based on toxicity of effluents rather than on total volume of pollutants discharged, polluters sometimes diluted the wastewater to lower toxicity below the level of regulatory standard. Inspectors from the regulatory agency became the target of bribery from noncomplying plants. To prevent illegal discharges, the Ministry of Environment inspects through the verification of effluent facilities and the identification of abatement process.

Most of the problems encountered in applying the modified effluent charge system in Korea, however, were stemmed not from the introduction of the charge system per se, but because of insufficient regulatory provisions and loose implementation of direct control. To attain targeted environmental standard within a specified region, not only toxicity but also total volume of pollutants discharge should be regulated. In the revised new five-year economic and social development plan of 1993-97, the introduction of total volume-based regulation is planned beginning 1997.

Introduction of total-volume based regulation implies the intensification of direct control in environmental protection. Intended effluent charge system which is closer to its original form will still function as a supplementing instrument. Whatever becomes the policy instrument in environmental protection, improvement of monitoring capacity of regulatory agency must be the determining factor for the attainment of target environmental quality level.

In the Waste Disposal Deposit-Refund System, the deposited amount comprises only 10 to 20 % of necessary costs to collect and treat wastes by manufacturer's own distribution channel. So the manufacturers just give up the deposit. As such, the present deposit-refund system can not give proper economic incentive for the manufacturers to collect and treat wastes voluntarily and take back the deposits.

To deal with the problem, the Ministry of Environment plans to raise the deposit rate about twice the present rate and is consulting with related ministries such as the Economic Planning Board and the Ministry of Health and Welfare. In addition to this, the government plans to revise the provision on the collection and treatment of wastes. In the revised provision, the manufacturers, sellers, and the users of designated items will be obligated to establish collection system and to operate treatment facilities. Items subject to this regulation would be all items designated in the deposit-refund system ; some items of waste disposal charge system such as insecticides and toxic substances containers, and fluorescent lamps ; and 9 other items such as refrigerator, gas-oven, electric range, VTR, computer, used plastic containers, used lubricant container, packing materials for electric home appliances, and used furnitures.

The introduction of direct regulation for waste collection and treatment implies that the market-based economic incentive system is not effective in itself in reducing waste discharge and raising resource reuse ratio. Presently, the deposit or charge rates are not sufficient to give incentives to the waste generators to voluntarily collect and treat the wastes. However, it is not easy to raise the rate sufficient enough to be effective because of the opposition from interest groups such as producers, sellers, consumers, and even from the government itself. Ministries in charge of economic development and the fostering of industries are opposing to the raise of deposit or charge rates because they fear the weakening of competitive power of related industries and the rise in general price level.

Beginning from the 1990s, new types of economic instruments

such as the environmental improvement charge system, the waste-disposal deposit-refund system, and the waste disposal charge system were introduced in Korea. These instruments are at initial stages of application and the primary purpose of introduction was revenue generation. However, various problems were pointed out already and some remedial actions are set in motion.

There are several reasons for the frequent revision of environmental policy instruments in Korea. When introducing a new law or a system, government officials first look at the reactions of general public. If the lawmakers who are sensitive to the response of their constituents do not cooperate, the proposed law cannot be enacted. In the process of lawmaking, bureaucrats and politicians become the target of strong lobbying groups. Lobbying groups can be consumers sometimes or manufacturers or sellers in other times. That is why there are quite a number of exemptions in the charge system in Korea. Second consideration is to secure revenue sources ahead of other branches of the government. When introducing a new law, various conflicts of interests should be overcome by the proposed ministry and the result becomes quite different from the original plan. If the new law is related to raising revenue source such as charge system, all the related ministries will try hard to make their share bigger. In case of extending the objects of the environmental improvement charge system to manufacturing facilities, the Ministry of Environment will face fierce opposition from the Ministry of Trade, Industry, and Resources, for example.

Reference

Lee, Jeong-Jun and Eui-Soon Shin, *Hwankyung Gaeseon Chokjinul Wihan Cheongchaek Balcheon Bangahn Yonku* (*Policy Instruments for Environmental Improvement*), International Trade and Business Institute, May 1991.

Lee, Sun-Yong, *Economic Incentives to Control Pollution : A Case Study of Korea's Non-Compliance Charge System*, a doctoral thesis submitted to Indiana University,1992.

Ministry of Environment, *Hwankyung Baekseo* (*Environmental White Paper '91*), 1992.

______, *Hwankyung Baekseo* (*Environmental White Paper '92*), 1993.

______, *Hwankyung Tujajaewon Jodalchaekye Jeongbimit Tujahwakchung Bangahn Yonku* (*A Study on the Improvement of Environmental Investment Revenue System and Investment Promotion Strategy*), June 1993.

Nam,Il-Chong, "Using Price Mechanism in Waste Management", mimeo, Korea Development Institute, June 1993.

Rhee, Hosaeng "The Use of Economic Instruments for Environmental Protection in Korea : Performances and Difficulties", a paper prepared for Informal Workshop on the "Use of Economic Instruments in Environmental Policies", Paris, 8 and 9 November 1993.

Shin, Eui-Soon, *Hwankyung Cheongchaekgwa Gonghe Bangji Biyongui Bundam* (*Environmental Policy and the Sharing of Pollution Control Costs*), Korea Economic Research Center, The Korea Chamber of Commerce and Industry, March 1991.

Sunwoo, Youngjoon, "Pollution Emission Charge System- Efficiency, Barriers, and Adjustment Requirement", Environment and Policy Institute, East-West Center, January 1989.

11. Economic Analysis and Valuation of Urban Environmental Problems*

I. Economic Analysis of Urban Environmental Problems

1. Urban Environmental Problems

World's urban population increased from less than 300 million in 1950 to about 1.4 billion by the late 1980s. By the turn of the century, the cities and towns of the developing world are likely to have absorbed another 600 million people or about two-thirds of the total population increase. Many of these new residents will live in so-called mega-cities, each with more than 10 million people. By the year 2000, there are expected to be nineteen such cities in developing countries.[1)]

---

* "ECONOMIC ANALYSIS AND VALUATION OF URBAN ENVIRONMENTAL PROBLEMS," *Regional Development Dialogue*, Vol. 15, No.2 (Autumn 1994), pp. 129-142.

1) Carl Bartone and Stephen K.Mayo, "Economic Trends and Macroeconomic Policies

|Figure 1| Interaction between the Environment and Urban Economic System

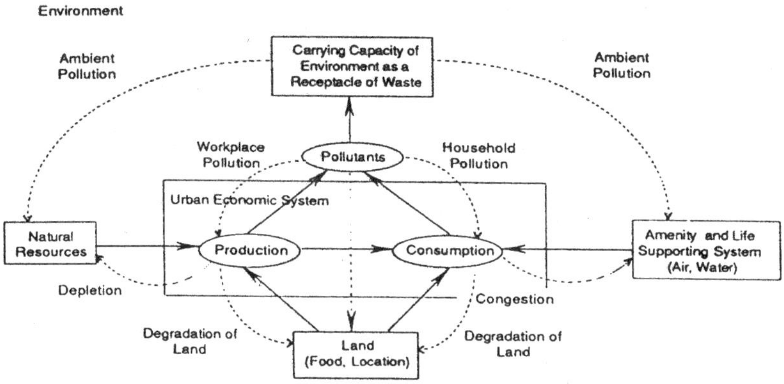

Notes : → Benefits from the environment.

⇢ Negative feedback to the environment.

* Natural resources together with land constitute natural capital.

Urban growth brings with it a degradation of the natural environment which hinders environmentally sound and sustainable development. Inadequate provision of infrastructure and poor management often aggravate the deterioration of the natural environment in addition to worsening urban living conditions, especially those affecting the urban poor.

Environment is the set of natural conditions which defines the human living space. Environment provides four functions for the economy as shown in Figure 1. Firstly, environment provides public goods for consumption such as air, water, the amenity of the landscape, and the recreational assets of nature. Secondly, environment

Affecting Urban Development in the Third World" (April 1990).

provides resources that are used as inputs in production activities, such as water, energy, minerals, and oxygen for combustion. Thirdly, environment absorbs the pollutants emitted from various production and consumption activities. Lastly, environment provides location for the economic system.

2. Scale and Typology of Urban Environmental Problems

The conventional approach to examining urban environmental issues is to follow sector-based categorization such as air, water, sanitation, and solid waste. This approach reflects the way data are classified and government agencies organized. However, the sector-based approach tends to ignore important socioeconomic and institutional considerations.

Alternative approach is to classify urban environmental problems on a spatial scale. In Figure 2, the sector-oriented urban environmental problems are spatially categorized into household/workplace, community, metropolitan area, region, and globe. At each step of the spatial scale, environmental problems and the related infrastructure and services needed to address such problems differ.[2]

Urban environmental problems in developing countries can be classified into three broad categories-pollution, congestion of urban systems, and the degradation of the natural support system. Major impacts associated with these environmental problems are shown in

2) Carl Bartone, "Annotated Outline of a Report on Strategic Options for Managing the Urban Environment" (draft), World Bank, 1991.

|Figure 2| Spatial Scale of Urban Environmental Problems

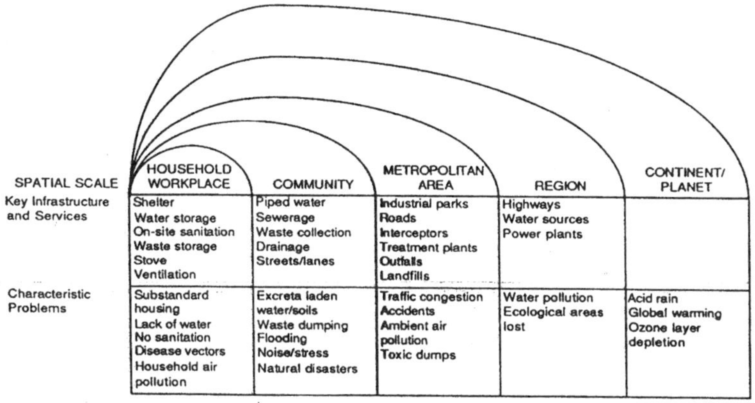

Source : Carl Bartone, "Annotated Outline of a Report on Strategic Options for Managing the Urban Environment"(draft), Washington, DC : World Bank, 1991.

Table 1.

Some of the major impacts associated with pollution include health and safety aspects such as health care costs, lost working days, and higher mortality rates. Other major impacts are productivity loss through destruction of organic systems in such areas as forestry, fishery, and agriculture as well as losses due to inorganic system destruction resulting in material corrosion and product quality reduction. Pollution can also lead to degradation of amenities in terms of reduced visibility, aesthetics, and recreational values.

Major impacts associated with congestion are extended travel time, secondary health effects, overcrowding of public facilities, and the loss of access to amenities.

|Table 1| Urban Environmental Problems and Their Impacts

Problems \ Impact	Health/Safety	Productivity	Amenity	Ecological Value
Pollution				
Indoor Air Pollution	X	X		
Ambient Air Pollution	X	X	X	X
Freshwater Pollution	X	X	X	X
Lake, Coastal Water Pollution	X	X	X	X
Solid Wastes Pollution	X	X	X	
Hazardous Waste Pollution	X	X	X	X
Fecal Contamination	X	X		
Noise	X	X	X	
Deterioration of Living Environment (Congestion)				
Traffic Congestion	X	X	X	
Congested Urban Amenities			X	
Occupation of High-Risk Land	X	X	X	
Degradation of Natural Support System				
Freshwater Depletion	X	X	X	
Degradation of Land and Ecosystem	X	X	X	X

Source : Euisoon Shin et al., *Economic Valuation of Environmental Problems-With Emphasis on Asia*, Washington, DC : Urban Development Division, World Bank, 1992.

Degradation of natural support system can result in the following impacts : increasing scarcity and higher supply cost of surface water, land subsidence from groundwater over-pumping, loss of recreational sites and cultural property, increased danger of natural disaster such as flooding and landslide, and the loss of biological diversity.

3. Cause of Urban Environmental Problems

Environmental deterioration in many cities can be attributed to ineffective institutional arrangements to deal with the myriad urban problems such as rapid population growth, over-concentration of industrialization, lack of urban infrastructure, and unplanned development taking place in an unintegrated manner.

The origin of urban environmental problems can be explained in terms of the following "excess scale hypothesis" :

> Population pressure together with direct and indirect institutional weaknesses leads to urban growth over and above the carrying capacity of a city's natural and living environments, causing congestion of urban infrastructure and environmental degradation.

Direct institutional weakness, which refers to the inadequate investment in urban infrastructure, constitutes the basic cause of urban environmental degradation together with population pressure. Indirect causes are such triggering factors as a lack of public information, education, and political will, and property rights uncertainties such as the absence of efficient market and pricing system.

Urban economic system depends on the natural support system, which includes life support elements, such as water, air, and land. As there is a limited carrying capacity of the environment, environmental problems will occur if proper care and management of the environment are not taken. Many urban environmental problems originate from overpopulation and the excess use of the natural environment beyond its carrying capacity.[3)]

The concept of "carrying capacity" was originally used by biologists. The carrying capacity concept in biology refers to the maximum supportable size of the population of a particular species in a given area. Maximum size depends on three factors : (a) environmental constraints ; (b) feedback from interactions with other species and with endogenous regulating factors ; and (c) population-driven feedback.[4)] Its application has extended to regional ecosystems and even to global issues described in the Brundtland Report as "environmentally sound and sustainable development."[5)]

In their study on the determinants of environmental degradation in three Latin American countries, Foy and Daly compared three causes, namely, misallocation of resources, unequal distribution of resources, and excess use of the regenerative and assimilative capacities of a country's environment, what is referred to as "excess scale".[6)] They concluded that the scale factor is the most important

---

3) "Carrying capacity" refers to the capacity of nature to support human populations and their activities within a certain geographical boundary of the national environment. This concept is sometimes ambiguous because it is specific to the areas applied and is also subject to technical and institutional choice.

4) Malin Falkenmark, "Regional Environmental Management : The Role of Man-Water-Land Interactions", Environment working paper no. 21, World Bank, 1991.

5) World Commission on Environment and Development (WCED), *Our Common Future* (The Brundtland report), Geneva, 1987.

determinant of environmental degradation.

Scale is a choice variable measured by a product of population and per capita resource use. Carrying capacity is a constraining factor, but it can be increased through investment and technology or reduced through a degradation of the natural capital. Hence, the optimality of scale should be judged in relation to the existing carrying capacity. At any point in time, there exists a maximum scale of a city's use of environmental capital which the natural environment can sustain without serious degradation. The maximum scale is a dynamic concept subject to technology and the natural conditions of the environment. In an urban setting, the implication of this is the need for better estimates of carrying capacity of cities and overall use of environmental capital.

It is misguided to assume that urbanization *per se* leads to environmental degradation. Discharge of pollutants into the natural environment does not necessarily lead to environmental pollution. Only when the use of environmental services exceeds the carrying capacity of nature, pollution and the degradation of the environment become a social problem.

Urban infrastructure and services are also hindered by congestion when total use exceeds carrying capacity. By expanding carrying capacity before expanding use, severe environmental problems which accompany urban growth can be avoided. However, most cities grow before the adequate expansion of carrying capacity is effected,

---

6) George Foy and Herman Daly, "Allocation, Distribution and Scale as Determinants of Environmental Degradation : Case Studies of Haiti, El Salvador and Costa Rica", *Environment working paper* no.19, World Bank, 1989.

thereby incurring environmental degradation and at the same time diminishing the assimilative capacity for the future. Basically, the cause of urban environmental problems is urban growth without proper consideration being paid to the adverse effects of excess scale. A prime example of this process is the case of Bangkok which shows severe environmental degradation in the face of extremely rapid urban development.[7)]

---

7) Environmental degradation in the Bangkok Metropolitan Region (BMR) is not so much a consequence of urban and industrial growth as the very predictable result of failure to supply urban and environmental infrastructure consistent with the demands for such economic growth.

- High density development without adequate provision of mass transit and road networks has led to traffic congestion.
- High water demand without adequate municipal water supply has led to excessive groundwater pumping and consequent land subsidence.
- High density development without adequate drainage and sewerage has led to flooding and water pollution.
- Industrial development without adequate pollution control investment and enforcement has led to increased air, water, and solid waste pollution.

These are not the inevitable consequences of urban and economic growth but the results of failure to develop adequate institutional mechanisms to ensure that those who benefit from new development also pay for the necessary infrastructure and the pollution controls needed to protect the environment.

Developers, manufacturers, and landowners are currently allowed to reap major benefits, not only from their own investments but from the public infrastructure which made it possible. Furthermore, they do so without shouldering the full cost that their development imposes on the environment. Failure to require landowners and developers to pay their full costs ultimately becomes a subsidy to destructive development. (See Thailand Development Research Institute, *Urbanization and Environment: Managing the Conflict*, December 1990).

II. Economic Valuation of Urban Environmental Problems

1. Purpose of Economic Valuation

To set priorities for urban environmental management, the costs of environmental degradation and the benefits of environmental improvement must be quantified. Economic valuation can provide information on the magnitude of economic costs of various types of environmental damage on a macro scale. This information can be used to guide overall environmental policy, including allocation of resources among major environmental categories, so relative magnitudes are of major concern.

Economic valuation can also provide information on the economic benefits of specific environmental improvement projects on a micro scale, such as air pollution control, drinking water supplies, or alleviation of urban traffic congestion. In this case, the absolute magnitudes are of greater importance.

Macroeconomic valuation has less stringent data requirements in identifying damage functions or dose-response relationships, than microeconomic valuation does. Careful adoption of does-response coefficients from developed countries is acceptable.

The theory of economic valuation has become quite sophisticated, but very little application has been done in developing countries. What is needed at the moment according to Munasinghe and Lutz, "is not for more theory or techniques, but for application of existing methodology and approaches to concrete problems, particularly in developing countries."[8)]

2. Overview of Valuation Methods

The justification for monetary valuation of environmental services lies with the function of money as a measuring rod for welfare change. People express their willingness to pay by exchanging money for goods in everyday life, thus revealing their preferences through market transactions.[9)] Unfortunately, well-defined property rights and markets from which the value of environmental degradation can be derived are nonexistent for most environmental goods. So indirect approaches are usually necessary.

We can classify existing economic valuation methods based on the role of individual preference in valuing environmental damage. According to this classification, all the existing valuation techniques can be broadly categorized into physical linkage and behavioral linkage methods.[10)] Physical linkage methods examine the technical relationships between environmental degradation and physical damage without paying attention to the subjective preferences of the affected population. For example, increased respiratory disease or

---

8) Mohan Munasinghe and Ernst Lutz, "Environmental-Economic Evaluation of Projects and Policies for Sustainable Development", *Environment working paper* no.42, World Bank, 1991.

9) David W. Pearce and R.Kerry Turner, *Economics of Natural Resources and the Environment*, Johns Hopkins University Press, 1990.

10) V.Kerry Smith, "A Conceptual Overview of the Foundations of Benefit-Cost Analysis" in J.D. Bentkover, V.T. Covello, and J.Mumpower, eds., *Benefit Assessment : The State of the Art*, Netherlands : Reodel, 1986.

crop damage can be attributed to diminished air quality, and the relationships are objectively determined, based on statistical analysis or crop production data.

On the other hand, the behavioral linkage methods assume that the value of environmental goods should be based on people's willingness to pay to secure better environmental quality or to escape environmental deterioration. The behavioral linkage methods can be subdivided further depending on whether preferences are indirectly evident through market behavior or stated directly, as in a survey. The revealed preference approach is based on Maler's "weak complementarity." Which occurs where an individual must consume a given amount of a market good in order to derive utility from a non-market good such as environmental quality.[11)]

Of the three different types of valuation methods listed in Table 2, the physical linkage method has been alternatively called the damage function approach ; the revealed preference method is also known as the surrogate market approach ; and the stated preference method is also called the survey or contingent valuation method.

Table 2 is based on the assumption that the major urban environmental problems are pollution, congestion, and the degradation of natural support system. These problems have negative impacts on health and safety, productivity, and amenity and ecological value.

Different environmental impacts necessitate different valuation

---

11) Karl-Goran Mäler, *Environmental Economics : A Theoretical Inquiry*, Johns Hopkins University Press for Resources for the Future, 1974.

|Table 2| Economy Valuation Methods for Urban Environmental Problems

Environmental Problems / Problems → Impact	Pollution (A),(B), (C),(D)	Congestion (A),(B),(C)		Destruction of Natural Support System (A),(B),(C),(D)
Valuation Methods \ Impacts	(A) Health/Safety	(B) Productivity	(C) Amenity	(D) Ecological Values
Resource or Opportunity Costs				
Cost of Productivity Loss	-	X	-	-
Cost of Illness	X	-	-	-
Human Capital	X	-	-	-
Replacement Costs	-	X	-	-
Revealed Preference				
Hedonic Pricing				
-Property Value Differential	X	-	X	-
-Wage Differential	X	-	X	-
Travel Cost	-	-	X	-
Averting/Mitigating Behavior	X	X	-	-
Stated Preference				
Contingent Valuation (cardinal preference)	X	-	X	X
Contingent Ranking (ordinal preference)	X	-	X	X

Source : Euisoon Shin et al., "*Economic Valuation of Urban Environmental Problems-With Emphasis on Asia*", Washington, DC : Urban Development Division, World Bank, 1992.

methods. However, each valuation method has its own advantages and disadvantages for specific application, and it is difficult to rank them in terms of overall performance.

For the valuation of environmental impacts on health and safety, most physical and behavioral linkage methods can be applied. In the case of productivity loss and materials damage, the physical linkage method seems to be the only applicable technique even if the averting/mitigating expenditure approach can be applied as a supplementary technique. Amenity values are estimated either by the revealed preference method or by the contingent valuation method. Ecological value refers mainly to the non-use values attached to the extinction of species or destruction of ecosystems, and its derivation is mostly based on the contingent valuation method.

III. Application of Valuation Methods

1. Damage Function Approach

There are four valuation techniques in the category of physical linkage or damage function approach. Two of them-cost of illness and human capital approaches-are used to value health and safety effects of environmental degradation while the costs of productivity loss and replacement cost methods are used to measure the economic cost of productivity losses and material damage. All of these require the estimation of a damage function or dose-response function which relates the exposure to environmental pollution and the effects on health or productivity. Such analysis usually entails an interdisciplinary approach.

The procedure for estimating health and productivity effects involves three steps. The first step is to relate the exposure associated with different levels of environmental quality to human mortality/morbidity rates, the productivity of living systems, and/or materials damage. Risk assessment studies for health effects or damage function studies for productivity loss are required at this stage. Information on the relationship between environmental quality and physical damage to health or productivity depends on scientific knowledge and data availability. As the core of the physical linkage method lies in the first step, the lack of scientific knowledge about cause-effect relationship is often a major drawback to this method. The second step is to measure the magnitude of physical damage using the dose-response coefficient estimated from the first step, and the third step is to evaluate the monetary cost of measured damage.

Before a meaningful valuation can be performed, a considerable amount of physical information must be collected and analyzed. However, even in developed countries, information on these physical relationships is inadequate in spite of extensive programmes of air and water quality monitoring and considerable laboratory and epidemiological research on the health effects of pollutants. The situation in developing countries is generally worse.

However, the Bangkok study of US Agency for International Development (USAID) shows that, with some ingenuity, limited data can at least be used to make rough approximations and generate ranges of values within an order of magnitude.[12] Although locally derived models are preferable, damage functions and dose-response relationships derived in developed countries can be adapted to the local situation, at least as a first approximation. A common mistake made in city-wide application is to aggregate air quality data into an average for the entire city. It is better, if time permits, to do separate does-response studies for areas around different monitoring stations since pollution concentrations and population density vary widely. It is also important to cross-check the results of dose- response models with empirical data to be sure that they do not differ greatly.

Because dose-response functions for health damage are confined to just a few of many air pollutants, physical linkage methods may capture only a part of total health damage from pollution-related illnesses. This should be indicated when reporting the estimated damage costs.

It is clear that any attempt to apply economic valuation techniques to environmental problems in Asian cities should involve a multidisciplinary team of environmental scientists, epidemiologists, biologists, chemists, physicists, hydrologist, engineers, and planners to work with economists in generating the information necessary for economic analysis.

---

12) US Agency for International Development (USAID), *Ranking Environmental Health Risks in Bangkok*, *Thailand* (Vols. 1 and 2) (Washington, DC : Office of Housing and Urban Programs, 1990)

2. Case Study : LNG Substitution in Korea

Republic of Korea has been substituting liquefied natural gas (LNG) for conventional energy sources since 1987 to alleviate urban air pollution in the Seoul Metropolitan Region (SMR). The SMR LNG project, which replaced the conventional energy sources such as briquettes and fuel oil with LNG, improved air quality in the region and reduced mortality and morbidity caused by respiratory disease. The benefit of the project was assumed to last for thirty years from 1987 to 2016.

Four steps were used to measure the benefits of air quality improvement in monetary value as shown in Figure 3.

|**Figure 3**| Urban Environmental Assessment and Valuation Process

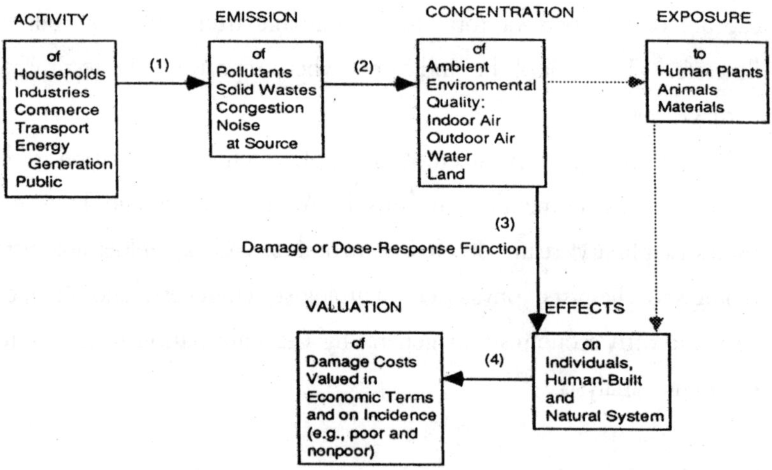

Step 1 : Activity analysis

This step involves calculating the reduced discharge of pollutants due to partial substitution of the conventional energy sources by LNG. The residual discharge coefficient for each energy source was used to calculate the residual discharge. By comparing the estimated quantities of residuals discharged between conventional energy sources and LNG, we can calculate the reduction rate of residuals through LNG substitution.

Step 2 : Residual discharge → Ambient concentration

Air quality is measured by the concentration of pollutants in the atmosphere. The output of the first step becomes the input for the analysis of effects on the ambient concentration of air pollutants in the SMR. The Gaussian continuous plume dispersion model was applied to estimate the ambient concentration of pollutants resulting from the discharges of gaseous residuals from point source. Daily maximum ambient concentrations of total suspended particulates (TSP) and sulfur dioxide (SO_2) in the atmosphere of eight cities in the SMR were calculated by this method.

As the quality of SO_2 concentration dominates TSP, average reduction rate of SO_2 was used to estimate the benefit of air quality improvement from LNG substitution.

To obtain the average reduction rate of SO_2, first the weighted average of SO_2 reduction rate for the estimated year was calculated using the population's share of each city as a weight. The average reduction rate of 4.37 per cent was obtained by taking the arithmetic mean of the yearly values which was estimated at five–year intervals.

Step 3 : Ambient environmental quality → Effects on receptors. Among several approaches to estimate the magnitude of the effects of environmental quality changes on environmental use, most commonly used empirical technique is the regression analysis. A good example of this approach is to estimate the following dose–response relationship :

$$M=a_0+a_1 P+a_2 S+a_3 Z+e ,$$

where M : mortality rate ; P : particulate concentration ; S : sulfate concentration ; and e : disturbance term.

With the dose–response relationship, it is possible to have separate estimates of the benefits from controlling each of the major air pollutants such as sulfurous oxides (SO_x), nitrous oxides (NO_x), TSP, and carbon monoxide (CO). However, as there is a high degree of correlation in the level of air pollutants, especially between TSP and SO_2, most studies consider TSP and SO_2 together. This tradition was followed and it was also assumed that the reduction rate of SO_2 represented the benefits of reducing the concentration of all the pollutants through energy substitution.

Best way to report the result of a dose–response relationship is to use elasticities. Elasticity gives the percentage change in mortality with respect to a 1 per cent change in pollution variable in ambient environment. Freeman reviewed the elasticity measurement from various studies on dose–response relationships.[13)] Of those studies, what was relevant for the present analysis was that of Lave and Seskin.[14)] They presented judgmental magnitudes of elasticities for all pollutants combined from their review of the literature and analysis of the data :

Bronchitis Mortality and Morbidity :	0.5–1.0
Lung Cancer Mortality :	0.5
Respiratory Disease Mortality and Morbidity :	0.5
Cardiovascular Mortality and Morbidity :	0.2
Cancer Mortality :	0.3

Proper dose–response coefficients between mortality and air pollution in the Republic of Korea were not available when the present case study was conducted. Thus, 0.5 was chosen as the elasticity of mortality and morbidity change with respect to the change in the level of combined air pollutants. In the second step, average annual reduction rate of air pollutants was calculated to be 4.37 per cent. By multiplying 0.5 by 4.37 per cent, the mortality and morbidity reduction rate of respiratory disease due to LNG substitution was determined to be 2.18 per cent. The estimated number of reduced mortality and morbidity was calculated by

13) A. Myrick Freeman III, *The Benefits of Environmental Improvement : Theory and Practice*, Johns Hopkins University Press, 1979 ; and Freeman, "The Benefits of Air and Water Pollution Control : A Review and Synthesis of Recent Estimate," Report prepared for the Council on Environmental Quality, December 1979.

14) Lester B. Lave and Eugene P. Seskin, *Air Pollution and Human Health*, Johns Hopkins University Press for the Resources for the Future, 1977.

multiplying 2.18 per cent by the estimated annual number of mortality and morbidity by respiratory disease in Table 3.

|Table 3| Estimated Mortality and Morbidity Caused by Respiratory Disease in the SMR

Year	Population (thousand)	Morbidity			Mortality
		Inpatient	Outpatient	Total	
1981	11,323	4,299	197,804	202,103	718
1986	12,337	4,684	215,518	220,202	782
1991	13,119	4,918	229,179	234,160	832
1996	13,725	5,211	239,765	244,976	870
2001	14,080	5,346	245,966	251,312	892

Step 4 : Effects on receptor → Economic value

After analyzing the dose-response relationships, the benefits of reduced mortality and morbidity from a reduced concentration of suspended particulates and sulfur compounds were evaluated. Economic measure of benefits is the value that people place on reducing the adverse effects of pollution. Several approaches have been developed to assign monetary values to mortality and morbidity. These approaches can be categorized according to either resource or opportunity costs, or according to individual preferences. The "willingness to pay" approach is theoretically consistent with the consumer surplus measure of benefit estimation. However, despite its theoretical weakness, the most common method of calculating the economic measure of human health has been the "human capital and the cost of illness" approach.

The human capital approach values each life lost as the present value of the expected amount of future earnings for that individual if that individual's premature death had been avoided. Morbidity is valued according to the loss of output as measured by earnings or imputed earnings. That approach is based on the validity of the theory of marginal productivity of labor, assuming that the earning reflects the individual's contribution to total economic output.

According to Mishan, the present value of a person's expected future earnings can be calculated as follows :[15)]

$$L_1 = \sum_{t=\tau}^{\infty} Y_t P_\tau^t (1+r)^{-(t-\tau)}$$

where

Y_t=Expected gross earnings by the person during the τth year

P_τ^t=The probability in the current or τ^{th} year of the person being alive during the τth year

r = The social rate of discount expected to rule during the τth year

Alternatively, net output approach can be taken by subtracting C_t, the individual's expected expenditure during τ^{th} year, from Y_t.

Air pollution can adversely affect the productivity of labor force through increased illness and death. Improvement in the level of ambient air quality would lead to an increase in productivity through a reduction in the morbidity and mortality rates. The

15) E. J. Mishan, *Cost-Benefit Analysis* (Third edition), London : George Allen and Unwin, 1982.

economic values of these increases in productivity and reduced costs associated with reductions in morbidity and mortality are the environmental benefits of the LNG project.

Monetary benefits from improved environmental quality are the savings of three major costs : (a) foregone earnings through premature death, sickness, or absenteeism ; (b) increased medical expenses such as the costs of the service of physicians and other medical personnel, and the costs of drugs, hospital facilities, and equipment ; and (c) the psychological costs of pain and discomfort.

Ostro estimated the effect of air pollutants on morbidity using damage functions.[16)] Restricted activity days (RAD) and work loss days (WLD) were regressed to particulates, sulfates, and several socioeconomic variables. Regression results showed that particulates affect both RAD and WLD significantly. The elasticity was 0.45 for WLD and 0.39 for RAD. His equation was used in a detailed study of environmental health risks in Bangkok.[17)]

Calculation of Economic Value

The monetary value of the improved air quality in the SMR caused by the fuel-switching project is the sum of the value of reduced mortality and morbidity over the project's lifespan.

---

16) Bart D. Ostro, "The Effects of Air Pollution on Work Loss and Morbidity," *Journal of Environmental Economics and Management* 10 (1983), pp. 371-82 ; and Ostro, "Air Pollution and Morbidity Revisited : A Specification Test," *Journal of Environmental Economics and Management* 14 (1987), pp. 87-98.

17) USAID, *Ranking Environmental Health Risks in Bangkok*.

Mortality

The willingness to pay to avoid premature death should be estimated based on the people's willingness to pay to reduce the risk of death using the hedonic wage differential or survey method. However, as no such analysis was undertaken in the country, the value of life estimated in the US was adopted and adjusted by comparing per capita income in the Republic of Korea and the US. The value of life in the Republic of Korea calculated by this method was 50 million won per death.

Valuation of Reduced Mortality :

(1) Reduction in pollution : 4.37 per cent

(2) Elasticity of respiratory disease-caused mortality due to pollution : 0.5

(3) Mortality caused by respiratory disease : table 3

(4) Reduced mortality : (1) × (2) × (3)

(5) Economic value : 50 million won × (4)

Morbidity

A. Direct cost

Direct cost is the expenditure on medical care such as doctors, hospitalization, and drugs. Insurance pays 80 per cent of charges for hospitalized patients and 70 per cent of medical costs for outpatients.

Inpatient : average hospitalization days (9.8 days) × daily hospitalization charges

(17,596 won/day) = 172,441 won per case

Outpatient : average visiting days (3.37 days) × average medical cost per visit

(3,407 won/day) = 11,482 won per case

B. Indirect cost

Indirect cost values lost labor productivity due to morbidity.

Inpatient : average hospitalization days (9.8 days) × daily working hours (8 hours/day) × hourly wage (968 won/hour) × share of population actively participating in economic activity (40 per cent) = 30,356 won per case

Outpatient : average visiting days (3.37 days) × daily working hours (8 hours/day) × 1/2 × hourly wage (968 won/hour) × share of population actively participating in economic activity (40 per cent) = 5,219 won per case

Valuation of Reduced Morbidity :

(1) Reduction in pollution : 4.37 per cent

(2) Elasticity of respiratory disease–caused morbidity due to pollution : 0.5

(3) Estimated number of inpatients : n_i

(4) Estimated number of outpatients : n_0

(5) Reduced morbidity : (1) × (2) × [(3) or/and (4)]

(6) Economic value :

[172,441 won + 30,356 won] × (1) × (2) × (3) + [11,482 won + 5,219 won] × (1) × (2) × (4)

3. Caveat

The case presented in this article is very rudimentary and the magnitude of the measured benefit is open to debate. The prime objective of this case study is to explain the necessary steps for monetary valuation of environmental degradation or improvement. The author feels that the application of proper valuation techniques backed up by dependable data will greatly enhance the acceptability of the monetary valuation of environmental quality change in developing countries.

12. Acid Rain Deposition and Impacts in Northeast Asia : Lessons from RAINS-Asia*

I. Overview of RAINS-Asia

In 1990, 12 of the 15 most polluted cities in the world were in Asia, imposing significant threats to human health. Integrated Assessment models help to structure the problem in a consistent way. Such models apply confirmed scientific evidence of the various disciplines to the specific situation in a region. By putting the various aspects into relation to each other such models are valuable tools for gaining insight into costs and benefits of alternative approaches to reduce impacts of air pollution. Therefore, they are most useful both on the nationl level and on the international level when considering international cooperative solutions to avoid or reduce environmental problems caused by air pollution.

RAINS (Regional Air Pollution Information and Simulation)-Asia

---

* "Acid Rain Deposition and Impacts in NEA : Lessons from RAINS-Asia," in Kap-Young Jeong et al. (eds.), *Dynamic Transition and Economic Cooperation in Northeast Asia*, 1997, pp. 165-187.

was aimed to be an integrated acid rain and emissions policy analysis model for the development of national and regional policy perspectives in Asia. RAINS-Asia Project has been carried out by a team of experts from Asia, Europe, and the United States. This broad-based effort has been coordinated by the Asia Technical Department of the World Bank and the Asian Development Bank. The model uses 1990 data as a base year and calculates future energy levels, and environmental impacts through the year 2020 in ten-year time steps.

The RAINS-Asia model covers the countries of East, South, South-East Asia, with particular focus on China, India, Thailand, South and North Korea. The temporal range of all the model is 1990-2020 with the time resolution of one year.

RAINS-Asia consists of four modules,each describing a part of the cause-effect chain. The four basic modules of the RAINS model are as follows :

1. Regional energy scenario generation module (RESGEN)

The RESGEN module estimates present and future energy supply and sectoral energy consumption for a wide variety of socioeconomic and technological assumptions. Using RESGEN, a user can select, review, and modify a number of key parameters at the sub-country (regional) level, including socioeconomic data ; growth rates of energy demand ; energy intensity ; mix of fuels used in each sector ; fuel characteristics ; and electricity supply systems characteristics.

2. Energy and emissions module (ENEM)

The ENEM module uses the information generated by RESGEN to estimate the resulting amounts and patterns of SO_2 emissions, and the costs of various control options. With ENEM, the model user can calculate SO_2 emissions and investigate a number of different emission control options, focusing on reducing the sulfur contained in fuel, either before, during, or after combustion. The following control measures are included :

- use of low sulfur coal, either from naturally occurring low-sulfur coal types, or by some degree of coal washing
- use of low sulfur heavy fuel oil, either from low sulfur crude or oil desulfurized during refining
- use of diesel oil with low sulfur content
- desulfurization during the combustion process
- desulfurization of the flue gas after the combustion

The RAINS model provides "national cost curves" that rank the abatement measures according to their cost-effectiveness. Due to country-specific factors such as energy use patterns and technical infrastructure, national cost curves show significant differences among countries.

3. Atmospheric module (ATMOS)

The ATMOS sub-module provides estimates of ambient levels of acid precursors and acid deposition loading throughout the region under study as a function of changing emission. The projection of acid deposition for future emissions scenarios is based on a transfer matrix for long range transport, which is calculated by using an atmospheric transport/deposition model. For Asia, the deposition fields are calculated with the National Oceanic Atmospheric Administration (NOAA) BAT (Branching Atmospheric Trajectory) model. As inputs, the BAT model requires the area and point source emission rates of SO_2 (from ENEM), meteorological winds and temperature, precipitation rates, and estimates of the dispersion coefficients, dry deposition velocities, and wet scavenging coefficients. The results are aggregated to provide source/receptor information for each of the 94 sub-regions, the acid deposition patterns in the study region, and further aggregated to provide country-to-country source/receptor information.

4. Impact module (IMPACT)

The IMPACT sub-module assesses the sensitivity of various ecosystems (their "critical loads") to acidic deposition, and compares this information to the deposition data generated by the ATMOS module. Critical loads are the maximum long-term deposition level which can be tolerated without damage. By estimating critical loads for various regions and ecosystems, and comparing these natural sensitivities to deposition levels, the IMPACT module allows users to assess the environmental effects of different energy and emisssion scenarios , answering such questions as :

- What regions and ecosystems are most sensitive to acid

deposition?

- What is the geographic scope and extent of ecosystem damage which results from a particular energy scenario?
- What environmental benefits would be realized if a particular emission control strategy were implemented?

In this paper, the World Bank report on "RAINS-Asia : An Assessment Model for Air Pollution in Asia (December 1995)" will be summarized and rearranged to see the impact of and strategies to reduce the deposition of acid rain in Northeast Asia. Northeast Asia here is comprised of China, Japan, South and North Korea, and Mongolia.

II. Energy Module

The results of the Base Case and Low energy scenarios are displayed in Table 1 for each of the 5 Northeast Asian countries and for 39 regions in Table 2. For the Base Case, energy consumption grows at an average rate of 4.0 % per year over the 30-year period in Asia. In aggregate, total energy consumption in Asia would be approximately 130 Exajoules(EJ) in the year 2000 and 275 EJ by 2020. China and India will continue to dominate the regional energy consumption. In 1990, China accounted for 36% of the total regional energy consumption. By 2020, the share will rise to 37% for the Base Case. However, Japan's contribution will fall from 21% in 1990 to 11% in 2020.

|**Table 1**| Total Energy Consumption by Country

(Petajoules/year)

Country	1990	2000		2010		2020	
		Base	Low	Base	Low	Base	Low
China	30,255	50,527	43,438	73,518	59,131	101,016	75,348
Japan	17,866	22,606	20,187	25,679	20,913	28,809	21,535
Korea S	3,594	6,264	5,814	9,497	7,794	13,448	9,743
Korea N	1,764	3,186	2,862	4,980	3,923	7,910	5,455
Mongolia	151	193	178	260	212	361	266
Total	53,630	82,776	72,479	113,934	91,973	151,544	112,347
Asia Total	83,594	129,468	114,669	188,528	154,476	274,121	207,431

Source : Wes Foell, Markus Amann, Greg Carmichel, Michael Chadwick, Jean-Paul Hettelingh, Leen Hordijk, Zhao Dianwu(eds.), *RAINS-Asia : An Assessment Model for Air Pollution in Asia*, Report on the World Bank Sponsored Project "Acid Rain and Emission Reductions in Asia," December 1995, Table 3.8.

The aggregate energy intensity in China is higher than any other large country. It was 2.5 times the level in India in 1990 and 3.5-4 times higher than levels in Indonesia and South Korea. The current and future structure of China's energy use is largely determined by the available indigenous resources. In 1992, coal production was 1,130 million tonnes representing nearly 30% of world production. The average thermal efficiency of China's coal-fired power plants is about 29%. This is due both to continued use of out-of-date technology and to plant sizes, which are too small to capture economies of scale. China has a substantial potential for

Table 2 Total Energy Consumption by Region

(Petajoules)

Country		1990	2000		2010		2020	
			Base	Low	Base	Low	Base	Low
China	Total	30255	50527	43438	73518	59131	101016	75348
	BEIJ	730	1272	1068	1809	1443	2561	1899
	CHON	412	697	605	1032	821	1403	1035
	FUJI	571	958	856	1296	1089	1769	1395
	GUAH	1135	2007	1725	3295	2633	4690	3513
	GUAX	627	1322	1140	1923	1565	2586	1964
	GUAZ	395	610	535	877	713	1120	810
	GUIY	192	267	233	353	290	453	352
	GUIZ	462	759	677	1090	907	1512	1157
	HEHE	4627	7435	6405	11092	8904	14259	10618
	HUBE	978	1906	1670	3106	2554	4721	3627
	HUNA	748	1303	1155	2000	1624	2821	2104
	IMON	1068	1329	1165	1927	1546	2861	2061
	JINU	2595	3961	3407	5917	4767	8726	6531
	JINX	489	866	758	1333	1077	1817	1342
	NEPL	5301	8766	7427	11110	8825	15195	11315
	SHAN	770	1090	927	1628	1295	2250	1589
	SHEN	256	447	379	623	482	890	624
	SHGA	1173	2014	1724	3042	2415	4151	3101
	SHND	1219	2024	1755	3088	2502	4230	3060
	SHNX	1223	1996	1617	2853	2262	3770	2858
	SICH	1653	2949	2581	4299	3536	5757	4437
	TAIY	387	812	667	1182	920	1659	1198
	TIAN	607	1007	841	1559	1224	2153	1546
	WEST	774	1443	1251	2047	1671	2783	2122
	WUHA	487	614	542	827	678	1038	780
	YUNN	718	1584	1398	2440	1991	3466	2600
	ZHEJ	658	1088	932	1768	1399	2377	1710

	Total	3594	6264	5814	9497	7794	13448	9743
	NORT	562	846	776	1310	1065	1920	1380
Korea S	PUSA	1311	1691	1585	2628	2211	3803	2871
	SEOL	1052	2584	2390	3799	3050	5155	3593
	SOUT	668	1143	1063	1761	1468	2570	1899
	Total	17866	22606	20187	25679	20913	28809	21535
	CHSH	2850	3502	3092	3788	3065	4046	3036
	CHUB	3229	4370	3893	5055	4062	5454	4050
Japan	HOTO	2087	2684	2435	3082	2590	3412	2624
	KANT	4277	5401	4831	6290	5115	7692	5709
	KINK	3111	3844	3438	4335	3535	4857	3635
	KYOK	2313	2805	2497	3128	2546	3346	2483
KoreaN	WHOL	1764	3186	2862	4980	3923	7910	5455
Mongolia	WHOL	151	193	178	260	212	361	266
Total		53630	82776	72479	113934	91973	151544	112347
Asia Total		83594	129465	114671	188527	154474	274116	207432

Source : Table 3.9 of the World Bank Report.

improvements in industrial energy efficiency. The most important energy consuming sectors-iron and steel, cement, and chemical-all have a much higher specific energy consumption than observed in developed countries. Main energy consuming equipment such as boilers and electric motors have much lower efficiency than could be obtained by using advanced international technology. Coal is the dominant fuel for urban space heating and cooking in China and the efficiencies are very low. There is a great room for the improvement of energy efficiency in China.

III. Emissions and Control

Developing an accurate and detailed picture of sulfur dioxide emissions in Asia is a crucial component of the RAINS-Asia project and serves multiple purposes. It is an output of the charaterization of the energy and industrial situation that links the economic development of the region with the damage it causes to the environment. By studying the use of fossil fuel for provision of energy services and production levels in industrial manufacturing it is possible to drive the atmospheric transport, transformation, and deposition model, which calculate the temporal and spatial fate of emissions. Subsequently, the impact module estimates the vulnerability of ecosystems to these patterns of deposition. Also, by projecting future change in energy and industrial development, future emissions can be estimated and future threats to the environment assessed.

The goal of ENEM (Energy, Emissions and Control Module) is the development of regional and LPS (large point sources) emission scenarios for 95 regions and 355 LPS included in the RAINS-Asia model and the estimation of the incremental costs of pollution control associated with scenarios that reduce emissions.

Table 3 shows anthropogenic emissions of sulfur dioxide by country, together with emissions from international shipping that comprise the gridded base-year inventory. Total Asian emissions of SO_2 in 1990 is 33.6 million tons, of which China contributed 21.9 million tons.

|**Table 3**| SO_2 Emissions in 1990 from Area Sources and LPS

(Unit : kt SO_2)

Country	Area sources	LPS	Total
China	18,548	3,360	21,908
Korea S	1,542	98	1,640
Japan	818	17	835
Korea N	343	0	343
Mongolia	78	0	78
TOTAL	21,329	3,475	24,804
ASIA TOTAL	28,247	5,428	33,675

Source : Table 4.11 of the World Bank Report.

A powerful feature of the RAINS-Asia model is its capability to explore the effects and costs of emission reduction strategies. Defining a control strategy means prescribing certain emission control measures for specific emission sources. The following groups of emission control options are considered in the RESGEN and RAINS-Asia models :

- energy conservation
- substitution of fuels containing sulfur by those with less or no sulfur
- desulfurization of fuels before combustion
- desulfurization before and after combustion

The first two emission control options are explored in the energy scenario generation module (RESGEN). But dusulfurization before, during, and after combustion is directly related to reducing SO_2

|**Table 4**| Total SO_2 Emissions by Region (Area Sources plus LPS) in 1990

(unit : kt SO_2)

Country	Region	Emission
	Beijing	270.3
	Chongqing	974.2
	Fuijian	297.9
	Guangdong-Hainan	705.6
	Guangxi	800.7
	Guangzhou	231.3
	Guiyang	340.2
	Guizhou	785.6.
	Hebei-Anhui-Henah	3084.9
	Hubei	426.4
	Hunan	394.3
	Nei Mongolia-Ningxia	689.8
	Jiangsu	2108.6
China	Jingxi	334.6
	Heilongjiang-Jilin-Liaoning	2491.1
	Shanghai	507.4
	Shenyang	102.3
	Shaanxi-Gansu	827.4
	Shandong	1061.9
	Shanxi	632.4
	Sichuan	2336.1
	Taiyuan	199.8
	Tianjin	231.8
	Tibet-Quinghai-Xinjiang Uygur	348.1
	Wuhan	316.1
	Yunnan	874.9
	Zhejiang	534.5

Japan	Chugoku-Shikoku	162.0
	Chubu	157.6
	Hokkaido-Tohoku	110.2
	Kanto	167.9
	Kinki	125.1
	Kyushu-Okinawa	112.7
Korea-North		343.1
Korea-South	Northern Province	246.2
	Pusan	606.0
	Seoul-Inchon	499.1
	Southern Province	289.0
Mongolia		77.7
Asia Total		33674.7

Source : Table 4.12 of the World Bank Report.

emissions. These options are treated in the energy and emissions (ENEM) module of RAINS-Asia.

|**Table 5**| Technical Options to Reduce SO_2 Emissions Considered in ENEM

Technical SO_2 Control Option	SO_2 Removal Efficiency or Final Sulphur % Achieved
Oil Desulphurization / Heavy Fuel Oil	0.6 % S
Oil Desulphurization / Diesel	0.3 - 0.05 % S
Low Sulfur Coal	0.6 % S
Coal Washing	50 %
Limestone Injection or Fluidized Bed Combustion	50 %
Wet Limestone Scrubbing (FGD)	90 %
Regenerative processes	98 %

Source : Table 4.13 of the World Bank Report.

In future work, it will be important to add emissions of nitrooxides, in order to obtain a complete picture of acidifying pollutants and to be able to assess the urban air pollution situation. This will necessitate new emphasis on the transportation sector. As the project moves into the phase of assessing costs and emissions under future scenarios, it is important that RAINS-Asia uses appropriate technologies for the Asian context and also appropriate cost, performance, and application data for these technologies. Note that in Phase I the technology characteristics are largely based on European and North American experience. An Asian technology characterization data base is needed that could be used within the model and also for stand alone analyses.

IV. ATMOS Module

The ATMOS module is a long range transport and deposition model which calculates the ambient concentrations, and the wet and dry deposition of SO_2 and sulfate resulting from emissions from area and large point sources. The matrix which provides annual deposition of sulfur as a function of SO_2 emissions is the product of ATMOS module. The calculation of this matrix requires the use of a long range transport model. Such a model was developed as a part of Phase-I effort.

The ATMOS module requires as inputs the emission rates of the species of interest and the location of the sources, meteorological winds, temperature, and precipitation rates. The model traces sulfur emissions from both area (surface) sources and large point sources (LPS).

1. ATMOS modeling results

The high sulfur deposition follow closely the spatial distribution and the density of the emissions. For example, the dense emission regions in eastern and southern China, South Korea, northern Thailand, and eastern India all show elevated sulfur deposition. The deposition patterns in Asia have a strong seasonal variation.

2. Source-recetor relationships

The ATMOS module calculates the deposition from each source directly and this information can be used to analyze a variety of policy-related questions. For example, the deposition from a specific LPS, region, or country can be viewed separately. This information can also be used to identify which sources contribute to the deposition at a specified receptor and this information can be aggregated to provide source-receptor information at a country-to-country or region-to-region level. Table 6 demonstrates the impact of China's sulfur deposition in the region. Column 2 shows 83% of the sulfur deposited in China is from Chinese sources and 97% of China's emissions fall either within China or on the region's oceans. The remaining 3% can account for significant percentages of the neighboring countries' total deposition as seen in column three. For example, 35% of the sulfur deposited in North Korea is due to

Chinese emissions. Table 7 shows that South Korea contributes 37% of North Korea's total sulfur deposition while North Korea contributes only 1.2% of South Korea's total sulfur deposition.

|Table 6| China's Contribution to Sulfur Deposition in the Region

Receptor	% of China's Deposition	% of Receptor's Total Deposition
China	83	96
Oceans	14	36
Korea S	0.4	13
Japan	0.5	10
Korea N	0.8	35
Mongolia	0.2	48

Source : Table 5.3b of the World Bank Report.

|Table 7| Other Country's Contribution to Sulfur Deposition in Receptor Countries

Receptor / Contributor	% of Receptor's Total Deposition (Korea S)	% of Receptor's Total Deposition (Japan)	% of Receptor's Total Deposition (Korea N)	% of Receptor's Total Deposition (Mongolia)
China	13	9.6	35	48
Korea S	83	7.1	37	0.01
Japan	0.5	36.8	0.05	0
Korea N	1.2	0.6	29	0.01
Mongolia	0.01	0.002	0.06	52

Japan : Volcano ⇒ 46%
Source : Calculated based on Table 5.3a of the World Bank Report.

The distribution of surface concentrations follow closely the emission distribution and density. Elevated SO_2 values are found throughout on Asia. Direct environmental impacts to sensitive forest and crops can occur at levels of 20 to 30$\mu g/m^3$. Vast areas of China and Korea exceed these levels.

3. Preliminary model evaluation

Calculated annual sulfate deposition amounts can be compared with available observational data in Asia. While the data for direct comparison is limited, it is possible to undertake a preliminary comparison. The most comprehensive data set on acid deposition in Asia exists in Japan. Japan Environmental Protection Agency has operated a country-wide network for many years. The model tends to underpredict the deposition. This is likely due to the fact that the monitoring sites are largely located in or near major urban areas. In the Phase-I of the RAINS-Asia project, it was learned that a meaningful model performance evaluation is not available because of lack of dependable observed data. For the Phase-I study, passive samplers were used to get ambient SO_2 data. The new passive samplers offer a low-cost means of obtaining long-term ambient average sulfur dioxide concentrations throughout Asia. These simple inexpensive (U.S. $35 per sampler including manufacturing, mailing, and analysis) devices can obtain weekly to monthly average sulfur dioxide levels.

V. Impact Module

This module has attempted to create maps of sensitivity and critical loads. The critical load signifies the exposure to one or more pollutants below which significant harmful effects on the specific elements do not occur according to present knowledge. In other words, the highest deposition of compounds that will not cause chemical changes leading to harmful effects on ecosystem structure and function is defined as the critical load.

Sufur deposition gives rise to acidification and, once critical loads have been exceeded, ecosystem damage may occur. Deposition of acidifying compounds such as $(NH_4)SO_4$, HNO_3, and $(NH_4)_2SO_4$ leads to ecosystem acidification, to a degree which is dependent on biological transformation and ion leaching.

Acidic deposition has caused acidification of surface waters, fish mortality and other ecological changes in large areas of central and northern Europe and eastern parts of North America. In Asia damage has been reported to forest and crops, although it is yet undetermined whether these occurrences should be attributed to indirect pollution processes such as acidification.

Comparison of critical loads with actual sulfur deposition shows the degree of exceedance. The areas with the largest excess when 1990 data were used were southeast China, Thailand, parts of Indonesia, Korea, the south of Japan and small areas in Phillipines. The 25-percentile critical loads were used for this comparison, meaning that in areas where no excess occurs at least 75% of the natural systems are 'protected'.

The present and projected high rates of economic growth in Asia, and the consequent increase in emissions of SO_2 and the excess of critical loads that would result, suggest that many natural and associated systems in Asia may eventually be at risk from acidification. Thus, the use of critical load values, as indicators of deposition limits, should enable some of the adverse effects, encountered in European lakes and forests, to be avoided.

Deposition alone is not the only cause of increased risk of damage. Atmospheric concentrations (of sulfur dioxide, nitrogen oxides and ozone) have been shown to cause direct damage to natural ecosystems and crops, as well as having health effects in large urban areas. In fact, in many parts of Asia, the concern for urban air quality is increasing and air concentration of SO_2 may already reach dangerous levels. Determination of critical levels for SO_2, along the lines of European work, needs to be undertaken. Critical levels (concentrations below which no damage is expected) have been formulated for ozone, sulfur dioxide and nitrogen oxides. The assessment of environmental benefits of emission reductions should include both levels and loads simultaneously.

VI. Scenarios of Future Acidification in Asia

RAINS-Asia explored the potential impacts on acidification of future scenarios of energy development in Asia. To provide a basis for the analysis of emissions and emission control strategies, the RESGEN module of the RAINS model was used to develop two alternative energy pathways : One of them is the base case energy pathway,resembling 'business as usual' practices. The other is an energy efficient pathway which explores the possible reduction of emissions through a strong effort to use energy more efficiently.

1. Reference emission scenario

This scenario assumes that there will be no additional control measures beyond what is required by current legislation in Japan and Taiwan. Due to the strong growth in economic activities and subsequent energy consumption, SO_2 emission in the region will increase significantly from 33.6 million tons in 1990 to more than 110 million tons in 2020, a 230 percent increase. The increase in SO_2 emissions is strongly connected to the use of coal. Coal combustion is responsible for about three quarters of the total emissions over the whole period under study. In Japan, SO_2 emissions would increase about 30 percent, while in other fast developing countries, the predicted expansion reach a factor of four to five.

The boost in SO_2 emissions resulting from the high growth in energy consumption will cause a strong increase in sulfur deposition throughout the region. In major areas in eastern and southern China and in some parts of Japan, sulfur deposition will increase by a factor of two to three, with places which increases up to a factor of five. A factor of five is also observed in many regions such as India, Korea and Thailand. Analysis shows that under the reference emission scenario, critical loads will be exceeded in many regions in

|**Table 8**| SO_2 Emissions in 1990 and for the Reference Scenario in the Year 2020

(1,000 tons of SO_2)

Country	1990	Reference Scenario 2020	Increase
China	21908	60687	177 %
Japan	835	1120	34 %
Korea North	343	1345	292 %
Korea South	1640	5537	238 %
Mongolia	78	168	115 %
Sea Lanes	243	511	110 %
Asia Total	33674	110477	228 %

Source : Table 7.1 of the World Bank Report.

Asia. In southern and eastern China, in Korea and in Northern Thailand, widespread serious excess deposition has to be expected. Highest excess deposition (up to 15 to 20 grams sulfur per square meter per year) is calculated for some ecosystems in Korea, the Bangkok metropolitan region, and in the Sichuan and Shanghai provinces. For comparison, total sulfur deposition in many of these areas is currently in the range of two to three grams. High deposition is always linked to sufficiently high levels of ambient concentrations. High ambient levels of SO_2 concentrations resulting from this scenario do not only imply serious risks to natural and agricultural ecosystems, but impose also serious threat to human health. Based on the above analysis,it can be expected that the growth in SO_2 emissions associated with the increased energy use gives reason for serious concern about maintaining sustainable conditions for natural and agricultural ecosystems in Asia. The following sections explore costs and environmental benefits of alternative strategies for reducing SO_2 emissions.

2. Best available technology (BAT) scenario

This scenario assumes the application of the best current available technologies in many developed countries. Measures assumed for the 'best available technology'(BAT) scenario are :

- Flue gas desulfurization (wet limestone scrubbing) for all (existing and new) large power stations (LPS) burning coal and oil
- Flue gas desulfurization (wet limestone scrubbing) for all large industrial boilers
- Use of low sulfur fuel (coal, heavy fuel oil, gasoil) for all other users

According to this scenario, SO_2 emissions from this region would decline from 33.6 to 16.3 million tons between 1990 and 2020. Declining emissions will result in reduced sulfur deposition and the sulfur deposition will decrease below the critical loads almost everywhere in the region. A major exception is the border area between Hunan and Jiangxi provinces in China, where sensitive ecosystems are located in regions with intense economic activity. Additional isolated 'hot spots' occur in India, Thailand and Korea. The reduction of SO_2 emission with BAT scenario has its price. The costs estimates here reflect annualized full life cycle costs.

In the year 2020, full application of advanced emission control technologies would require 90 billion US $ per year, which is about 0.59 percent of the regional GDP assumed for the underlying energy scenario. For comparison, the relative costs for the latest aggreement on reducing sulfur emissions in Europe (the Oslo protocol) were only about one third of this level (0.21 percent of the GDP).

3. Advanced emission control technology (ACT) scenario

BAT is costly way of achieving lower sulfur deposition. A more cost effective way would be to reduce the overachievement of the critical loads by selecting only the most cost effective measures to reduce emissions. ACT scenario assume the application of advanced control technologies (wet flue gas desulfurization) only for new large emission sources in the power plant, the industrial and refinery sectors. Emissions from existing power stations and from small sources in the industry are assumed to be controlled through the use of low sulfur fuels. Measures for ACT scenario are :

- Flue gas desulfurization for all new power stations
- Flue gas desulfurization for all large industrial boilers in refineries
- Low sulfur fuels for boilers in industry (100% of liquid fuels and 50% of coal consumption)
- Low sulfur fuels for the domestic and transport sectors (100% of total consumption)

The ACT scenario produces 50 percent increase of emissions at level of 50.4 million tons. However, this level is still less than half of the unabated level of 110 million tons. Selecting only the most cost-effective measures reduces costs. From more than 90 billion US $ per year (costs for the BAT scenario in 2020) costs drop to 39 billion US $ per year. Consequently, compared to GDP the strategy would only take a share of 0.25 percent, which is already close to the 0.21 percent level currently discussed in Europe. In China, where the BAT strategy would consume 1.7 percent of GDP, limiting measures to the more cost-effective technologies will reduce the share to 0.59 percent of GDP. ACT scenario shows that Korea and some Chinese provinces would have excess deposition, whereas in most other regions the critical loads could be achieved.

4. Basic control technology (BCT) scenario

Experience shows that developing countries often have limited access to the necessary technical and financial resources needed to implement advanced technological solutions. Consequently, preference is often given to less advanced approaches readily available on the domestic market. BCT scenario assumes that in China, India, and Pakistan emissions from new large point sources are controlled by domestic technology (with a typical removal efficiency of about 50 percent) rather than by advanced flue gas cleaning methods (with efficiencies of more than 90 percent). Due to the applications of less efficient control technologies, the remaining emissions in all three countries will be higher than in the advanced technology scenario. For China, SO_2 emissions in the year 2020 would amount to 38.1 million tons (an increase of 77 percent) while the growth rate was 37 percent in the ACT scenario. Most interesting, however, is the fact that total costs are close to the levels of the ACT scenario. This can be explained by the fact that the RAINS model calculates and compares total life cycle costs of emission control equipment. Table 9 summaizes emissions and costs from the three emission control scenarios discussed up to now. Obviously, there is a clear trade-off between emission levels, control costs and eco-systems's protection.

|**Table 9**| Emissions and Control Cost for the BAT, ACT and BCT Scenarios in the Year 2020

Country	SO_2 Emissions (thousand tons of SO_2)			SO_2 Control Costs (million US $/yr)		
	BAT	ACT	BCT	BAT	ACT	BCT
China	6672	29932	38124	34230	11975	12712
Japan	393	1047	1047	6132	3458	3458
Korea N	75	7075	7075	3087	1089	1089
Korea S	552	1469	1469	3769	3214	3214
Mongolia	13	81	81	138	56	56
Asia Total	16321	50396	62822	90424	38877	40108

Source : Table 7.3 of the World Bank Report.

5. Local application of advanced technologies (LCAT) scenario

Earlier versions of the RAINS model implemented for Europe

contain optimization of emission control measures and have been used to identify optimized abatement scenarios as a starting point for international negotiations. By directing advanced control measures to ecologically sensitive areas and relaxing control requirements at less sensitive locations, it is possible to reduce control costs further without increasing environmental damage. China is currently exploring similar approaches by requesting only power stations in ecologically sensitive regions to reduce emissions. Table 10 shows that significant cost reduction is possible in China with the LACT scenario. In this scenario, the emission from low income countries remain uncontrolled and the countries with higher per capita income control their emissions as in the ACT scenario.

|**Table 10**| Emissions and Control Costs in 2020 for China in the LACT Scenario

Country	Emission (thousand tons SO_2)			Costs (million US$)		
	LACT	BCT	ACT	LACT	BCT	ACT
China	37904	38124	29932	8505	12609	12063

Source : Table 7.4 of the World Bank Report.

From Table 10, it can be derived that focusing advanced emission control measures on ecologically sensitive regions would result in emissions roughly comparble to the basic technology case, at only two thirds of the costs. In the LCAT case, ecosystems protection is slightly lower than in the ACT scenario, while costs decline substantially. The scenario demonstrates that targeting control measures could substantially increase the cost-effectiveness of strategies.

6. Relocation of plants in sensitive regions

An alternative approach to protect sensitive ecosystems-or to avoid the occurrence of 'hot spots', i.e., areas with peak excess deposition-would be to locate new power stations in less sensitive regions.Point sources make a significant,and often dominant, contribution to local deposition. Consequently, measures that focus on a few specific sources could significantly improve the local situation. The RAINS model could be used to explore the impact of reducing emissions at these power stations by introducing various emission control options. Another way to limit environmental impacts could be to move individual stations to less sensitive areas.

7. Energy efficiency pathway

SO_2 emission level is crucially dependent on the energy scenarios, and the energy policies promoting energy efficiency and use of cleaner fuels are important instruments to reduce pollution and pollution control costs. With control strategy based on the energy efficiency pathway, SO_2 emissions would be consistently lower than in the base case energy path. Consequently, emission control strategies based on the energy efficiency pathway provide better protection for the ecosystems than would result from the base case. Furthermore, Table 11 shows that, despite the lower emission levels resulting from the various control scenarios, the costs for achieving the lower emissions are also about 30 percent below the costs of the base case energy pathway.

|Table 11| Comparison of Emission Control Costs for the Base Case Energy Pathway and the Energy Efficiency Pathway

Energy Pathway		Emission Control Scenario			
		No Further Control (NFC)	Basic Control Technology (BCT)	Advanced Control Technology (ACT)	Best Available Technology (BAT)
Emissions (million tons SO_2)	Base case	110.5	62.8	50.4	16.3
	Efficiency	80.1	47.1	39.1	12.4
Costs (billion $/yr)	Base case	3.9	40.1	38.8	90.4
	Efficiency	2.0	26.9	25.5	65.6

Source : Table 7.6 of the World Bank Report.

VII. Conclusion

As the economic cooperation dialogues at the so called natural economic territories in Northeast Asia increase, the concerns and discussions on environmental cooperation as well as on improvement of mutual political and economic relations have been increasing. However, the size and impact of transboundary acid rain in the region had not been seriously investigated so far due to lack of monitoring stations and ecological research.

The application of RAINS–Asia model in this region indicates that currently observed trends in energy consumption will impose significant environmental threats to a variety of ecosystems in many areas of Asia, if no countermeasures were taken. The observed and expected future growth of economic activities and energy consumption will increase SO_2 emission and it will severely threaten the sustainable basis of many natural and agricultural ecosystems in the region.

There is a variety of measures that can be taken to reduce SO_2 emissions and thereby avoid widespread excess deposition in the region. The analysis also shows that carefully designed energy policies could promote energy efficiency and reduce SO_2 emission.

The RAINS-Europe model has been used in the negotiations that led to the signing the Second Sulphur protocol. This protocol contains SO_2 emission reduction requirements for the 33 signatories which have largely been based on calculations with RAINS-Europe. For the time being it will be difficult to replicate the experiences of Europe to Northeast Asia to reduce SO_2 emission. Especially China is reluctant to discuss the transboundary air pollution problems and Japan has a reservation on establishing new regional environmental cooperation body and on assuming the financial burdens.

The experiences accumulated so far show that specialists meeting or nonofficial meetings were more effective channel of exchanging useful informations than the official intergovernmental meetings.

Even though the RAINS-Asia is useful for the integrated assessment of strategies to keep SO_2 emissions from energy use at acceptable levels, the model still is in a development stage. Special attention should be devoted to validation of the various models and data bases developed in the first phase of the RAINS-Asia project.

It will be worthwhile to improve the Rains–Asia model and application in the Northeast Asia for regional environmental cooperation.

13. Economic Analysis of Transboundary Air Pollution in Northeast Asia*

I. Introduction

There is a growing concern over the transboundary air pollution problems such as acid rain and global warming. Acid rain has the ecological consequences in that it affects the soil, vegetation, especially forests and lakes. It causes economic damage to manmade structures and it also affects human health. The western countries, however, dealt with the acid rain issue properly and the damage from it has been decreasing. On the other hand, Northeast Asia, surrounded by the fast growing, most populous countries, confronts growing risk from the acid deposition.

Most of the countries have predominantly relied on non-market policy instruments to reduce the levels of sulphur dioxide emissions into the atmosphere. The most common instruments implemented

* "Economic Analysis of Transboundary Air Pollution in Northeast Asia," in Kap-Young Jeong and et al. (eds.), *Toward New Dimensions of Cooperation in Northeast Asia*, Institute of East and West Studies, Yonsei University, 1998, pp. 163-196.

are emission standards for large point sources, fuel quality standards, and national emission ceilings such as those set down by the Oslo Protocol in Europe. However, in recent years, market instruments for sulphur emission control have been introduced in the U.S. while Scandinavian countries introduced charges upon the emissions of a number of air pollutants including sulphur dioxide.

Not all environmental problems are amenable to market-based solutions. What makes acid rain such a good candidate for applying market-based mechanism is its large geographic scale. The long distances and great number of sources support the underlying environmental premise of the acid rain trading programme. Sensitive ecosystems will be protected and improved by reductions in deposition regardless of which particular sources are controlled or to what specific degree.

There are basically two positions in dealing with regional acid rain control proposals. One is cost-sharing principle and the other is strict "polluter pays" principle. The cost-sharing position stems from the view that the acid rain is a regional problem, solution of which can be found through cooperation among countries within the same atmospheric region. "Polluter pays" position sees the problem as simple externality and insists that the polluter should compensate for the loss inflicted upon the polluted countries. To understand the potential contribution of economic instruments, it is necessary to study the current institutional framework for handling the problems. Experience shows that economic instruments are usually applied as supplements to existing regulations and the form they take is affected by the existing institutional structure.

In this paper we will study the economic instruments and cooperative mechanisms applied to the acid rain problems in the U.S. and Europe to get some lessons for Northeast Asia. In the following chapter, the U.S. sulfur emission trading programme will be evaluated and the development of cooperative mechanism in Europe will be surveyed in some detail. In chapter 3, the energy consumption and sulfur emission trends in Northeast Asia will be reviewed first and then the source-receptor relationship with acid deposition will be introduced. Chapter 4 utilizes the survey of Chapter 2 to shed a light on finding optimal cooperative approach toward Northeast Asian acid rain problem. Chapter 5 is Summary and Conclusion.

II. Cooperative Mechanism to Control Sulfur Deposition in Western Countries

1. U.S. Sulfur Emission Trading Programme

1) Background and Objective

On November 15, 1990, the U.S. Clean Air Act Amendments became law. Title IV of this eleven-title Act contains the acid rain control programme which directly addresses the problems of long range transport and transformation of air pollutants. The objectives of the acid rain programme are to reduce the adverse impacts of acid deposition through a 10 million ton reduction in the annual SO_2 emission and an NOX reduction of around 2 million tons from the 1980 levels ; and to achieve these reductions at the lowest costs by employing traditional methods and an emission allowance trading system (Klaassen 1996, p. 145). The outstanding features of the acid rain control programme are its relative stringency and its market-based implementation scheme. The acid rain control programme and its emissions allowance trading system provide an interesting case study in public policy development and offer useful lessons for the greenhouse gas debate. The emission trading scheme allows utilities to choose the most cost-efficient way to reduce emissions. Each allowance permits an emission unit to emit one ton of SO_2 during or after a specific year. An allowance is defined as a limited authorization to emit SO_2. However, it does not constitute a property right and does not limit the authority of the U.S. to terminate or limit such authorization (U.S. Congress 1990, pp. 2591-2592).

The environmental community's support for emissions trading depends on the integrity of both the reduction targets and the trading system itself. The most important provision uniting the government with the environmentalists was the cap on total SO_2 emissions. The "cap-cum-trading" deal forged an alliance that effectively disarmed acid rain control opponents and paved the way to the first acid rain control legislation and the first extensive market-based provisions in U.S. environmental law (Kete 1992, P. 83).

Although SO_2 emissions in the United States had declined from their peak of 33 million tons in 1973 to 25.9 million tons in 1980, the 1990 Clean Air Act Amendments set a goal of further reducing SO_2 by 10 million tons below the 1980 level to protect public health and the environment. Total SO_2 emissions were around 23 million tons in 1985. In the same year, electric utilities emitted 16 million tons. The acid rain program establishes a national cap on the SO_2 emissions of all utilities of 8.95 million tons/year. This is a reduction of around 10 million tons, comparable to the 1980 level of the electric utility emissions. This cap is to be implemented in two phases. Phase I starts in 1995 and requires the 110 highest emitting electric utility plants in 21 eastern and midwestern states to meet an interim ceiling of 5.7 million tons. Phase II begins in 2000 and will include not only these 110 units but also smaller, cleaner plants throughout the U.S. With Phase II, a national cap of 8.95 million tons of SO_2 is placed on the number of allowances. Initial allowances are allocated for each year beginning 1995. At the end of each year, each unit must hold allowances at least equal to its annual emissions. Furthermore, regardless of the number of allowances a unit holds, it is never entitled to exceed the ambient air quality standards for public health. The unit is free to buy the allowances, but it might not be able to use them to increase emissions if this threatens to violate ambient standards (Klaassen 1996, p. 146).

2) Evaluation

It is too early to evaluate the success of sulfur trading scheme in the U.S., because Phase I only started in 1995. However, it is possible to study the expected cost savings, to compare expected market activity and prices with reality, and to analyze the circumstances that have influenced the market so far. Table 1 shows that sulfur trading programme has the potential to cut costs by

US$9.4 to $13.4 billion over the life time of the program. This is a reduction in costs of 40 to 45 percent. Here, costs consist of direct pollution control cost measures and the administrative implementation costs. The pollution control cost estimates are based on a linear programming model and assume a perfect permit market. Implementation costs consist of allowance system, monitoring, and permit costs (Klaassen 1996, p. 148).

|**Table 1**| Expected Cost Savings of Sulfur Trading (1995-2010)

(million US$, 1990 value)

Type of costs		Traditional control	National trading program	Cost savings
Pollution control		19,000 to 30,900	9,500 to 17,100	9,600 to 13,800
Implementation	Allowance system	0	207 to 416	−207 to −416
	Monitoring	2,512	2,395	117
	Permits	0	68	−68
Total costs		21,612 to 33,412	12,170 to 19,979	9,442 to 13,433

Sources : ICF (1991, 1992), quoted from Ger Klaassen, *Acid Rain and Environmental Degradation : The Economics of Emission Trading*, IIASA, 1996, p. 149.

The evidence thus far indicates that the program has been largely successful. However actual allowance trading was not so much as expected. There are various ways to achieve compliance under Title IV in addition to allowance trading. Those are intra-firm reallocation of emission allowances, fuel switching and/or blending, installing scrubbers (flue gas desulphurization), retiring plants, repowering plants, energy conservation, reduced utilization, and substitution among facilities. In principle an active allowance market is neither a necessary nor sufficient condition for cost effectiveness. However, under Title IV, allowances are allocated on the basis of historic emissions without reference to cost, so one might anticipate ample trading. In fact not much allowance trading has occurred, but the prices of abatement options available to utilities have undergone dramatic changes since 1990. These changes stem from changes in the prices of rail transport of low sulfur coal and increased productivity in mining as well as from innovations in the use of fuel blending and in the design and use of scrubbers. However we can hypothesize that the changes in compliance costs are to a significant degree attributable to regulatory innovation embodied in Title IV. Even in the absence of robust allowance trading, the program has empowered utilities with the flexibility to take advantage of exogenous changes in input markets, such as a decline in the cost and an increase in the availability of low sulfur coal. Moreover this flexibility has promoted competition between input markets, which in turn has encouraged innovation and amplified cost savings. Hence, success to date is the result of fundamental regulatory reform of environmental regulation that has promoted efficient implementation through economic competition. Nonetheless, future performance standards may not be sufficient if low sulfur coal markets become constrained, especially after the year 2000 when phase II of Title IV will greatly expand the program's coverage. Firms then may face widely disparate marginal costs for compliance, and allowance trading may become essential to the program's success (Burtraw 1996, p. 81).

Next question is why the price of allowance has been far below forecast. Table 2 presents the range of price forecasts and realizations over the last few years. Before the passage of the Clean Air Act, estimates of marginal abatement costs were as high as $1,500 per ton, which is the figure stipulated in the Act for direct allowance sales by the EPA. In debates surrounding the 1990 amendments, the EPA cited estimates of marginal abatement costs about half as high, and these costs became the basis for estimates of allowance process. Since passage, estimates have fallen further. Thorough the first half of 1995, the price of allowances traded privately was about $179 and fell to the low $100s by year's end. The marginal price of 1995 allowances in the EPA auction administered by the Chicago Board of Trade (CBOT) has ranged from $122 to $140 (Burtraw 1996, p. 83).

|Table 2| Marginal Cost Estimates and Realizations for Compliance Options

Industry Estimates Pre-1989	EPA 1990 Estimate	Early Allowance Trades	Early 1995 Allowance Trades*	1993 CBOT Allowance Auction	1994 CBOT Allowance Auction	1995 CBOT Allowance Auction
$1500	$750	$250	$170	$122	$140	$126

*Rico, 1995.

Table 3 presents three estimates of the phase I compliance activities of utilities. Over half of the plants affected by phase I are fuel switching and/or blending. The next most common strategy is intra-utility offsets among facilities and pre-phase I actions. Compliance is achieved by either over-compliance in one facility (accompanied under-compliance in another facility) and/or reaching compliance criteria prior to phase I in order to earn bonus allowances. Scrubber installations have been less common. Inter-utility allowance trading also has been less common. As of 1995, only 12 utilities have bought more than 5,000 emission allowances from other companies. From March 1994 through March 1995, the first year of the EPA's Allowance Tracking Program, about 28.9 million allowances were transferred between utilities or from brokers or fuel companies to utilities (USEPA 1995).

|**Table 3**| Comparison of Compliance Strategies Estimates

Compliance Strategy	GAO (94)	Rico (95)	EIA (94)
Switch and/or Blend Coal	55%	63%	59%
Purchase Allowances[a]	3%	9%	15%
Install Scrubbers	16%	11%	10%
Pre-Phase I Compliance[b]	18%	15%	10%
Switch to natural Gas/Oil	5%	1%	3%
Retire Plants/Repowering	3%	1%	2%
Total	100%	100%	99%

a. The EIA find that 15 percent of utilities are using allowances in combination with other strategies.
b. For Rico (1995) and GAO (1994), this includes reduced utilization, and substitution of Phase II sources.

3) Lessons from the Experience

Following observations were made available after almost two years of operating experience with the sulfur emission trading in the

United States (McLean 1996, pp. 148–149).

First, traditional operating permits can be greatly simplified with rigorous emission monitoring and flexibility of an allowance system. There is no need for setting source–specific emission limits, specifying control technology, or requiring detailed compliance schedules.

Second, transaction costs can be made very small because the government involvement in an allowance transation simply involves recordation, not case–by–case review of approval, and the source has numerous venues in which to transact allowances.

Third, the ability to bank allowances can reduce cost and lead to significant early emissions reduction.

Fourth, continuous emission monitoring can be expensive, particularly for installation of elevators and platforms for tall stacks and for frequent quality assurance, but accurate monitoring and timely reporting are also critical to the credibility of the entire trading program and their cost is modest when compared to the overall cost savings. The cost of monitoring at over 2000 sources for SO_2, NO_X, and CO_2 has been estimated at about $200 to $300 million per year compared to the cost savings for the SO_2 program alone of $2 to $3 billion per year.

Fifth, phasing in the participation of sources can complicate administration and undermine achievement of emission reduction goals and has been perhaps the most serious flaw of the SO_2 allowance program. Approximately 75 percent of the cost of developing and implementing the permitting provisions of Title IV and at least one third of the cost of developing and operating the allowance tracking system, or about $6.6 million, can be attributed to the complexity of Phase I. In retrospect, all affected sources should have been included from the outset in Phase I with emission limitations tightened in Phase II to accomplish the goals of the program.

Sixth, capping total emissions coupled with allowance system compliance flexibility are compatible with electric power industry restructuring. The power industry in the U.S. is currently undergoing a major restructuring from regulated monopolies to the one open to national competitions on price and availability. A cap and trade program accommodates a dynamic market situation by ensuring that total emissions will not increase and by allowing costs of emissions control to follow shifts in production and emissions.

Seventh, cost savings can exceed expectations. Since 1990, the projected cost of compliance with the full SO_2 emission reductions has declined from $4 billion per year to less than $2.0 billion per year, against an annualized cost of compliance without trading of $4.9 billion.

Eighth, governmental administrative costs can be much lower than traditional programme. By streamlining permitting, eliminating case-by-case review of trades, removing government participation in compliance decisions, and focusing instead on the measurement of emissions produced by affected sources, considerable public resources can be saved. One governmental decision not eliminated by the allowance system is the need to allocate allowances. This usually requires some consideration of historical utilization and emissions information. For an allowance trading program this activity occurs once for all participating sources at the beginning of the program.

Initial allocation process in the SO_2 allowance program was made unnecessarily costly and long, and provoked litigation. Approximately one third of the cost of developing and supporting the allowance trading program, or about $1.4 million, can be attributed to this factor. Allowance formulas and data requirements can and should be kept to a minimum with requirements defined clearly and consistently.

2. Regional Cooperation to Control Sulfur Emissions in Europe

1) Acidification in Europe

The European Monitoring and Evaluation Programme (EMEP) was set up in 1978 to monitor the movement of pollutants, and to determine where the deposition of pollutants released from each source occurs. The surface of Europe is divided into squares with grid lines 150 km apart. There are about 100 monitoring sites which are used in the EMEP model and, which are termed arrival points (Newbery 1990, p. 302). The information generated by EMEP is remarkably useful, not only in quantifying the level of pollution, but also in identifying efficient and feasible abatement policies. The information on deposition can be used to draw maps showing the average acidity of precipitation over Europe using contour lines of increasing levels of acidity. The EMEP tables can also be used to throw light on the political economy of pollution control.

Next question one can ask of the EMEP data is whether there are significant opportunities for bilateral bargaining between pairs of countries over pollution levels. One way to identify such opportunities is to look for instances where the volume of bilateral pollution exchange is large relative to total depositions, and where trade is bilateral rather than unilateral. Bilateralism can be measured by the difference between exports and imports. Another possible question to ask is which pairs of countries have large net trade balances in pollution which might lead to financial negotiations over pollution levels. The following countries have net imports from another country which are greater than 5 percent of total depositions : Poland from GDR (19%) ; Denmark from GDR (12%) ; Scandinavia from GDR (10%) ; Scandinavia from Poland (9%) ; USSR from Poland (9%) and so on (Newbery 1990, p. 306).

2) Regional Cooperation

(1) The Convention on Long-range Transboundary Air Pollution (CLRTAP)

It was not until the 1972 United Nations Conference on the Human Environment that the threat posed by acid rain was put on the international agenda. The UN conference accepted the principle that states must ensure that activities within their jurisdiction of control do not cause damage to the environments of other states. A Swedish case study in 1972 confirmed the damaging impact of sulfur and acid precipitation on materials and ecosystems. OECD (Organization for Economic Cooperation and Development) conducted an international study to estimate the local and foreign contribution to each country's deposition of sulfur in 1977 and 1979. This study came to the conclusion that long-range transport of sulfur compounds was indeed occurring. It showed among other things that more than 50 percent of the atmospheric sulfur deposition in Austria, Finland, Norway, Sweden, and Switzerland came from foreign sources. Although not all countries agreed with the result, the OECD study provided a strong impetus to the call for international policies to control transboundary sulfur pollution. The UN/ECE based in Geneva, provided a unique forum where both West and East could meet on equal footing to find solutions to control acid deposition in Europe, and a meeting of the ministerial level was held in Geneva in November 1979. This meeting resulted in the signing of the Convention on Long-range Transboundary Air Pollution (CLRTAP). This convention constitutes a framework within which contracting parties identify the problems posed by transboundary air pollution and accept the responsibility for taking appropriate steps. The convention was signed by 35 parties, including all the countries in Europe and two republics of the Soviet Union, Bellarus and Ukraine. It was put into force in March 1983 after it had been ratified by 24 parties. The convention establishes an Executive Body as the supreme policy-making assembly. The second institutional layer consists of intergovernmental working groups as well as the Steering Body to EMEP (Klaassen 1996, p. 188).

(2) The First Sulfur Protocol

In March 1984, ten countries agreed to reduce emissions by 30 percent. Because at that time there was limited knowledge on abatement options, the 30 percent was taken as a percentage that was feasible. This 30 percent club was extended in June 1984 to a group of 18 at the conference in Munich. The First Sulfur Protocol was opened for signatures in Helsinki in 1985 and has been signed by 20 parties. The basic provision of the Protocol is that parties are to reduce their annual sulfur emissions or their transboundary fluxes by at least 30 percent as soon as possible, or at the latest by 1993, using 1980 as a basis for calculating reductions.

(3) The Second Sulfur Protocol

Negotiations on the Second Sulfur Protocol started in 1991. They came to a close in June 1994, when the Protocol was signed by 26 parties in Oslo. At the end of 1994, 27 parties signed. A major new element in the Second Sulfur Protocol is the intention to apply an effect-oriented approach by basing the extent of emission reductions on the susceptibility of natural ecosystems to avoid acid deposition. The ultimate goal is to reduce emissions so that critical loads and levels are not exceeded. Critical loads are defined as the maximum level of deposition below which no damage to sensitive ecosystems occurs. Critical levels refer to the concentrations of pollutants above which adverse effects on receptors may occur.

Economic, technical, and other constraints may make it difficult to achieve the necessary reduction everywhere and immediately. So interim steps might be needed. An accepted step in this approach is the generation of target loads that not only take into account environmental sensitivity (critical loads) but also technical, social, economic, and political considerations. Critical loads remain a long-term objective toward which the Second Sulfur Protocol makes a gradual move. As an interim target, the difference between the sulfur deposition in 1990 and the five-percent critical loads must be reduced by at least 60 percent (Amann et al. 1993). The resulting targets for the deposition of sulfur have to be attained in a cost-efficient way, minimizing total European costs subject to the condition that countries carry out at least those reductions that they were planning to undertake anyway. The scenario, called A5, formed the basis for further negotiations. The A5 scenario would require an average reduction of 59 percent over 1980 levels. Although A5 served as the reference point, further negotiations led to a slightly different schedule for emission ceilings. A5 scenario intends to reduce sulfur deposition to protect 95 percent of all ecosystems in each singular grid. Several countries did not agree to carry out the required reductions in the year 2000 as scenario A5 proposed. The reductions of several countries were therefore postponed until 2005 or 2010 (Klaassen 1996, p. 197).

The differentiated national emission ceilings are one of the two tiers of the Second Sulfur Protocol. In principle, these ceilings were based on an effect-oriented (critical-loads-based) approach combined with political horse trading. Broadly speaking, the critical load refers to the amount of acidic deposition which can fall on a given area before harmful environmental impacts occur (For a summary of European studies on estimates for the costs of different types of damages, see pp. 311-313 of Newbery 1996).

The relationships between emissions and depositions are calculated by the EMEP programme as part of the CLRTAP. Emissions are accumulated within national geographical boundaries. Deposition d_j is mapped onto each 100 by 100 km square according to the formula :

$$d_j = b_j + \sum_i e_i t_{ij}$$

where b_j is the background deposition on the jth square, e_i is the emission from the ith country and t_{ij} is the "transfer coefficient" from the ith country to the jth square. For the most part, actual deposition levels in Europe considerably exceed critical loads. The Oslo Protocol set national emission ceiling-i.e. limits to e_i for each country i - with the declared aim of reducing the gap between existing deposition levels and agreed critical loads. So, for example, these deliberations resulted in emission ceilings for the U.K. which require 50% reduction in sulfur emissions by the year 2000. 70% by the year 2005 and 80% by the year 2010, relative to 1980 emission levels (Jackson and Bailey, p. 71).

The second tier of the Oslo Protocol is a source-based approach consisting of emission standards for new large combustion plants and fuel standards specifying the maximum sulfur content in gas oil.

The fuel standards require parties to lower the sulfur content in gas oil to 0.05 percent for on-road vehicles (diesel oil) and 0.2 percent otherwise, no later than two years after the Protocol enters into force. In the case of limited supply, the lowering of the sulfur content may be postponed by 10 years (Klaassen 1996, p. 198).

|Table 4| Sulphur Emission Ceilings and Percentage Emission Reductions in the Second Sulfur Protocol

	Emission levels (kt SO_2/year)		Sulphur emission ceiling (kt SO_2/year)			Percentage emission reductions (base year : 1980)		
	1980	1990	2000	2005	2010	2000	2005	2010
Austria	397	90	78			80		
Belarus	740		456[j]	400	370	38	46	50
Belgium	828	443	248	232	215	70	72	74
Bulgaria	2,050	2,020	1,374	1,230	1,127	33	40	45
Canada								
−national	4,614	3,700	3,200			30		
−SOMA	3,245		1,750			46		
Croatia	150	160	133	125	117	11	17	22
Czech Republic	2,257	1,876	1,128	902	632	50	60	72
Denmark	451	180	90			80		
Finland	584	260	116			80		
France	3,348	1,202	868	770	737	74	77	78
Germany	7,494	5,803	1,300	990		83	87	
Greece	400	510	595	580	570	0	3	4
Hungary	1,632	1,010	898	816	653	45	50	60
Ireland	222	168	155			30		
Italy	3,800		1,330	1,042		65	73	
Liechtenstein	0.4	0.1	0.1			75		
Luxembourg	24		10			58		
Netherlands	466	207	106			77		
Norway	142	54	34			76		
Poland	4,100	3,210	2,583	2,173	1,397	37	47	66
Portugal	266	284	304	294		0	3	
Russian Federation[c]	7,161	4,460	4,440	4,297	4,297	38	40	40
Slovakia	843	539	337	295	240	60	65	72
Slovenia	235	195	130	94	71	45	60	70
Spain	3,319	2,316	2,143			35		
Sweden	507	130	100			80		
Switzerland	126	62	60			52		
Ukraine	3,850		2,310			40		
United Kingdom	4,898	3,780	2,449	1,470	980	50	70	80
European Community	25,518		9,598			62		

* The sulphur emission ceilings listed in the table shows the obligations referred to in the Oslo protocol. The 1980 and 1990 emission levels and the percentage emission reductions listed are given for information purpose

only.

- If, in a given year before 2005, a party cannot comply with its obligations under this annex, it may fulfill those obligations by averaging its national annual sulphur emissions for the year in question, the year preceding that year and the year following it, provided that the emission level in any single year is not more than 20% above the sulphur emission ceiling.
- For Greece and Portugal, percentage emission reductions given are based on the sulphur emission ceilings indicated for the year 2000.

c : European part within the EMEP area.

Source : United Nations, "Protocol to the 1979 Convention on Long-Range Transboundary Air Pollution on Further Reduction of Sulphur Emissions," 1994. 6.

3) Joint Implementation and Emission Trading

(1) Joint Implementation

There is a difficulty in designing a system of joint implementation that helps parties to the Protocol meet their emission reduction targets in a cost-effective manner that is also consistent with the critical load concept. Sulphur emissions cannot be traded on a simple one-to-one basis in Europe. It has been argued that it is possible to convert sulphur emissions into a quantity that can be traded by using a sulphur emission "exchange rate" r, defined according to a formula of the following kind :

$$\triangle e_D = -r_{DH} \cdot \triangle e_H ,$$

where $\triangle e_D$, the allowable increase in emissions above the target level in the donor country D, is some fraction, r_{DH}, of the decrease in emissions below the target level achieved in the host country H, $\triangle e_H$. The exchange rate r is supposed to capture the spatial differences which characterize deposition as a result of emissions from the donor country as compared with emissions from the host country (Jackson & Bailey, 1996, p. 72). It is not an easy task to come up with agreeable exchange rates. In general, the value of the exchange rate will depend crucially on a number of other potential constraints which might be imposed upon the situation.

(2) Possibilities of Sulphur Emissions Trading in Europe

While emission trading is one of the main policy instruments used to reduce emissions of sulphur dioxide in the Clean Air Act Amendments of 1990 in the U.S., European countries have not introduced sulphur emission trading yet. The principal difficulty faced in designing sulphur emissions trading schemes is the spatial nature of the pollution. In mathematical language, the transfer coefficients t_{ij} are not identical for all countries i, for all squares j. Thus a unit of sulphur emission abatement in one country cannot be equivalent to a unit of sulphur abatement in another country, and one-to-one trading of emissions is generally invalid. The sulphur trading system introduced in the U.S. ignored the spatial characteristics of sulphur pollution in pursuit of simplicity. U.S. expected a bad spatial pattern of emission after the emission trading and prepared a range of safeguards and political adjustments. In Europe, these compromise would be both scientifically and politically more problematic.

III. Acid Deposition and Source-Receptor Relationship in NEA

1. Energy Consumption and Sulfur Emission in NEA

Total energy consumption in Northeast Asia (NEA) was 43 EJ (exajoules or 10^{18} joules) in 1990. This represents 51% of total primary energy consumption of Asia and 12% of the world. As shown in Table 5, Northeast China comprises 45%, Japan 42%, South Korea 8%, and the North Korea 4%. It is expected that the share of Northeast China will increase to 55% by 2020.

|**Table 5**| Total Energy Consumption by Country

(10^{18} joule/year)

Country	1990	2010		2020	
		Base	Low	Base	Low
N.E. China (China)	19.4 (30.3)	44.5 (73.5)	35.6 (59.1)	61.0 (101.0)	45.0 (75.4)
Japan	17.9	25.7	20.9	28.8	21.5
South Korea	3.6	9.5	7.8	13.4	9.7
North Korea	1.8	5.0	3.9	7.9	5.5
Total	42.7 (53.6)	84.7 (113.7)	68.2 (91.7)	111.2 (151.1)	81.7 (112.1)
Total in Asia	(83.6)	(188.5)	(154.5)	(274.1)	(207.4)

* Figures in parentheses are calculated using the energy consumption of China as a whole instead of Northeast China.

Source : Wes Foell, Markus Amann, Greg Carmichel, Michael Chadwick, Jean-Paul Hettelingh, Leen Hordijik, Zhao Dianwu (eds.), *RAINS-*

ASIA : An Assessment Model for Air Pollution in Asia, A report on the World Bank sponsored project 'Acid Rain Emission Reduction in Asia,' December 1995.

For the analysis of acid rain problem in Northeast Asia, we need to estimate the future energy consumption. Major factors which determine energy consumption are economic growth and energy intensity which shows how efficiently the energy is used. In many of the Asian countries, the energy is used inefficiently now. We can slow down the energy consumption with the improvement of energy efficiency without undermining the sustained growth in the region. Table 6 shows the energy intensity of industrial sector in each country.

|**Table 6**| Industrial Energy Intensity Assumptions for the Base Case

(Gigajoules per US $1,000(1990) Industrial GDP)

Country	1990	2000	2010	2020
China	109.9	81	60	44.2
Japan	4.78	4	3.37	2.85
South Korea	11.5	9.5	8	6.7
North Korea	85.5	120.7	139.9	158
Asia Average	17.1	17.1	15.9	14.6

Source : Wes Foell et al., *op. cit.*, Table 3.7.

Table 7 shows the pattern of final energy use by end-use sector. In Northeast Asia, 45% of energy was used in the industrial sector, 19% in the power generation sector, 16% in the domestic and commercial sector, and 10% in the transportation sector. It is expected that the share of the industrial sector will decrease to 40% by 2020.

|**Table 7**| Energy Consumption in Northeast Asia by End-Use Sector

(10^{18} joule/year)

Use	1990	2010		2020	
		BAS	HEF	BAS	HEF
Industrial Fuel Combustion	19.3(45%)	36.0	28.7	45.0	33.9
Domestic/Commercial	6.9(16%)	12.8	11.1	16.1	12.8
Transportation	4.1(10%)	10.3	8.0	15.5	9.9
Power Generation	8.2(19%)	17.5	13.7	24.4	17.3
Non-energy Uses	1.8	3.4	3.0	4.2	3.8
Other (Conversion and Loss)	2.3	4.7	3.6	5.9	4.1
Total	42.7(100%)	84.7	68.2	111.1(100%)	81.7

Source : David G. Streets, "Energy and Acid Rain Projections for Northeast Asia," mimeo, 1997, p. 7.

Table 8 shows the energy consumption in Northeast Asia by fuel type. Coal was the principal fuel with 48% of primary energy use, heavy and medium oil followed with 20%, and light fuel oil with 15%. The share of natural gas and nuclear was about the same with 7%. The high reliance on fossil fuel such as coal and oil contributes the main reason for the high levels of sulfur dioxide and nitrogen oxides emissions that lead to acid rain. It is expected that the energy consumption in Northeast Asia will increase from 43 EJ in 1990 to 111 EJ in 2020, and coal is expected to increase more than twice from the 1990 level of 21 EJ to 59 EJ in 2020. If the increased energy use is satisfied by nuclear or renewable energy sources, there will be no danger of air pollution in this region. However, coal will remain as the dominant energy source because it is richly endowed in this region and cheap, easy to exploit and use.

|Table 8| Energy Consumption in Northeast Asia by Primary Fuel Type

(10^{18} joule/year)

Use	1990	2010		2020	
		BAS	HEF	BAS	HEF
Coal	20.6(48%)	44.8	34.1	58.8(53%)	39.8
Heavy and Medium Oil	8.7(20%)	15.1	11.8	19.3	13.3
Light Fuel Oil	6.6(15%)	10.6	8.8	12.6	9.2
Natural Gas	3.0(7%)	6.1	5.3	8.8	7.5
Renewables	0.1	0.2	0.2	0.3	0.3
Hydroelectric	0.8	2.7	2.7	3.8	3.8
Nuclear	2.8(7%)	5.2	5.2	7.6	7.6
Total	42.7(100%)	84.7	68.2	111.1(100%)	81.7

Source : David G. Streets, ibid.

China has vast coal deposits in Shanxi / Hebei / Shandong area with 700 billion tons. This coal has the sulfur contents ranging from 0.3% to 3%. Heilongjiang province has the estimated coal reserves of 40 billion tons with the sulfur content of 0.4%. Inner Mongolia is also endowed richly with coal. China's coal industry has expanded rapidly and produces 1 billion ton of coal annually, becoming the number one coal producer in the world. It is expected that the coal consumption in China will increase up to 2.2 billion tons by next century. The imports of coal by Japan and Korea will grow steadily but the surplus from China, Australia and Indonesia will be enough not to bring supply shortage in this region. Table 9 shows the estimates of coal trade in the Northeast Asia.

|Table 9| Regional Coal Trade in Northeast Asia

(million ton/year)

Country	1993			2010		
	Production	Consumption	Net Trade	Production	Consumption	Net Trade
China(Total)	1,141	1,123	+18	2,000	1,975	+25
Japan	7	118	−111	1	150	−149
South Korea	9	40	−31	4	77	−73
North Korea	34	35	−1	50	58	−8
Australia	-	-	+132	-	-	+230
Indonesia	-	-	+18	-	-	+37
Vietnam	-	-	+2	-	-	+7

Source : Intarapravich et al., "Asia-Pacific Energy Supply and Demand to 2010," *Energy*, 21, 1996, pp.1017-1039.

The estimate of total sulfur dioxide emission in Northeast Asia in 1990 was 14.7 million metric tons (mt). Northeast China was responsible for 81% with 11.9 mt, South Korea 12% with 1.7 mt, Japan 5% with 0.8 mt. and North Korea 2% with 0.3 mt. Major areas of heavy sulfur dioxide emissions in China are China's industrial centers : Hebei-Anhui-Henan areas with 3.1 million tons, Northeast Plain with 2.5 million tons, and Jiangsu province with 2.1 million tons. Under the Bussiness-As-Usual (BAS) energy scenario, sulfur dioxide emissions will rise to 31.3 mt in 2010 and 40.5 mt in 2020. While there would be a slight increase of sulfur dioxide emission in Japan, significant increase was projected to occur in Northeast China and South and North Koreas until 2020. Under High-Efficiency (HEF) scenario, which assumes improved energy efficiency and fuel substitution away from fossil fuels, sulfur dioxide emissions would grow to 24.7 mt in 2010 and 28.8 mt in 2020.

It is expected that sulfur dioxide emissions would decline from 24 mt in 1990 to about 17 mt in 2020 in North America and from 37 mt in 1990 to about 16 mt in 2020 in Europe. These two regions realized the importance of regional acid rain problems and had taken necessary measures to reduce sulfur dioxide emission arduously. This signifies the situation that it is not sufficient to just improve the energy efficiency in Northeast Asia to significantly reduce the emissions of sulfur dioxides. It is required to utilize various emission control technologies additionally. Otherwise the Northeast Asia will become the major emitter of sulfur dioxide in the world soon or later.

In Asia, very little research has been conducted to investigate the levels and impacts of acid deposition. However available monitoring data confirms that the acid rain is in fact increasing in many parts of Asia. Some of the ecosystems of the Asia region are similar to the U.S. and Europe where significant amount of economic as well as scientific studies have been performed to bring a noticeable change in acid deposition. Thus, in some cases, it is possible to extrapolate the potential effects found in these western nations to the corresponding ecosystems of Asia (Wes Foell et al. 1995, pp.1-5). RAINS-Asia project was performed to analyze and assess the relative vulnerability of anthropogenic and natural environments

|**Table 10**| Emissions of Acidic Air Pollutants in Northeast Asia by Country under Base Case Scenario

(million ton/year)

Country	SO_2			NO_X		
	1990	2010	2020	1990	2010	2020
Northeast China	11.9(81%)	25.3	32.5	6.9	N/A	26.8
Japan	0.8(5%)	1.0	1.1	2.6	N/A	4.6
South Korea	1.7(12%)	4.1	5.6	1.1	N/A	5.1
North Korea	0.3(2%)	0.9	1.3	0.5	N/A	2.4
Total	14.7(100%)	31.3	40.5	11.1	N/A	38.9

N/A=Values not calculated.
Source : David G. Streets, *op. cit.*, p. 12.

to acid deposition. According to the summary report of the RAINS-Asia project, Northeast China, Japan, and Korea are highly vulnerable to acid deposition and are expected to be at a greater risk in the future.

2. Source-Receptor Relationship in NEA

Columns in Table 12 show the source countries of sulfur dioxide emission and the rows show the receiving countries. For example, China received 5,990 thousand tons of SO_2 from herself and received 21.6 thousand tons from North Korea. South Korea received 175 thousand tons of sulfur from herself and 28 thousand tons from China.

|Table 11| Vulnerability of Various Asian Regions to Acid Deposition Risk Factor

	High emission		High deposition		Sensitive soils	Sensitive vegetation and materials	High risk
Region	Current	Future	Current	Future			
NE China	×	×		×		×	
Japan Korea			×(winter mostly)	×(winter mostly)	×	×	×
S China		×	×(winter mostly)	×(winter mostly)	×	×	×
SE Asia	×	×	× (local area summer mostly)	× (local area summer mostly)	× (mountain area)	× (mountain area)	× (mountain area)
SE Asian Islands	×	×	×(isolated, local)	×(isolated, local)	×(mounta in area)		
N India	×	×		×(summer)		×(Himalayan foothills)	
SW India			(borderline acidity)	×(winter)	×	×(mountain area)	(borderline acidity in mountain area)
NE India		×		×(summer)	×		
Sri Lanka, Maldives			(borderline acidity)	×(winter)			
Siberia, N Mongolia				×(summer)		×	

Source : Wes Foell et al., *op. cit.*, Table 1.2.

|Table 12| Country-to-Country Source-Receptor Matrix for Sulfur

(thousand sulfur ton/year)

Receptor \ Source	China	Japan	S. Korea	N. Korea	Total	Asia Total
China	5,990.0(83%)	0.2	4.6	21.6	6,016.4	6,140.0
Japan	38.8(0.5%)	149.0	28.8	2.5	219.1	405.0
S. Korea	28.0(0.4%)	1.2	175.0	2.6	206.7	211.0
N. Korea	59.6(0.8%)	0.1	62.8	49.3	171.8	172.0
Total	6,116.4	150.4	271.2	76.0	6,614.0	6,928.0
Asia Total	7,220.0(100%)	291.0	513.0	111.0	8,135.0	12,300.0

Source : Constructed by the author based on Wes Foell et al., *op. cit.*, Table 5.3.a.

Table 13 shows the percentage of sulfur deposition on Northeast Asian countries which are originated from China. China emitted 7,220 thousand tons, 83% of which (5,990 thousand tons) fell on China, 0.4% fell on South Korea, 0.5% fell on Japan, and 0.8% fell on North Korea. Even if only a small portion of sulfur emitted from China reach neighboring countries, they contribute significant share of sulfur deposition in those countries. For example, North Korea receives only 0.8% of China's total sulfur emission, but it comprises 35% of total sulfur deposition in North Korea.

Table 14 shows the country-to-country, source-receptor relationship among Northeast Asian countries. South Korea is responsible for 7.1% of Japan's sulfur deposition and 3.7% of North Korea's sulfur deposition. In case of Japan, anthropogenic emission from Japan takes only 37%, while volcano is responsible for 46% of sulfur deposition. North Korea's own contribution is 29%, while

|Table 13| China's Contribution to NEA Countries

Receptor	% of China's Deposition in Asia	% of Receptor's Total Deposition
China	83	98
South Korea	0.4	13
Japan	0.5	10
North Korea	0.8	35

Source : Wes Foell et al., *op. cit.*, Table 5.3.b.

China is responsible for 35% of sulfur deposition in North Korea.

Table 15 is constructed based on "Regional Source-Receptor

|Table 14| Country-to-Country Source-Receptor Relationship

Source \ Receptor	% of Receptor's Total Annual Sulfur Deposition			
	South Korea	Japan	North Korea	Mongolia
China	13	9.6	35	48
South Korea	83	7.1	3.7	0.01
Japan	0.5	36.8	0.05	0
North Korea	1.2	0.6	29	0.01

* Volcano is responsible for 46% of total annual sulfur deposition in Japan.
Source : Constructed by the author based on Wes Foell et al., *op. cit.*, Table 5.3.a.

Relationships for Northeast Asia" produced by Streets and et al. (Streets and et al. 1997). It shows the sources of sulfur deposition of ten areas in South Korea and Japan. According to the analysis, 13% of acid deposition in Seoul-Incheon areas originates from China. The contribution from China is smaller in southern part of Korean peninsula. The most vulnerable areas to China's sulfur

|Table 15| Sources of Acid Deposition for South Korea and Japan

Receptor \ Source		Northeast China (%)	Japan (%)	South Korea (%)	North Korea (%)
S. Korea	North	14%	0	80%	3%
	Seoul-Incheon	13%	0	84%	2%
	South	9%	0	88%	0
	Busan	4%	1%	93%	0
Japan	Chukoku-Shikoku	28%	56%	13%	3%
	Chubu	3%	90%	3%	0
	Hokkaido-Tohoku	9%	79%	9%	1%
	Kanto	11%	78%	9%	1%
	Kinki	13%	66%	18%	1%
	Kyushu-Okinawa	32%	37%	29%	0

Source : Constructed by the author based on 'Relationships for Northeast Asia' in David Streets, Gregory Carmichael, Markus Amann, and Richard Arndt, "Energy Consumption and Acid Deposition in Northeast Asia : Taming the Tigers," mimeo, 1997.

emission are Chukoku-Shikoku and Kyushu-Okinawa areas of Japan. Almost one third of acid rain is caused by sulfur transported from China. It is alarming to see that South Korea is responsible for 29% of sulfur deposition in Kyushu-Okinawa area. On the other hand, Japan's contribution to South Korea's sulfur deposition is almost none.

In Japan, the Air Pollution Control Law was enacted in 1968 and strictly regulated the emissions of SO_2 from thermal power plants. As a result, the SO_2 concentration in urban areas has significantly decreased since 1970. The Environment Agency of Japan initiated a comprehensive assessment of acid deposition in Japan and CRIEPI investigated the transport of air pollutions from neighboring countries intensively. Japanese CRIEPI divided the Northeast Asia which includes China, Japan, Korea, Taiwan, Mongolia, and the Far East Russia into 54 by 54 grids, with each grid 80 km apart. This study investigated the distribution of anthropogenic SO_2 emissions for 1990. Total anthropogenic SO_2 emission from East Asia was about 25 million tons in 1990, 21 million tons from China, 1.0 million tons from Japan, 1.6 million tons from South Korea, 0.7 million tons from North Korea, 0.6 million tons from Taiwan, and 0.3 million tons from the remaining areas. The SO_2 emission from volcanoes was estimated to be approximately 1.5 million tons a year. According to CRIEPI study, the emissions from both volcanic and anthropogenic source in Japan accounted for about 60% of the annual sulfur deposition. In winter, the contribution of Asian continents to western coast of Japan reaches more than 80%. For the Japan as a whole, the contributions of China, Japan, and Korea are estimated to be 50%, 35% and 15% respectively. During the winter season, the predominant wind system is northwesterly from China to Korean peninsula and to Japan, while in the summer season the winds to Japan come from various directions. The contribution of Asian continents to west coast of Japan amounted to more than 80% in winter times (Hye-Sook Park Ono, "Air Pollution Problems in Japan," a Paper "Presented at the Workshop on Atmospheric Issues in North-East Asia," September 25-27, Yonsei University, Seoul, Korea).

IV. Optimal Framework toward Acid Rain Problem in NEA

1. Environmental Cooperation in NEA

Regional environmental cooperation became one of the top priorities in every region of the world recently. In the Asia-Pacific region, there are several sub-regional environmental cooperative bodies at the intergovernmental level. These include the ASEAN Senior Officials on the Environment (ASOEN), South Asia Cooperative Environment Program (SACEP), South Pacific Regional Environment Program (SPREP), and Lower Mekong Basin Development Environment Program (LMBDEP). In Northeast Asia, however, it was not until 1993 that an intergovernmental forum on environmental cooperation was established. The main hindrance to the establishment of such a forum came from the military and political confrontation which had dominated international affairs in Northeast Asia. However, the end of Cold War made the formation of a forum for regional environmental cooperation possible.

Cooperative mechanism to deal with environmental problems in Northeast Asia can be broadly classified into multilateral-cooperation and bilateral-cooperation as shown in Table 16. The multilateral cooperation is operated through the regional cooperative bodies such as ESCAP and APEC ; or through intergovernmental meetings such as Northeast Asia Sub-regional Programme for Environment Cooperation (NEASPEC), Northwest Pacific Action Plan (NOWPAP), and Tuman River Area Development Plan (TRADP) ; or through

|Table 16| Northeast Asian Environmental Cooperation

Multilateral Cooperation	Through Existing Regional Cooperation Bodies	ESCAP	· Asia-Pacific Environment Ministers' Meeting(Every 5 years) · Asia-Pacific Environment and Sustainable Development Commission · Regional Action Programme for Environmentally Sound & Sustainable Development, 1996-2000
		APEC	· APEC Environment Ministers' Meeting · APEC Marine Preservation Meeting
	Inter-Governmental	NEASPEC	· Members : China, Japan, Korea S, Korea N, Mongolia, Russia · First Meeting ; Seoul(1993) · ESCAP functions as temporary secretariat
		NOWPAP	· Members : China, Japan, Korea S, Korea N, Russia · First Meeting ; Seoul(1994)
		TRADP	· Members : China, Korea S, Korea N, Mongolia, Russia · Initiative : UNDP
	Inter-Agency or Non-Governmental	ECO-ASIA	· Initiative : Japan · Met 5 times during 1991-96
		Northeast Asia Acid Rain Specialists Meeting	· Initiative : Japan EPA · Met 3 times during 1993-95
		Workshop on Transboundary Air Pollution	· Initiative : Korea Environmental Research Institute
		NEACEC	· Members : China, Japan, Korea S, Mongolia, Russia · Meet annually since 1992
Bilateral Cooper-ation	Japan-Korea		· Agreement : 1993. 6
	China-Korea		· Agreement : 1993. 10
	Korea-Russia		· Agreement : 1994. 6

Source : Eui-Soon Shin, "Acid-Rain Problem and Environmental Cooperation in Northeast Asia," *Korea Journal of Resource Economics*, September 1997, p. 136.

other cooperative bodies such as Environment Congress for Asia and the Pacific (ECO-Asia) and Northeast Asian Conference on Environmental Cooperation (NEACEC). Bilateral cooperation is operated between the two interested countries such as Korea-China, Korea-Japan, and Korea-Russia.

2. Market-based and Cooperative Approach

1) Economic Rationale

Acid rain differs from greenhouse gases like carbon dioxide and CFCs in that it is not a pure public good (or bad) in the Samuelson sense. Acid rain causes damage where it is deposited, and there appears to be a reasonably linear relationship between emissions and depositions. It is possible to predict a stable relationship between the location of the source and the deposition, at least averaged over a year. A large fraction of SO_2 can be accounted for by individually identified large stationary sources, predominantly power stations. Technically, acid rain appears to be a depletable or rival good in consumption, in that if one ton of sulfur falls on a given local area, then that cannot fall elsewhere, and reduces the amount which will harm others by that amount. It might appear to be a simple bilateral externality of the kind considered by Ronald Coase. But there are two important differences from the simple case of bilateral externality. If one country emits sulfur into the air, then more than one country will be affected. If the recipients are to bargain over reductions in acid rain, they will have to agree among themselves how to coordinate their bargaining, and how to share any costs involved.

Let us consider the efficacy of bilateral or multilateral bargaining over pollution abatement, in the spirit of Coase. One can imagine two possible allocations of property rights. The status quo is one in which each country is free to pollute its neighbors. The alternative is one in which each country agrees to a certain annual level of emissions – for example, 70% of the 1980 measured level. In the second case, the polluter would have to pay for increased emissions, and a natural offer would be an amount between the marginal cost of abatement and the marginal damage done to the recipients. This principle is termed the Polluter Pays Principle, or PPP. In the status quo situation, new polluting sources could set up and pollute at no apparent cost. The costs of damage would be borne by the recipients (the Victim Pays Principle, or VPP). In this case, the first task would be to agree on a reference path of pollution in the absence of any cleanup–presumably based on a forecast of energy demand and emissions per unit of energy used. In the second case, the recipient would pay the polluting country the damage cost of the difference between 70% of 1980 levels and the reference emission path (Newbery, 1990, p. 328).

Licenses to pollute which are tradable and are auctioned off have several attractions. The first is that they are the natural instrument to meet international agreements which constrain total emission levels. Second, they can overcome organized resistance from the industry affected, since firms can be allocated licenses proportional to current emission levels. The costs of abatement fall on consumers and on new entrants, who have to buy licenses from incumbents. Third, other countries can negotiate further reductions by buying up licenses. Licenses work well for large stationary sources which are the main source of SO_2, but are not immediately applicable to small mobile sources. An important experiment with the license system was the U.S. Environment Protection Agency's sulfur emissions trading policy, with its various components allowing firms to meet firm level or area level standards by either internal reorganization or by external trading or bargaining. The resulting cost-saving has been substantial as analyzed above.

2) A Possible Strategy

Inter-governmental negotiations so far have been guided by the principles of uniform reduction in emissions from a benchmark level or uniform standards. However, there are two serious problems with this approach. The first is political, and may be sufficient to derail the negotiations-some countries are net loser from such negotiations. The second objection is economic-the reduction in aggregate pollution damage is done at higher than least cost. Both problems can be solved by the natural solution which allows beneficial and efficient bargaining. This would involve first agreeing to a benchmark trajectory of allowable emissions (not necessarily equal for all countries), and then facilitating bargaining over deviations from this level. This might be done by first estimating the marginal damage costs (or willingness to pay for abatement, if higher) by each cell or square, then calculating the appropriate cost sharing formula for the group of countries affected by polluter *j*. Thus for country i, its share of the payments to polluter j would be

$$\alpha_i = MD_i \cdot t_{ij} / \sum_k MD_k \cdot t_{kj}$$

The recipients would then appoint a negotiator with powers to levy charges on recipients proportional to these cost fractions, up to the total damage level. The negotiator could then bribe the polluting country to make additional reductions (Newbery 1990, p. 334). The current tax rate would be the amount offered by the recipient negotiator. The main problem is that FGD requires a large fixed investment to amortize over up to 40 years, and thus requires the investor to calculate the future benefits of installation. If these future benefits are uncertain, then abatement may be deferred. It would pay the recipient negotiator to offer formal contracts, possibly indexed to recipient GNP, in order to reduce uncertainty and thus induce greater abatement for the same cost.

V. Summary and Conclusion

Even though not enough time has passed since its enactment, the SO_2 allowance program of U.S. provides useful lessons and serves as a benchmark against which other pollution control and market-based programs can be compared (McLean 1996, p. 149). Following is the lessons learned from the experience of U.S. SO_2 allowance trading program :

First, actions prior to program design are important. Market-based instruments are tools to solve problems, but first the problem must be defined, goals set, and the economic, social, and environmental implications of alternative solutions should be evaluated. Public's acceptance and support of proposed solutions should also be assessed.

Second, the design of the program is critical because it determines whether effective and efficient implementation is possible. The goals and responsibilities should be clearly stated, and there should be unequivocal consequences for not complying or for delaying implementations. From the beginning of the program, the emission of all potentially affected sources should be accounted for and a maximum allowable emission level, the cap, should be established and sustained. Accurate measurement of emissions is the key to environmental accountability, market credibility, and operational flexibility. Allowance allocation is primarily a political process, not an environmental one. Overall, the design should be simple.

Third, in implementing the program, government should stay focused on achieving the goals in the legislation, resolving issues promptly, and improving operational efficiency. Government should refrain from trying to participate in, control, or fine tune the market, particularly since many changes, such as restructuring, may occur outside the regulator's domain.

It is hard to imagine any politically-acceptable policy that assigns varying reduction requirements to specific countries based on the results of large scale source-receptor modelling in Northeast Asia at this time. It is even harder to imagine the political acceptability of ambient-based trading which theoretically would be more efficient than the emissions trading programme adopted in the U.S. Thus, emission trading, while only a crude substitute for ambient trading, is more politically feasible and at least as effective as ambient targeting. The question is how to devise a mechanism to introduce a cost-effective market-based emission trading mechanism in Northeast Asia.

The concept of joint implementation (JI) or activities implemented jointly now appears within the policy frameworks of a number of international conventions. These include the Framework Convention on Climate Change (FCCC), the Biodiversity Convention, the Montreal Protocol, and the Convention on Long-range Transboundary Air Pollution (CLRTAP). The general intention under each of these initiatives is to develop mechanisms which allow two or more parties to meet their obligations to the conventions through activities implemented jointly. The main argument for such a procedure has been from economic efficiency : the costs of transboundary pollutants abatement might be lowered by seeking out the least cost options first, irrespective of geographical boundaries. Climate change is a problem that may be even more amenable to market-based solutions than acid rain, mainly because greenhouse gas emissions do not cause local and regional "hot spots" which need to be guarded against. To slow the overall greenhouse effect, it may be better to concentrate on the total set of greenhouse gases, rather than focusing on individual greenhouse gases.

While Europe and the U.S. found ways to control transboundary transportation of sulfur dioxides, they are struggling to cope with the global warming problem, which is technically and politically more difficult and problematic than the acid rain problem. Northeast Asia is in an infant stage in establishing a regional cooperative institution comparable to that of Europe now. So the first task for the Northeast Asian countries is to establish a permanent cooperative body which would deal with transboundary problems in Northeast Asia or in Asia-Pacific region, if it is more proper geographical boundary. Then some kind of conventions and protocols will be derived based on the agreed total emission limit in the region, and specific country's reduction target will be negotiated. Perhaps integrated approach toward all transboundary pollutants including SO_2, NO_X, and CO_2 could be more cost-effective because all the transboundary problems are not properly dealt with in this region yet. It is important to keep in mind here that the regional acid rain programme would be "in addition to," not "in lieu of," existing protection measures taken by each country.

References

Burtraw, Dallas, "The SO_2 Emissions Trading Program : Cost Savings without Allowance Trades," *Contemporary Economic Policy*, vol. XIV, April 1996, pp.79-94.

Dowlatabadi, Hadi and Winston Harrington, "Uncertainty and the Cost of Acid Rain Control," *Contemporary Policy Issues*, vol. VIII, July 1990, pp. 43-58.

Foell, Wes, Markus Amann, Greg Carmichel, Michael Chadwick, Jean-Paul Hettelingh, Leen Hordijik, Zhao Dianwu (eds.), *RAINS-ASIA : An Assessment Model for Air Pollution in Asia*, A report on the World Bank sponsored project 'Acid Rain Emission Reduction in Asia,' December 1995.

Jackson, Tim and Peter Bailey, "Transboundary Initiatives for Controlling Sulphur and Possible Lessons for CO_2," in Royal Institute of International Affairs, *Controlling Carbon and Sulfur : International Investment and Trading Initiatives*, Proceedings, 5-6 December 1996, Chatham House, London, pp. 69-80.

Kete, Nancy, "The U.S. Acid Rain Control Allowance Trading System," in OECD, *Climate Change : Designing a Tradable Permit System*, 1992, pp. 78-108.

Klaassen, Ger, *Acid Rain and Environmental Degradation : The Economics of Emission Trading*, Edward Elgar, IIASA, 1996.

McLean, Brian, "Evolution of Marketable Permits : The U.S. Experience with Sulphur Dioxide Allowance Trading," in RIIA, *Controlling Carbon and Sulfur : International Investment and Trading Initiative*, Proceedings, 5-6 December 1996, London : Chatham House, pp. 136-150.

Newbery, David, "Acid Rain," *Economic Policy*, October 1990, pp. 297-346.

Shin, Eui-Soon, "Acid Rain Deposition and Impacts in NEA : Lessons from RAINS-Asia," Kap-Young Jung et al. (eds.), *Dynamic Transition and Economic Cooperation in Northeast Asia*, The Institute of East and West Studies, Yonsei University, 1997, pp. 165-187.

______ (in Korean), "Acid Rain Problems in Northeast Asia and Environmental Cooperation," *Korea Journal of Resource Economics*, vol. 7,

No. 1, February 1997, pp. 119-150.

Streets, David G., "Energy and Acid Rain Projections for Northeast Asia," mimeo, 1997, p. 7.

Streets, David, Gregory Carmichael, Markus Amann, and Richard Arndt, "Energy Consumption and Acid Deposition in Northeast Asia: Taming the Tigers," mimeo, 1997.

14. Environmentally Sound and Sustainable Economic Cooperation between South and North Korea*

I. Introduction

When the economic integration between South and North Korea is studied, environmental ramification of the development should also be considered. According to the environmental capital flight hypothesis, dirty industry is shifted to the countries where environmental standards are lax and little financial sources are available to care for the environment. It has been considered that the North Korean environmental pollution was not serious in general as the industrial sites were restricted to limited areas. However recent researches report that in some parts of North Korea pollution problems are serious. The environmental pollution will be more serious as the North Korea accelerates economic development

* "Environmentally Sound and Sustainable Economic Cooperation between South and North Korea," paper presented at the 'Seminar on Structural Adjustment of Industry and Environment, Institute of Unification Studies, Yonsei University, November 23-24, 2000.

following the opening up of her economy.

The accompanying environmental cost will be an additional burden to the South Korea in the long run. Unification cost includes not only the development cost but also the environmental protection and recovery costs. That is why we need to look into the effect of fast economic development on environment in advance and integrate the developmental and environmental considerations at the same time.

We have limited information and data on the environmental situation of North Korea. So the experiences of former socialist countries and the Central and Eastern Europe would give us precious lessons in pursuing environmentally sound and sustainable economic cooperation between North and South Korea. The purpose of this study is to investigate the following three issues. Firstly, we will study the economic and environmental situation of North Korea based on government documents and existing research outputs. Secondly, we will predict the impact of economic transformation to the environment in North Korea by investigating the experiences of Central and Eastern European Countries, together with that of South Korea. Thirdly, we will study the possibility of environmentally sound and sustainable economic cooperation between South and North Korea.

II. Economic and Environmental Situation of North Korea

1. North Korea's GDP and Comparison with South Korea

North Korea's GDP growth turned positive after nine consecutive years of negative growth, but real GDP in 1999 was equivalent to only about three quarters of that of 1989.

The shares of the agriculture, forestry & fishing industry (31.4%) and the electricity, gas & water industry (4.5%) in North Korea were higher than South Korea. In contrast, the shares of the mining & manufacturing industry (25.6%), the construction industry (6.1%), and the service industry (32.4%) were lower than those in South Korea.

North Korea's economic scale (nominal GNI) in 1999 was

|**Table 1**| South and North Korea's Industrial Structure

(Unit : nominal basis, %)

	North Korea			South Korea	
	'97	'98	'99	'98	'99
Agriculture, forestry & fishing	28.9	29.6	31.4	4.9	5.0
Mining & manufacturing	25.5	25.6	25.6	31.2	32.2
Electricity, gas & water	4.3	4.2	4.5	2.4	2.6
Construction	6.3	5.1	6.1	10.1	8.8
Services	35.0	35.6	32.4	51.2	51.4
GDP	100.0	100.0	100.0	100.0	100.0

Source : Bank of Korea, *Gross Domestic Product of North Korea in 1999.*

estimated to have been one twenty-sixth of that of South Korea, and its per capita GNI was about one twelfth of South Korea.

2. Environmental Situation of North Korea

North Korea lies between Eastern Europe and China in the composition of industrial structure. Environmental pollution problems were raised since 1980s and severe pollution incidences

|**Table 2**| Comparison of Major Economic Indicators between South and North Korea in 1999

	Unit	North Korea(A)	South Korea(B)	B/A(times)
1.Population	1,000 persons	22,082	46,858	2.1
2. Nominal GNI[1]	₩billion	18,741.0	478,251	25.5
	(US$100mil.)	(158)	(4,021)	(25.5)
3. Per capita GNI[1]	₩10,000	84.9	1,020.6	12.0
	(US$)	(714)	(8,581)	(12.0)
4. GDP growth rate	%	6.2	10.7	-
5. External economy				
Trade total	US$100mil.	14.8	2,634.4	178.0
(Exports)	〃	5.2	1,436.9	276.3
(Imports)	〃	9.6	1,197.5	124.7
(Trade amounts/ nominal GNI)	%	9.4	65.5	-
Exchange rate	₩/US$	2.17	1,189.48	-
Foreign debt	US$100mil.	123.0	1,364.5	11.1
6. Budget volume[2]	US$100mil.	92.2	703.5	7.6

	Unit	North Korea(A)	South Korea(B)	B/A(times)
7. Energy industry				
Coal production	10,000 tons	2,100	420	0.2
Power generation capacity	10,000 kW	739	4,698	6.4
Actual power generation quantity	100 million kWh	186	2,393	12.9
Crude oil imports	10,000 tons	32	11,816	369.3
8. Agricultural & fishing goods production				
Grain	10,000 tons	422.2	600.0	1.4
(Rice)	〃	162.9	526.3	3.2
Fishing products	〃	66.4	291.1	4.4
9. Mining goods production				
Iron ore	10,000 tons	378.6	18.8	0.5
Nonferrous metals	〃	11.7	102.1	8.7
10. Heavy & chemical industry production				
Automobiles	10,000 vehicles	0.73	284.3	389.5
Steel	10,000 tons	124.3	4,104.2	33.0
Cement	〃	410.0	4,815.7	11.7
Fertilizer	〃	77	370.1	4.8
11. Light industry production				
Textiles	100 mil. m^2	1.0	84.0	84.0
Synthetic fiber	10,000 tons	2.7	258.5	95.7
12. Infrastructure				
Railroad length	Km	5,214	6,683	1.3
Road length	Km	23,479	87,534	3.7
Harbor loading and unloading capacity	10,000 tons	3,501	41,756	11.9
Ship possession	10,000 tons	79.0	607.6	7.7

Notes : 1) The figures in ( ) indicate the numerical value calculated according to the South Korean Won-US dollar exchange rate.
2) Settlement of accounts basis for North Korea, the central government's general accounting budget(including supplementary budgets) basis for South Korea.

Source : Bank of Korea, *Gross Domestic Product of North Korea in 1999*.

were reported in the 1990s. North Korean economy depends on heavy industry and the coal is her main energy source. North Korean metal and chemical plants are old and produce large polluting materials. Faced with increasing pollution problem, North Korea introduced the Enforcement Ordinance in 1995 to implement 'the Law of the Democratic People's Republic Korea on the Protection of the Environment' which was adopted on April 6, 1986. However it is uncertain whether the endeavor would bring real effect considering the difficult economic situation of North Korea. In addition to the industry-related structural problem, human-caused environmental destruction is also very serious in the North. The loft fields developed under the instruction of Kim Il Sung destroyed the forests and caused increased damage during the 1995 flooding.

(1) Deforestation

The development of loft fields started from 1976 and has destroyed the forest environment and ecological system. The exploitation of forest for fuel use was the primary cause of the problem as well as the construction of a tunnel for military purpose. The degradation was worse in a cease-fire line and the south of Pyongyang than other regions.

(2) Water pollution

The water quality of the major rivers, the Daedong River, the Tuman River, and the Chungchun River, is in poor condition. They were polluted by untreated factory waste water. For example, the

|Table 3| Environmental Overview of North Korea

Total Energy Consumption (1998E)	1.8 quadrillion Btu (0.5% of world total energy consumption)	Energy-Related Carbon Emissions (1998E)	42.7 million metric tons of carbon (0.7% of world carbon emissions)
Per Capita Energy Consumption (1998E)	77.7 million Btu	Per Capita Carbon Emission (1998E)	1.8 metric tons of carbon
Energy Intensity (1997E)	71,200 Btu / US $1990	Carbon Intensity (1997E)	1.7 metric tons of carbon / 1000 US $1990
Sectoral Share of Energy Consumption (1997E)	Industrial (57.1%), Transportation (42.5%), Residential (0.4%)	Sectoral Share of Carbon Emissions (1997E)	Industrial (74.7%), Transportation (24.9%), Residential (0.4%)
Fuel Share of Energy Consumption (1998E)	Coal (84.0%), Oil (4.0%)	Fuel Share of Carbon Emission (1998E)	Coal(96.6%), Oil (3.4%)
Major Environmental Issues	Localized air pollution attributable to inadequate industrial controls ; water pollution ; inadequate supplies of potable water		

Source : U.S. Energy Information Administration, *North Korea*. (http://www.eia.doe.gov)

Moosan plant that is located in the upper reaches of the Tuman River has discharged 15 million tons of ore dust in a year. The quality of major rivers is not fit to drink and cause waterborne diseases.

(3) Air pollution

The DPRK at present has neither the financial resources nor the expertise to simultaneously solve its environmental problems and to promote economic recovery without substantial cooperation from outside. Of the many environmental concerns currently facing the nations of Northeast Asia, acid rain problem presents perhaps the most serious combination of immediate and ongoing impacts. Acid rain, caused primarily by emissions of nitrogen and sulfur oxides, is already having an environmental and economic impact in the countries of Northeast Asia. Acid gas emissions from the DPRK affect both the DPRK and other countries of the region, and the DPRK is also the recipient of acid rain exported from its neighbors. (Source : David Von Hippel and Peter Hayes, "DPRK Energy Sector : Current Status and Scenarios for 2000 and 2005", Nautilus Institute.

III. Economics of Korean Unification

The Institute for International Economics (IIE) constructed a Korean Integration Model (KIM), a two-country computable general equilibrium (CGE) model which links the North and South Korean Economies, and simulated the impact on the two economies of economic integration.

"In the simulation, the factor mobility is of critical importance. If factor markets do not integrate, the macroeconomic impact on South Korea of economic integration with the North is relatively small, while the effects on North Korea are large. With a unified exchange rate and factor market integration, there is a significant impact on the South Korean income and wealth distribution. If investment flows from South to North and labor flows from North to South, there is a shift in the South Korean income distribution toward capital, and within labor toward urban high skilled labor, suggesting growing income and wealth inequality in the South. Similarly, the specific form of technological transfer is important : if North Korea succeeds in adopting South Korean technology, it experiences a tremendous boost in productivity in the traded goods sector, which tends to increase the magnitude of change in macroeconomic aggregates and distributional shares exhibited by south Korea. If integration is accompanied by large capital inflows, there is a significant appreciation of the real exchange rate with deleterious implications for the South Korean traded-goods sector."

The study by Noland, Robinson, and Scatasa (NRS, 1997) also obtained the following results : (1) the static gains from trade liberalization for North Korea are potentially huge – on the order of 25 to 35 percent of GDP depending on specific assumptions about factor market adjustment ; (2) total factor productivity could increase by 18 percent, leading to a roughly 50 percent increase in national income in the complete liberalization scenario ; and (3) that North Korea could absorb up to an approximately 50 percent "obsolescence shock" reduction in the capital stock before national income fell under successful economic reform.

The study also indicated that there would be an enormous shift in the composition of output and employment towards the light industry, while agriculture and capital goods sector would tend to contract as factors were reallocated in a more economically rational way. The NRS model calculated the "cost of unification" defined as the addition to the North Korean capital stock necessary to increase

North Korean per capita incomes to 60 percent of those of the South, a target thought adequate to suppress incentives for mass migration. In 1990 this "cost of unification' was $319 billion, rose to $754 billion in 1995, and $1,721 billion in 2000 as the gap between North and South Korean incomes grew with delay in the initiation of reform.

The authors asserted that the situation of Korea is somewhat different from the case of German unification. First, the dissimilarity of factor endowments is far more significant in the Korean case than in the German case. So the integration would bring more dramatic implications in Korea. They suggested that NAFTA model might be more relevant to the Korean case because the economic size between South and North Korea is far larger compared to East and West Germany before the unification. Second, Korea can learn the lessons from the experience of German unification. For example, the wage equalization policy of Germany is considered as a mistake and can be avoided in the process of Korean unification.

IV. Economic Transformation and Environment in Hungary

1. Environmental and Economic Reforms in the Central and Eastern European Transitional Economies

Following lessons relevant to managing environmental problems can be learned from more than five years of experience with the transition process towards market economies in the Central and Eastern Europe :

(1) Environmental protection matters

(2) Setting priorities is challenging

- There is general uncertainty about scientific and economic data needed to evaluate environmental problems
- There is a continuing uncertainty about the extent to which environmental problems will ebb as a consequence of economic restructuring
- Priority setting is complicated by the need to respond to both domestic needs and objectives that reflect regional interests. Under these complications and uncertainties, following is a rule of thumb guidelines for priority setting :
  - Addressing problems that are widespread and not that costly to ameliorate
  - Isolating and addressing local disasters
  - Seeking to avoid damages that are large scale and irreversible
  - Identifying targets that are managerially feasible given the limited regulatory capacities

(3) Economic restructuring is essential

(4) Cost-effectiveness is important

2. Direct Impacts of Industrial Restructuring on Air Pollution and Hazardous Waste Emissions in Hungary

According to the predictions, the decreasing importance of metallurgy is expected to have the biggest positive impact on pollution emissions. The most striking feature of the results is the imbalanced nature of the overall picture on emission changes with a few sectors playing an influential role. Except for the case of SO_2 which has a more balanced picture, the iron and steel, aluminum and lime and cement industries are responsible for the majority of decreases in air pollutant emissions, while the oil, sugar and plastic industries are responsible for the major increases in emissions. According to the study, an overall 6–7 per cent decrease in industrial hazardous waste emissions could be a result of restructuring itself.

In his 1991 paper, Hughes cautiously stated that there might have been the potential environmental gains from economic restructuring in Hungary. The study by Kaderjak confirmed the findings of Hughes. The result supported the hypothesis that the industrial adjustment process that characterized the first period of economic transition (1989–92) was advantageous from an environmental point of view in Hungary. The study found that, independent of economic growth or recession, decreases in emissions that are attributable solely to structural change occurred for all pollutants investigated. The estimated emission reductions ranged from 3–29 per cent of total emissions for these pollutants, which was far below the reduction goals required by both domestic regulations and international conventions. Thus the study did not indicate that the structural shift in manufacturing could be expected as a major and cheap source of pollution abatement for Hungary in the future.

3. Environmental Impacts of Industrial Privatization in Hungary

1) Opportunities and problems created by industrial privatization to the environment

(1) Opportunities that industrial privatization brings to the environmental problems

a. Private ownership of enterprises, with a simultaneous elimination of widespread subsidies, is a necessary precondition for the successful implementation of market-based environmental regulations.

b. The privatization of formerly state-owned companies frequently involved the transfer of properties having contaminated sites.

c. Host country could enjoy a positive externality stemming from strict environmental regulations typical for the home countries of multinationals.

d. Privatization could help mobilize significant financial resources (parts of privatization revenues) into the cleaning-up of contaminated sites all around the country.

(2) Problems that industrial privatization brings to the environment

a. Historically, the State Property Agency (SPA)-the seller-wanted to set aside environmental problems in the course of privatization. Raising environmental liability concerns was considered to potentially slow down privatization. Later on the privatization process, the strategic use of environmental information in price bargains encouraged the SPA to look more closely to the environmental issues in a more systematic way.

b. As smaller business units are developed and sold, responsibility for past pollution became even less clear and past polluters even further distanced from any responsibility.

c. The relatively cheap environmental services of the country might attract polluting activities and revitalize pollution intensive production via Foreign Direct Investment (FDI).

2) Environmental concerns of potential investors

Foreign Direct Investment (FDI) has played an outstanding role in the Hungarian privatization process, and environmental considerations influence the investment decisions of foreigners, although this influence was moderate.

The principal problem faced by foreign investors was how to deal with the uncertainties surrounding the value of environmental liabilities resulting from the past activities of the enterprise under sale. In order to get reliable information on the actual level of contamination at an enterprise being sold, investors usually have to employ environmental consultants, because environmental authorities have limited information in this respect. It is very complicated to estimate the value of necessary investments required to comply with existing and expected environmental standards.

3) Connecting privatization and the environment

(1) 1990-July 1992

In the first three years of economic transition (1990-July 1992) the environmental issue did not appear directly in the regulations concerning privatization. In this first privatization period the government did not declare its responsibility for environmental damages incurred by state-owned enterprises, and did not even attempt to regulate the management of such environmental problems.

(2) Post July 1992

The privatization law, adopted in July 1992 contained some elements regarding environmental problems. The law on privatization declared that the legal successor of the former state enterprises was the company established by the transformation. The legal succession refered not only to the duties but also to the rights of the new company, which had the potential to compound future liability cases. As part of the privatization process, the enterprises had to obtain a declaration on their environmental condition from the Minister for Environment. This declaration could be issued on the basis of a plan for the remediation of environmental damages. However, the obligation of preparing such a plan was not applied to the whole mass of state property foreseen for privatization.

4) Environmental guarantees of the SPA

The two ways in which the SPA and the legislature have typically contributed to the financing of the clean-up of past contamination as a part of the privatization process were : (a) price discounts in exchange for pre-specified environmental abatement activities on the part of new owners, and (b) environmental clean-up guarantee funds provided for certain investors, both being a part of sales contracts.

The environmental clean-up guarantees of the SPA functioned as escrow funds. The buyer paid only the price subtracting the foreseeable cost of the remediation of the environment was deducted. The difference was put into a separate account of the company as a guarantee of the seller. The clean-up costs were covered from this account after the authorization by the SPA. The money left after the clean-up or at the deadline of the guarantee was reimbursed to the SPA.

4. Cheap Environmental Services in Hungary : How Attractive Are They for Foreign Investors?

How will the differences in environmental endowments (including assimilative capacity of nature, population density and people's preferences towards the environment) affect the trade specialization of an open economy? In the short run, the most obvious manifestation of this 'environmental capital flight' (ECF) is through foreign direct investment (FDI). The principal explanation for such capital movements lies in cost differences for enterprises, which are implied by differences in the strictness of environmental regulations across countries. Environmentalists like to refer to this phenomenon as eco-colonialization.

With the notable exception of Kolstad and Xing (1995), the empirical literature did not provide much support for the ECF hypothesis.

Compared with the home countries, Hungary was typical 'pollution haven', reflected by lax environmental regulation and thus low relative prices of environmental (waste disposal) services. Also, Hungary aggresively attracted foreign investment since the beginning of 1989, most of which was direct investment. If the ECF hypothesis holds, a certain fraction of this capital inflow was most probably induced by differential environmental regulations. So if it is supposed that a certain part of FDI was attracted by environmental considerations, then it can be assumed that the environmental motive should play some role in the sectoral choice of investors.

Of all the Central and Eastern European countries(CEECs), Hungary emerged as the most attractive country for foreign investors : starting from a position of essentially no FDI in 1988, at the end of 1994 the stock of registered FDI reached $9 billion. According to survey results, there are two groups of explanations on why Hungary became so attractive for FDI. The first concerns the lack of certain obstacles to FDI in Hungary and includes a stable economic and political situation and more liberal regulation regarding the foundation and operations of joint ventures. Other important reasons are sufficient infrastructure compared to other countries in the region, the strong cultural links to the nations of the EU and geographic location of the country in the center of greater Europe.

An empirical study in Hungary gave a partial support to the

environmental capital flight hypothesis, and was in accordance with the findings of Kolstad and Xing (1995).

5. Introduction of Economic Instruments in the CEECs Countries

After some preliminary experimentation, Russia introduced an extensive pollution fee system in 1991. While Poland had maintained a system of standards and emission charges for many years prior to 1989, the role of economic instruments, especially that of emission fees, has become more important since 1990. The Environmental Protection Funds were mostly financed from the emission fees revenues on SO_2, NOx and particulate matter emissions. Emission charge system was also proposed or introduced in Hungary and Czech Republic. However, evidences on practical experience with the application of economic instruments in CEECs are still scarce. Following are the collection of observations from the experiences.

Basic government authorities such as environment ministries and inspectorates had been set up and basic legal regulations were established across the countries in the Central and Eastern Europe. Following the western trends, command-and-control type regulatory regimes were established with the key elements of emission/performance standards and corresponding non-compliance fines. However the vehicle of environmental regulation, while it looked similar, served somewhat different goals and functioned in a somewhat different way from its western prototype. The concept of the rule of law is not as firmly established in the CEECs society as it is in most western democracies. Society was socialized in a system where behavioral rules, norms and possibilities were formed mostly in informal ways and had little to do with legal norms. And the CEECs regulatory system is not equipped with proper investments. Without significant investments into data gathering and improvement of the environmental information network, an important precondition to the application of economic instruments will be missing in these countries.

V. Economic Development and Environmental Sustainability

We want to discuss here on whether the achievement of environmental sustainability necessarily mean a reduction in rates of economic growth. If not, under what conditions can the two objectives be met simultaneously?

1. The Concept of Environmental Sustainability

Most of the economists call GDP growth an "economic growth' and closely relate GDP to welfare. This concept however was reputed by Hueting (1986), who contends that welfare is affected not only by GDP, but environment, employment, leisure, working conditions, income distribution, and safety of the future as well. Assuming that GDP and environmental quality are both important components of welfare, we need to know the trade-offs between the two. Even if GDP growth could be reduced in the process of pursuing environmental protection, this could increase rather than reduce welfare, depending on the relative weight given to the components of welfare.

Sustainability literally means the capacity for some state or condition to be continued more or less indefinitely. For economic development to be termed sustainable, the level of economic welfare must be sustained. Non-decreasing welfare requires that the stock of capital which includes manufactured, human and natural capital, be maintained. Concerning the role of environment for sustainability there are two lines of thought. 'Weak' environmental sustainability condition derives from the perception that welfare is not constrained by specific form of capital. 'Strong' sustainability condition is derived from the fact that the substitutability of manufactured for natural capital is seriously limited by special characteristics of environment such as irreversibility, uncertainty and the existence of 'critical' components of natural capital. Fewer environmental goods can be permanently transformed into human-made capital under strong sustainability than under weak sustainability.

2. Environmental Impacts of Growth

The key consideration in evaluating whether a certain GDP-growing investment can be environmentally sustainable is the extent to which production process can add value without increasing associated environmentally negative biophysical throughputs. Following is the equation expressing the relation between environmental impact and human activity :

$$I = P \times C \times T,$$

where I is environmental impact, P is population, C is consumption per head, and T is impact per unit of consumption, which is analogous to the environmental impact coefficient (EIC) of output, which is average unit impact on the environment through the consumption of resources and production of wastes. T can be thought of as indicating the technology of consumption (and production). In some cases it will mainly reflect the inputs of production, the processes of transformation of production and consumption, and the disposal of wastes ; in other cases it may be influenced by social arrangements such as property rights and the effectiveness of legal systems.

Reducing the EIC provides the basic physical condition for the compatibility of sustainability and growth. But there is also an economic condition. Reducing the EIC is likely to require resources in new capital and often in more expensive inputs. So the net costs of reducing EIC must be neutral or negative for sustainability not to constrain GDP growth. There are two broad ways where the environmental efficiency of production might also involve raising general productivity, that is, where policy for environmental sustainability will also promote GNP growth :

(1) Situations in which governments change policies which are economically inefficient as well as environmentally damag-

ing

(2) Situations in which public or private sector businesses introduce changes in methods, processes of products, including systems of resource and waste management, which both improve environmental quality and turn out to be cost-saving or product-improving.

There are two requirements for growth not to conflict with environmental limits : First, the average environmental impact coefficient must be reduced ; second, this must be cost-neutral or must positively increase general productivity.

In a background paper for the World Bank's World Development report 1992, Anderson asserted that so long as the correct policies are put in place, growth over the next thirty years need not be constrained, and indeed can be enhanced by protection and improvement of the environment.

One of the good examples of governmental lose-lose policies is the Common Agricultural Policy (CAP) of the European community. The basic mechanism of the CAP is price support of marketed farm products, which has led to a number of adverse environmental effects including soil degradation, water pollution and the loss of amenity and diversity. Just as price supports for output can inefficiently increase both output and associated environmental damage, so can subsidies for inputs. Both economic and environmental benefits will be achieved by removing subsidies that encourage the use of coal, electricity, pesticides and irrigation and promote expansion of grazing and timber extraction on public lands.

In a competitive market, there are many opportunities for profitable investment that appear to have been overlooked. Business managers have been widely unaware of the economic, let alone the environmental, costs of resource use and waste disposal. In this situation, public pressure is needed to encourage the business to take actions that could bring economic as well as environmental benefits. Environmental pressure can also achieve economic benefits by stimulating creativity and innovation that results in new products or new business opportunities.

3. South Korea's Experience

Economic growth brings with it the structural and technical changes, which have independent effects on the environment. If the structural and technical changes geared toward the right direction, they can offset the adverse impact of growth on the environment.

"Countries at different stages of development show different patterns of environmental problems. These problems tend to decline as income increases. In low-income economies, the main environmental problems concern natural resources, especially deforestation and soil erosion, and lack of access to safe water. In middle-income economies, the main environmental problems are those created by industrialization such as airborne and water-discharged pollutants arising from power generation, land transformation and industrial production. These second-phase problems tend to worsen initially but then improve as income rises, although the improvement is not automatic. The third-phase environmental problems are associated with developed countries. Those are toxic wastes, municipal wastes, pesticide runoff and emissions of COx and Nox."

South Korea was no exception from this trend. The rapid economic growth in the '60s made it possible to solve such first-phase problems as deforestation, safe water supply and sanitation. However the rapid industrialization has created second-phase pollution problems due to the structural and technical changes associated with industrialization. The emission of sulphur dioxides increased nine times during 1965-1979 period while GDP increased 3.5 times. In the late 1980s, solid industrial waste and wastewater increased at about 20 percent per annum. South Korea was fairly successful in dealing with the first-phase environmental problems. However as long as the second and third-phase environmental problems are concerned, it was not so successful. South Korea pursued growth maximization strategy instead of welfare maximization, intensively utilizing imported materials and energy and neglecting proper environmental protection. Being a resource-poor country, South Korea artificially created the comparative advantage in resource intensive industries by neglecting or keeping low environmental standards. The artificial comparative advantage is reflected by the fact that disproportionately large share of major pollutants were generated in the export sector. Foreign direct investment was also concentrated in pollution-intensive industries in Ulsan-Onsan industrial complexes. In the 1960s the bulk of foreign investment went to such pollution-intensive industries as chemical/petrochemical and metallurgy. This trend went on to the 1970s and 1980s, with the addition of transportation equipment sector.

VI. Concluding Remarks

We have learned that economic growth need not necessarily bring environmental degradation in return. It is possible to reduce economic costs and at the same time to improve environmental condition simply by changing lose-lose governmental policy. In a socialist country there should be more cases of inefficient resource use and government subsidy program. So the first step towards environmentally sound and sustainable economic cooperation is to improve the efficiency of North Korean industry by renovating inefficient plants and by introducing environmentally sound technology. Introduction of private property rights and market mechanism will significantly reduce inefficiencies caused by the lack of incentives for efficient resource use.

During the process of economic transformation in North Korea, foreign direct investment will play a dominant role as South Korea experienced. In South Korea the growth objective frequently overrode the environmental concerns and economic planners considered the economic growth as utmost goal. The strategy of 'growth first, environment later' however can be cost inefficient, since it is often cheaper to prevent environmental degradation than to cure it later. The World Resources Institute also commented that the NICs' experiences do not show the model of sustainable development, even though they are often cited as a model of economic development. Taking South Korea's experience as a predecessor's lesson, North Korea should set the goal of welfare maximization, where economic growth is pursued with proper environmental care at the same time.

References

Bank of Korea, *Gross Domestic Product of North Korea in 1999*, 2000.

Bhaskar, V., and Andrew Glyn eds., The North, the South, and the Environment : Ecological Constraints and the Global Economy, UN University Press, 1995.

Chung, Hoe-sung, *North Korea's Environmental problems and the way to encourage environmental cooperation between South and North Korea*, Korea Environmental Technology Research Institute, 1995.

Hetzel, Nancy K., *Environmental Cooperation among Industrialized Countries : The Role of Regional Organizations*, University Press of America, 1979.

Jameson, Kenneth P., and Charles K. Wilber eds., *The Political Economy of Development and Underdevelopment*, 1996.

Kaderjak, Peter, and John Powell, "Economics for Environmental Policy in Transition Economies : An Analysis of the Hungarian Experience", Edward Elgar.

Kim, Byoung-lo Philo, *Two Koreas in development : a comparative study of principles and strategies of capitalist and communist third world development*, Transaction Publishers, 1992.

Ko, Ill-dong, *New approach toward economic cooperation between South and North Korea*, Korea Development Institute, 1997.

Koo, Bon-Hak, *Political economy of self-reliance : juche and economic development in North Korea, 1961-1990*, Research Center for Peace and Unification of Korea, 1992.

Korea Legislation System Research Institute, *North Korea's legislation related to the conservation of environment*, 1995.

McMillan, John, and Barry Naughton eds., *Reforming Asian Socialism : the growth of market institutions*, University of Michigan Press, 1996.

Tay, Simon S. C., *International Trade and Environment in Asia : Business and Environmental Cooperation across Regions : a Survey of the Issues*, National University of Singapore, 1996

Tisdell, C.A., *Economic Development in the Context of China*, Macmillan, London, 1993.

______, and Joseph C. H. Chai, *China's Economic Growth and Transition : Macroeconomic, Regional, Environmental and Other Dimensions*, University of Queensland, Brisbane, 1997.

______, "Asian Development and Environmental Dilemmas," *Contemporary Economic Policy*, 13 : 38–44, 1995.

World Bank, *World Development Report : Development and the Environment*, Oxford University Press, New York, 1992.

World Resources Institute, *World Resources 1992–93*, Oxford University Press, 1992.

Wu, B. and Flynn, A., "Sustainable Development in China : Seeking a Balance Between Economic Growth and Environmental Protection," *Sustainable Development* 3(1) : 1–8,1995.

15. Climate Policy Options and Their Implications on Korean Economy*

This paper compares the economic effects of climate policy options in Korea. The impacts and implications of carbon and Btu tax schemes are analyzed using the META-Net modeling system, which was developed at the Lawrence Livermore National Laboratory (LLNL). Findings indicate that carbon tax is more cost effective compared to Btu tax, but this does not necessarily mean the former is more desirable than the latter. Energy market stability and national energy security is equally important in choosing policy options

I. Introduction

As Marrakech COP 7 meeting reached an agreement to activate

---

* "Climate Policy Options and Their Implications on Korean Economy," paper presented at the 25th IAEE Annual Conference, Aberdeen U.K., June 26-29, 2002.

the Kyoto Protocol from 2002, CO_2 mitigation became not only the issue of international negotiation, but of the vital economic issue affecting the future of developed as well as developing countries. Possible climate policy instruments that have been studied so far are now passing through the final examination of their practical applicability. It is expected that the developing countries might have to join the mitigation obligation in the next decade, and they also need to find some policy schemes to minimize the socio-economic impacts.

Korea introduced various strategies for CO_2 emission reduction, but they are not for actual reduction but for capacity building to reduce possible shock in the near future. The purpose of this study is to evaluate and compare the impacts of introducing carbon and Btu tax schemes in Korea as a possible climate policy option.

II. Energy Use, GHG Emission and Climate Policy in Korea

Korea's energy consumption has doubled every ten years since 1970s and GHG (greenhouse gas) emission increased steadily in the 1990s. This trend is caused by rapid economic growth and energy intensive industrial structure of Korea. Table 1 shows the trends of energy consumption and GHG emission statistics in the 1990s. In the latter half of 1990s, there was a significant slowdown of economic growth, energy consumption, and GHG emission. The slow down of energy use and GHG emission might have been caused by industrial transformation to less energy intensive industry such as information and telecommunication, and government's efforts to encourage energy conservation, together with the impact of 1997 financial crisis. The share of information and telecommunication industry was only 11.1 % in 1990, but the share increased to 34.4% in 2000.

|Table 1| Recent Trends of Energy Consumption and GHG Emission in Korea

	Unit	1990	1995	2000	Annual Avg. Growth (%)	
					90-95	95-2000
GDP (A)	Trillion won	263.4	3774	476.3	7.45	4.77
Energy Consumption (B)	Million TOE	93.2	150.4	192.9	10.05	5.10
GHG Emission (C)	Million TC	83.0	119.5	134.9	7.55	2.46
B/A	TOE/million won	0.354	0.399	0.405	1.349[a]	1.069[a]
C/A	TC/million won	0.315	0.317	0.283	1.013[b]	0.516[b]

* 1995 constant
a. energy consumption growth rate / GDP growth rate
b. GHG emission growth rate / GDP growth rate

Even though energy efficiency improvement and industrial restructuring have improved the situation, Korea's energy consumption and GHG emission level is still above OECD average. Figure 1 shows that Korea's energy consumption per unit of GDP in 1998. While average OECD countries used 0.25 TOE of energy to produce 1000 dollars worth of GDP, Korea used 0.42 TOE. The share of imported energy in final energy use has reached 97.2% in 1999. The amount used to import energy was 22.7 billion dollars,

|Figure 1| Energy Consumption per unit of GDP in 1998

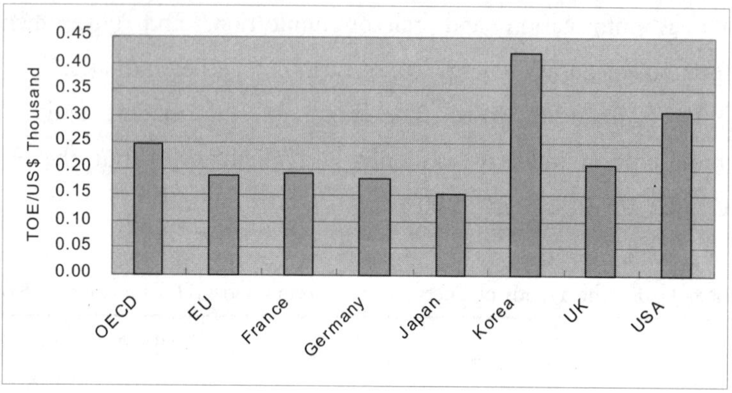

Source : OECD

which is 18.9% of total imports of Korea. This means that the conservation of energy and improvement of energy efficiency has to be the main policy goals in pursuing GHG reduction policy schemes in Korea.

Korean government announced the second comprehensive policy scheme to deal with UNFCCC in March 2002. It emphasized the need for enhanced capacity building to prepare for a sudden economic impact from the climate change negotiation. Detailed strategies mostly depend on government's direct intervention, large research fund, and voluntary actions of private sector. To structure a robust economic system, however, we need to introduce market-based incentive system which provides a right signal to the users of energy. That's why we chose to compare the effectiveness and policy implications of carbon and Btu taxes as possible climate policy options in this analysis.

|Figure 2| CO_2 Emissions per unit of GDP in 1998

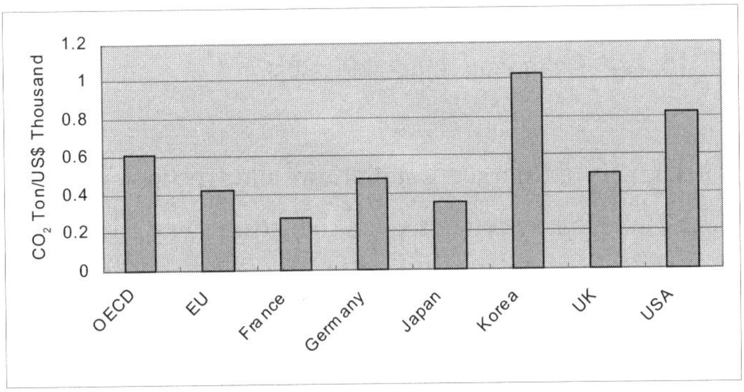

Source : OECD

Figure 2 compares the CO_2 emissions per unit of GDP among OECD countries in 1998. Compared to France, Korea emits nearly four times of CO_2 to produce same amount of GDP. If Korea is assigned a reduction target comparable to developed countries, she would have to bear heavy economic burden. The largest source of CO_2 emission in Korea is the industrial sector. It's share was 38% in 1998, and the share of transportation sector was 21%, and the share of residential and commercial sector was 16%. The share of industrial sector is getting larger, and the residential and commercial sector's share decreased from 30% in 1990. The total energy efficiency has improved in the residential and commercial sector, and the fossil fuel use, such as coal and petroleum, has been decreasing in this sector.

III. The Model

1. META-Net Economic Modeling System

The META-Net (Market Equilibrium and Technology Assessment Network) modeling system used in this study was developed at the Lawrence Livermore National Laboratory (Lamont, 1994). META-Net is a partial equilibrium modeling system that allows a user to represent and build an economic system as a network of nodes representing economic process such as resources, conversion process, markets, and end-use demands. The model is designed to compute multi-period equilibrium prices and quantities demanded for every energy source along with the capacity additions/retirements for each conversion process, and the resource extraction trajectories.

To design a model, the user specifies nodes for each type of process, their economic parameters which represent costs and technological characteristics, and their relationships to other nodes. Then, the system computes price-quantity equilibrium through a sequence of iterations passing quantities demanded down from the end-use nodes and prices up from the resources nodes. Finally, the system computes a multi-period solution for the entire network using an iterative algorithm.[1)]

1) See Lamont (1994) for more detailed descriptions of META-Net modeling system.

2. The Korean Model

Korean energy system in this analysis is composed of end-users, energy markets, conversion process, and energy resources. Final demand has four sectors : industrial, residential and commercial, transportation, and public. The types of final energy use are categorized into two-heat and electricity. Each component of the energy system is represented by one of the nodes installed in the META-Net modeling system. There are five basic node types available in the modeling system : top, end-use, conversion, market, and resource. In the modeling system, networks are designed so that resources are placed at the bottom of the network and end-use nodes at the top. Various type of energy flows from the bottom to the top, and the end-use demands and demand for primary energy or resource flow from the top to the bottom. Conversion nodes in the middle of network determine how much resource is required to meet the demand, and market nodes control and allocate demands among different supplier nodes.

The base year used for the analysis is 1998, and the projection and simulation was calculated up to the year 2043. Fifty years are divided into 10 periods. Final energy demand flows into market nodes, and each market node computes equilibrium prices and quantities of each energy source. The supply capacity of energy in each market depends on resource reserves, capital and O&M costs. Under the given final energy demand, the META-Net modeling system calculates the energy price and consumption by fuels for each period as well.

3. Carbon and Btu Tax Scenarios

The GHG mitigation target for this study was set at an 18.5% reduction of CO_2 emission from the reference case by the year 2043. We intended to compare the result of this analysis to the preceding analysis which applied the same model to the Japanese economy.[2] After several simulations with the Korean model, we came up with the carbon tax rate of $72/tonC and the Btu tax rate of $3.0/mmBtu which reduce the CO_2 emission to the targeted 186mmTC (million metric tons of carbon) in 2043. To achieve an 18.5% reduction target, 62mmTC of emission had to be eliminated from the energy system. Both taxes were introduced gradually over time and reached their highest rate in 2043.

Table 4 shows the CO_2 emission projection under different tax rates. Based on this simulation we determined the following three policy scenarios :

- Reference scenario : carbon emission increases from 115mmTC to 228mmTC between 1998 and 2043
- Carbon tax scenario : carbon tax of 72 dollars per tonC is levied and the carbon emission reaches 186mmTC in 2043
- Btu tax scenario : Btu tax of 3 dollars per mmBtu is levied and the carbon emission reaches 186mmTC in 2043

2) Nakata and Lamont (2000)

|Figure 3| Network for Korean META - Net Model

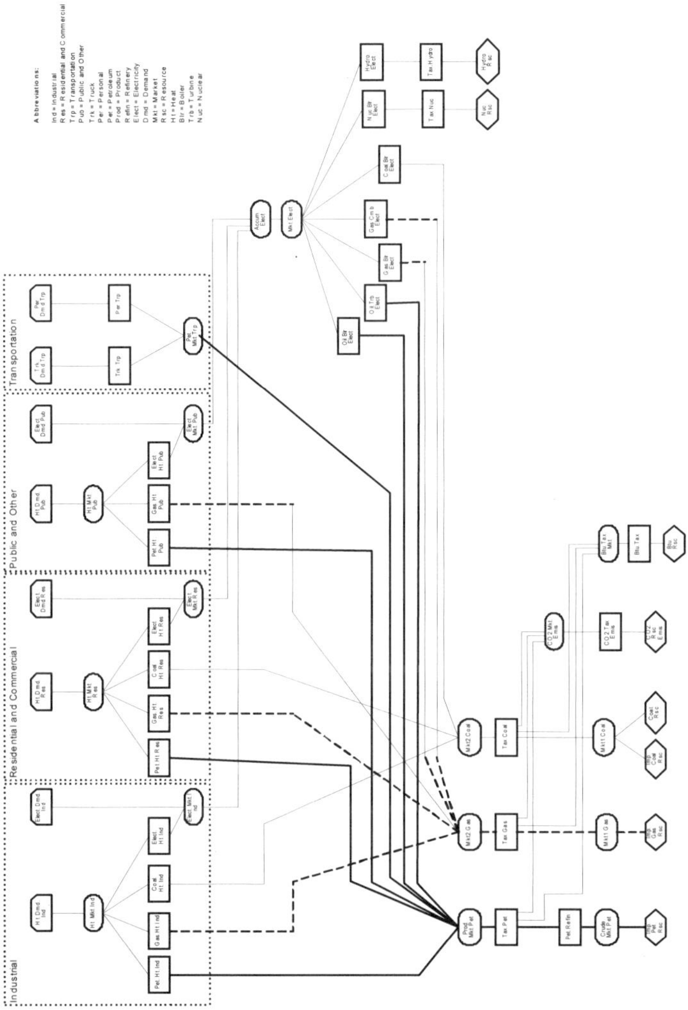

|Table 4| CO_2 Emissions under Different Levels of Carbon and Btu Tax in 2043

(Unit : mmTC)

Carbon tax	\$0/tonC	\$72/tonC	\$100/tonC	\$200/tonC	\$300/tonC
CO_2	228	186	176	158	150
Btu tax	\$0/mmBtu	\$1.5/mmBtu	\$3.0/mmBtu	\$6.0/mmBtu	\$9.0/mmBtu
CO_2	228	202	186	167	155

IV. The Impacts of Taxes

1. Energy Use

Main impact of the carbon or Btu tax scheme is the increase in the price of energy and the accompanying decrease of energy consumption. Table 5 shows the projected prices of four energy sources in 2043 under different scenarios. The increase in energy price is higher in the case of Btu tax than the carbon tax in general. So the energy consumption would decrease more under Btu tax scenario. The Btu tax increases the price of coal by 91% compared to the reference case.

Figure 4 shows the projected final energy consumption under different scenarios. Final energy consumption under Btu tax scenario decreased 10.75% compared to the reference scenario in 2043 while it decreased only 5.66% under carbon tax scenario. The annual average growth rate of final energy consumption was 1.75% under reference case, 1.54% under carbon tax scenario, and 1.35% under

|Table 5| Energy Price Changes with Three Scenarios

	Reference	Carbon Tax		Btu Tax	
	A	B	B/A	C	C/A
Petroleum	5.59	7.10	1.27	8.59	1.54
Gas	5.25	6.40	1.22	8.25	1.57
Coal	3.29	5.23	1.59	6.29	1.91
Electricity	15.70	17.54	1.12	20.88	1.33

Btu tax scenario.

In both tax policy scenarios, the heat demand of residential and commercial sector decreased significantly compared to other sectors. Carbon tax reduced the heat demand of residential and commercial sector by 14% compared to the reference case and the Btu tax reduced the demand 25% in this sector. The higher reduction rate was due to greater price elasticity. The heat demand of residential and commercial sector requires less capital cost in utilizing energy appliances compared to industrial or transportation sectors, which explains the greater price elasticity of this sector.

The most remarkable nature of the carbon tax is its heavy burden on high carbon emitting fossil fuel. The carbon tax increases the relative price of coal much higher than other energy sources. Accordingly, heavy substitution occurs from coal to gas under carbon tax scheme. Figure 5 shows the projected primary energy consumption in 2043 under different scenarios. We can easily observe that most of coal reduction was accompanied by the increase in gas consumption under the carbon tax scenario. This

|**Figure 4**| Projection of Final Energy Use in the Scenarios

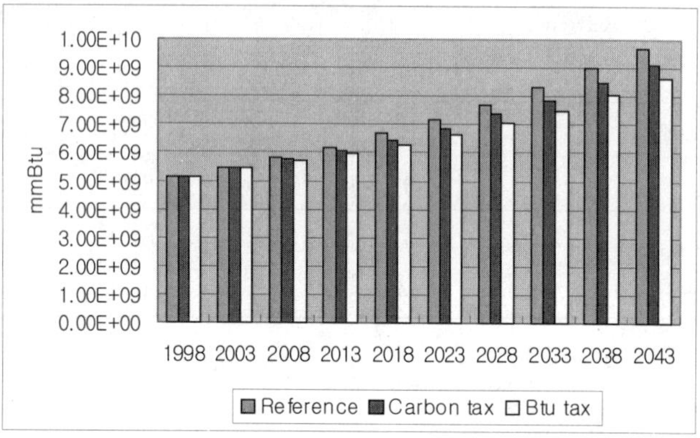

signifies the cost effectiveness of the carbon tax scheme in reducing carbon emission.

|**Figure 5**| Primary Energy Use in 2043

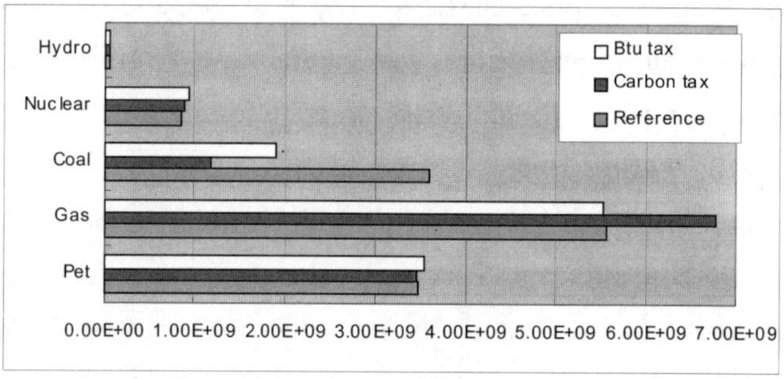

The demand for petroleum products, however, was only slightly affected by both tax schemes. There are two explanations for this unusual situation. One is that the coal-fired generation could be replaced partly by oil-fired electric generation. The other is that there will be limited room for fuel substitution in the petroleum consuming activities, mostly in industrial and transportation sectors for the time being.

2. Direct Energy Costs and Tax Revenue

Conversion nodes in the META-Net model are described by their technical and cost parameters. There are 29 conversion nodes in the Korean model, which are described by their capacity, efficiency, capital cost, and O&M cost. When equilibrium is reached, the capacity addition is determined, and the capital cost is recalculated.

Table 6 summarizes the direct costs and tax revenues computed in the Korean model. Each cost is the sum of present values between 1998 and 2043 using 5% interest rate. The capital and O&M costs of the three scenarios are not much different. However, as we noted before there is a significant difference in fuel cost. Final consumers should pay 37.8 billion dollars more under carbon tax scenario and 74.6 billion dollars more under Btu tax scenario, compared to the reference case. Strikingly, the difference in tax revenue turned out to be greater than expected. The revenue of the Btu tax was 899 billion dollars, which is about 70 times of carbon tax case. The tax base of Btu tax was much broader than the carbon tax, and Btu tax provided little room for fuel substitution in reducing GHG emission. The higher tax revenue together with high fuel cost signifies less cost effectiveness of the Btu tax compared to the carbon tax in meeting the targeted reduction.

|Table 6| Total Direct Costs and Tax Revenues under Three Scenarios (1998-2043)

(Unit : US$ billion)

	Reference	Carbon tax $72/tonC	Btu tax $3.0/mmBtu
Capital cost	134.5	131.1	131.2
O+M cost	167.8	167.9	163.9
Fuel cost	250.2	288.0	324.8
Total direct cost	552.4	587.0	619.9
Tax revenue	0	1.3	89.9

V. Concluding Remarks

This paper attempted to analyze and compare the impacts of carbon tax and Btu tax policies to Korea. The summary and policy implication of the study are as follows :

- Carbon tax is more cost effective than Btu tax in the sense that the former causes less burden to the consumers compared to the latter. But this is an incomplete assessment of the two tax schemes because we did not fully consider the externality and market distortion effects in the general equilibrium context. To find the optimal tax level, we should have the information on external cost of environmental pollution, together with the macro and dynamic effects of different tax schemes to the Korean economy.

- The long-term stability of natural gas supply plays a crucial role for energy security in Korea. When carbon tax is levied on carbon intensive fuels, rapid substitution will occur from coal to natural gas. Such an abrupt substitution might jeopardize optimal energy mix and cause the Korean energy system vulnerable to the international gas market situation. Therefore, without a secured supply of natural gas in advance, Korea's energy security could be threatened.
- Carbon tax is more effective in reducing carbon intensive energy sources. It is specifically targeted to reduce carbon-the main source of green house effect. However, Btu tax is more effective in reducing energy consumption in general. It reduces not only carbon intensive energy sources, but non-fossil fuel like electricity. Korean economy consumes too much energy and energy efficiency is very low compared to other OECD countries. So the reduction of energy demand growth should be the first priority of the national energy policy in Korea. In this sense, Btu tax might be preferred to the carbon tax for the time being.

References

Cline, William R., *the Economics of Global Warming*, Washington, DC : Institute for International Economics, 1992.

DeCanio, Stephen J., Richard B. Howarth, Alan H. Sanstad, Stephen H. Schneider, and Starley L. Thompson, *New Directions in the Economics and Integrated Assessment of Global Climate Change*, Pew Center on Global Climate Change, 2000.

Fullerton, Don, "A Framework to Compare Environmental Policies," NBER Working Paper 8420, Cambridge, MA : National Bureau of Economic Research, 2001.

Gaskins JR., Darius W. and John P. Weyant, "Model Comparisons of the Costs of Reducing CO_2 Emissions", *AEA Papers and Proceedings* Vol.83 No.2, 1993.

Harrington, Winston, Richard D. Morgenster, and Peter Nelson, "On the Accuracy of Regulatory Cost Estimates," Resources for the Future Discussion Paper 99-18, Washington, DC : Resources for the Future,1999.

IPCC, *IPCC Second Assessment Report : Climate Change 1995*, Intergovernment Panel on Climate Change, UK : Cambridge University Press, 1996.

Lamont, Alan, *User's Guide to the META-Net Economic Modeling System Version 1.2*, Lawrence Livermore National Laboratory, 1994.

______, "Analysis of Market Penetration Scenarios of Clean Coal Technologies in China Using the LLNL China Energy Model," Lawrence Livermore National Laboratory, 1998.

Nakata, Toshihiko and Alan Lamont, "Analysis of the Impacts of Carbon Taxes on Energy Systems in Japan," *Energy Policy* 29, 2000.

Stavins, Robert N., "Policy Instruments for Climate Change : How Can National Governments Address Global Problems?" RFF Discussion Paper 97-11, Washington, DC : Resources for the Future, 1997.